★ ★ ★ ★ *A* ★ ★ ★ ★

BRIEF HISTORY *of*
PUBLIC
POLICY
SINCE THE
NEW DEAL

★ ★ ★ ★ ★ ★ ★ ★

ANDREW E. BUSCH
CLAREMONT McKENNA COLLEGE

★ ★ ★ ★ ★ ★ ★ ★

ROWMAN & LITTLEFIELD
Lanham • Boulder • New York • London

Executive Editor: Traci Crowell
Editorial Assistant: Charlotte Gosnell
Executive Marketing Manager: Amy Whitaker
Interior Designer: Rosanne Schloss

Credits and acknowledgments for material borrowed from other sources, and reproduced with permission, appear on the appropriate page within the text.

Published by Rowman & Littlefield
An imprint of The Rowman & Littlefield Publishing Group, Inc.
4501 Forbes Boulevard, Suite 200, Lanham, Maryland 20706
www.rowman.com

6 Tinworth Street, London SE11 5AL, United Kingdom

British Library Cataloguing in Publication Information Available

Library of Congress Cataloging-in-Publication Data
Names: Busch, Andrew, author.
Title: A brief history of public policy since the New Deal / Andrew Busch,
    Claremont Mckenna College.
Description: First edition. | Lanham : Rowman & Littlefield, 2019.
    | Includes bibliographical references and index.
Identifiers: LCCN 2019016012| ISBN 9781538128268 (cloth : alk. paper)
    | ISBN 9781538128275 (pbk. : alk. paper) | ISBN 9781538128282 (electronic)
Subjects: LCSH: Policy sciences—United States. | United States—Politics and government.
Classification: LCC H97 .B865 2019 | DDC 320.60973—dc23 LC record available
    at https://lccn.loc.gov/2019016012

∞™ The paper used in this publication meets the minimum requirements of American National Standard for Information Sciences—Permanence of Paper for Printed Library Materials, ANSI/NISO Z39.48–1992.

Printed in the United States of America

To Roman and Serenity

Brief Contents

★ ★ ★

Contents

★ ★ ★

Acknowledgments

★ ★ ★

I WOULD LIKE TO ACKNOWLEDGE the research assistance of Hannah Burak, Aseem Chipalkatti, and Ian O'Grady; the graphing assistance of Nicholas Federochko; and the support provided by the James Madison Program in American Ideals and Institutions at Princeton University.

About the Author

★　★　★

ANDREW E. BUSCH is Crown Professor of Government and George R. Roberts Fellow at Claremont McKenna College. He is coauthor of several Rowman & Littlefield books, including *The Imperial Presidency and the Constitution, Defying the Odds: The Elections of 2016,* and *After Hope and Change: The 2012 Elections and American Politics.*

Introduction

★   ★   ★

A LARGE PART OF WHAT government does is to devise and implement "public policy." Public policy is an attempt by government to address some public issue, primarily through law, regulation, or administrative action.

This book will examine public policy since the New Deal, or roughly the beginning of the 1930s. The New Deal, as we will see, was a crucial turning point in the relationship between government and citizens in the United States. You cannot really understand economic policy, social welfare, energy or environmental policy today if you do not know how the debate has developed over time.

We will focus on domestic policy—that is, policy aimed primarily at problems within the United States. We will also focus on policy determined at the federal level by the legislative and executive branches, though it is often useful to think about what is going on at the state and local levels of government at the same time. And although public policy is not primarily about the judiciary, courts can come into play.

There are several themes that will serve to organize our study.

INPUTS AND OUTPUTS

First, we will think of public policy in terms of policy inputs and outputs. The **main output** we will consider is **the policy itself**—the collection of laws, regulations, administrative actions, and (occasionally, in practice) court decisions applied to a particular problem or set of problems. **Another important output**, which is often not sufficiently considered in studies of policy, is the effect on key **governing institutions and constitutional understandings** of the nation.

This book will feature a narrative examining the major domestic policy outputs of each era. Then we will summarize those outputs in **seven specific (though sometimes overlapping) policy areas:**

1. Economic policy, or overall policies regarding spending, taxing, and regulating, including the underlying economic principles driving those decisions[1]
2. Social welfare, or policies having to do with alleviating poverty and providing economic security
3. Civil rights, specifically policies seeking to promote racial equality
4. Education, at preschool, K–12, or higher education level
5. Environment, or policies having to do with conservation of natural resources or limitation of pollution or other environmental hazards
6. Moral/cultural issues, or non-tangible questions having to do with the moral framework of society
7. Federalism or intergovernmental relations—that is, the constitutional and practical relationship between the federal, state, and local levels of government

These summaries will allow us to trace a handful of key substantive policy areas over time as they come in and out of prominence in the policy agenda. These seven areas of public policy cross over political scientist Theodore Lowi's framework that identified four basic types of policy: distributive, redistributive, regulatory, and constitutive. In distributive policies, costs are assessed broadly but direct benefits are more narrowly focused; construction of highways, aid to education, and agricultural subsidies are all examples. Redistributive policies deliberately shift resources from one group to another; social welfare programs for the poor supported by progressive income taxation are a chief example, as are programs redistributing funds from working-age people to retirees. The archetype of a regulatory policy imposes costs on a narrow portion of society in order to benefit all or most people; environmental rules imposed on factories and rules regulating food safety would be examples. Finally, constitutive policies are constitutional or rule making in character.[2] Although the typology offers useful insights, subsequent attempts to apply it have shown that the categories are not clear-cut and that most policies have redistributive effects, whether intended or not.[3]

There are four active inputs, plus another important passive input that is a given: the **policy baseline**, or the existing trajectory of policy. One framework for studying public policy, **path dependence**, emphasizes the importance of what has happened already. Policy makers are seldom free to simply invent a policy from scratch. Indeed, "particular courses of action, once introduced, can be almost impossible to reverse."[4] Even when there are no laws, programs, or regulations yet, refraining from acting is its own policy, around which develops expectations and networks of interests. The policy baseline has such influence over the options available to policy makers that, as we will soon see, an entire understanding of how policy usually operates is built around it. However, path dependence too rigorously defined minimizes the importance of other factors, such as institutions or acts of political leadership.[5] Since we can observe that policy change can and does occur, path dependence is only part of the story.

Within the context established by the policy baseline, there are four sets of more active factors that contribute to the policy output. One is **ideas** or, more broadly, **belief systems**.[6] The existing policy context may be a given, but whether citizens and policy makers view it as a good thing that should be preserved or a bad thing that should be upended partly depends on the intellectual framework through which they view it. That framework also helps determine what options might be considered legitimate in the future. Some broad ideas—such as individual liberty, equality, democracy, and respect for constitutional norms—are foundational, and are common to most Americans, though we often disagree vehemently about what they mean or how to apply them. It is these disagreements that often serve as a backdrop for policy departures. The New Deal, for example, was preceded by nearly half a century of political thinking by populists, progressives, socialists, and new-style liberals who criticized the status quo and laid the intellectual groundwork for a major expansion of the power and scope of the federal government. Sometimes the ideas driving policy are new; sometimes they are recycled or recombined.

A second is external **events**.[7] New political ideas may be interesting but have little impact if they do not seem to be validated by real events. The more dramatic the event and the more people it affects, the greater its policy impact is likely to be. Events can not only validate ideas but can concretely change the **political circumstances**—especially the relative balance between competing political forces—which are a third factor. Scholar John Kingdon identifies three key aspects of the politics of policy making: national mood, pressure group campaigns, and administrative or legislative turnover.[8] Without the shock of the Great Depression, the New Deal would not have happened when and how it did, and may not have happened at all. The Depression changed the way many Americans thought about the responsibilities of government, and it also gave liberal Democrats control of the federal government for a time. The assassination of President Kennedy in 1963 was a spur to the enactment of his program, and also aided the election of Lyndon Johnson with a big Democratic congressional majority which then passed other far-reaching legislation.

The economic and foreign policy troubles of the 1970s seemed to many Americans to validate conservative criticisms of liberal governance and led to both a renewed legitimacy for conservative ideas and the victory of Ronald Reagan and a Republican Senate in the 1980 election. Reagan then gained enactment of major policy changes. The financial crisis of 2008 and the "Great Recession" that came with it gave Barack Obama and congressional Democrats power and the opportunity for a time to advance long-sought liberal policy aims such as expanded government health care programs.

Finally, **people** matter. Individual policy makers, whether presidents, members of Congress, or administrative appointees, come to their jobs with particular backgrounds, values, capacities, cognitive styles, and levels of risk tolerance.[9] It made a great deal of difference that Franklin Roosevelt was president in 1933 rather than Al Smith or John Nance Garner—two very different Democrats who also might have been nominated by their party. If George H. W. Bush or Howard Baker rather than Ronald Reagan had taken office in January 1981, the policy outcome would probably have been different.

So, within the context of existing policy, it is the interplay of ideas, events, politics, and individuals that produces new policy. Not only do they interact (think of the effect of events on politics), but there can also be a feedback loop. Changes in policy can affect the political circumstances, which can contribute to further policy changes. In the 1930s, Franklin Roosevelt's eventual embrace of workers' rights brought the American labor movement firmly into the Democratic coalition, which had political and policy consequences down the road. Or policy can go further than the public desires, leading to negative feedback, such as the Republican takeover of the House in 2010, which forced a serious adjustment of Obama's fiscal policies.

Students of the policy process have suggested a number of frameworks to help us understand why policy develops as it does—specifically, how the inputs outlined above come together to produce policy outcomes. This is primarily a book on policy history, not a rigorous empirical examination of alternative public policy models, but these frameworks can be useful for understanding the history of public policy.

The first framework to consider is called **incrementalism**.[10] Incrementalism is a way of understanding policy development that is closely related to the concept of path dependence. It is based on the observation that the American political system has a number of features that have the effect, many by design, of slowing the formation of new policy and making radical change difficult. These features include separation of powers between the federal executive, legislative, and judicial branches; federalism, or the division of powers and responsibilities between the federal, state, and local governments; bicameralism in Congress, or the division of Congress into House and Senate; the multiplication of competing interests in a large republic; and an electoral system that encourages dominance by two relatively moderate political parties. All of this means that there are multiple veto points in the American system, as well as a relatively moderate political culture, though there is evidence that Americans are becoming more ideologically polarized.[11] The consequence for policy makers is that, most of the time, the system will be much more receptive to smaller modifications of existing policy than to radical new departures. Additionally, certain psychological features of the electorate reinforce the institutional biases favoring slow change. In particular, voters are affected by "loss aversion," or the tendency to fear the negative consequences of a policy change more than they look forward to its positive consequences.[12]

Although incrementalism describes what happens in the policy world most of the time, it cannot explain the occasions when there is a burst of significant policy change. As a descriptive matter, policy development might be illuminated by Thomas Kuhn in *The Nature of Scientific Revolutions*.[13] Kuhn, who was writing about natural science, observed that science does not progress in a gradual, linear fashion. Instead, it experiences brief moments of radical improvement in knowledge, followed by a long period of consolidation and small accretions to knowledge. As time goes on, anomalies in the reigning "paradigm" (or belief system) accumulate, until they become impossible to ignore any longer. Then, and only then, is the way opened to a new paradigm that significantly changes the way we look at science. Similarly, long periods of small policy change finally give way to big changes when the shortcomings of the dominant paradigm become too great to sustain.[14]

Two frameworks proposed by scholars take into account such moments. One is called **punctuated equilibrium**. In this view, most of the time, there is an equilibrium characterized by incrementalism. That equilibrium can, however, be overcome when circumstances are right. Opponents of the status quo (policy entrepreneurs) construct new "policy images" and take advantage of the character of the US system, turning an obstacle (multiple veto points) into an opportunity (multiple policy venues).[15] The new images exist in the realm of ideas, and are activated both by events and by the politics of the moment; national politics forces change on previously stable policy subsystems, sometimes referred to as "iron triangles" or "issue networks." The policy entrepreneurs are the people.

Policy entrepreneurs => New policy image + Events/politics => Policy
(people)   (ideas)

The **multiple streams framework** similarly looks to a confluence of forces to occasionally open a **window of opportunity** for major policy change: when problems (often in the form of events), policy (ideas), and politics align, there is an opportunity for policy makers to go beyond merely incremental change.[16]

> **Problems + Policy + Politics => Opportunity for policy makers**
> (events)   (ideas)   (people)
>
> => **Policy**
> (outcome)

These "change frameworks" differ, particularly in respect to the role of the policy entrepreneurs or leaders. Where in punctuated equilibrium policy makers actively construct new ideas, in multiple streams they merely take advantage of ideas that have already been introduced. However, when applied to broad departures in policy, the distinction between these two notions can blur. The New Deal, for example, inherited and was built upon a set of preexisting ideas dating back as many as four decades. In that sense, Franklin Roosevelt took advantage of an opportunity. Yet he also played a proactive role, positively fashioning those building blocks into a new policy image. Where FDR as opportunist ends and FDR as builder begins is not easy to say. At their most fundamental, both of these frameworks propose understanding major policy change as an output of a fortuitous combination of events, ideas, politics, and people.

As originally proposed, the "multiple streams" framework applied to early stages of the policy-making process, specifically agenda setting (determination of which issues will receive the most attention from policy makers) and specification of alternatives (what policy options are put forward as reasonable ways of confronting those issues). "Punctuated equilibrium" was initially applied to legislation. However, the application of both "multiple streams" and "punctuated equilibrium" frameworks has been broadened by scholars. Subsequent scholarship, for example, has contended that the multiple streams framework could be extended to the full policy process. In other words, ultimate policy decisions, and perhaps whole broad trends of policy—not just agenda setting and alternative specification—are the product of ideas, politics, events, and people.[17] "Punctuated equilibrium" has also been expanded, to long-term analysis of the federal budget.[18] As we survey the history of public policy since the New Deal, these concepts can help illuminate broad trends in policy, even if they were originally developed to explain discrete policy decisions.[19] Overall, one could say that when events, ideas, people, and politics line up in just the right way, a New Deal, a Great Society, or a Reagan Revolution is possible. Once one or more of the key inputs falls out of place, the "window of opportunity" for major change closes.

THE IMPORTANCE OF EARLY STAGES OF POLICY MAKING

Students of the policy process were long taught to think in terms of the stages of the policy-making process. Those stages begin with agenda setting and problem definition and continue to assembling and considering alternatives, enacting and then implementing policy, evaluating performance, and modifying the policy, where the cycle begins anew. It is evident that control of agenda setting and problem definition are extremely valuable, as they "set the table" for subsequent policy adoption.

One theme we will follow is how, in the press of ideas, events, politics, and people, domestic policy issues rise and fall on the national agenda. Some issues are always, or almost always, at or near the top of the national agenda. The best example is the economy. It affects every American, and policy makers are (rightly or wrongly) held accountable by Americans for the economic performance of the nation. However, the specific economic issues that are of greatest concern shift—sometimes the issue is recession, sometimes inflation, sometimes both at once, sometimes international competitiveness, sometimes equality, sometimes reconversion to a peacetime economy after war. Other issues come and go, often in response to crises or other events. Energy, for example, was not a major national issue until the Arab oil boycott of 1973, was a matter of concern for the rest of the 1970s, and then mostly disappeared until 2000, when prices started rising again and environmental concerns led many Americans to hope for new energy policies. The environment was itself a nonissue, for the most part, until the 1960s; while it ebbs and flows, it has never fully receded from public view since then.

Moreover, the ability to define the public policy problem you are seeking to address is absolutely crucial, and scholar Eugene Bardach lists it as the first step in effective problem solving.[20] If you cannot do so, it is very difficult to know what to do next. On the other hand, once the problem is defined, the range of potentially useful remedies is narrowed considerably.

In some ways, it seems as though it should be relatively easy to define the problem that public policy needs to address. In the 1930s, everyone knew that the problem was the Depression. However, problem definition is not as easy as it seems. Policy makers often operate in an environment of ambiguity.[21] Most of the time, the nation is not facing a single overriding problem but rather a variety of lesser problems competing for attention. Moreover, no matter how few or many problems there are, problem definition frequently becomes quite contentious once one gets below the obvious surface. In the 1930s, the Depression was the prime problem, but that only led to the next question, which sought to get at the root of the problem and hence to possible solutions: Why did the Depression happen?

Franklin Roosevelt and liberal Democrats concluded that the Depression was the result of the free market running amok. In this view, too much greed, speculation, and income inequality led to a stock market crash and the subsequent contraction of the economy.[22] Given this interpretation of the cause of the Depression, their solution—more powerful centralized government to regulate the economy and guarantee economic rights and well-being to those at the bottom of society—followed logically. However, other interpretations have blamed the Depression on poor monetary policy by the Federal Reserve Board, protectionist trade policy, or other government interventions gone awry.[23] If one accepts these theories, the New Deal solutions begin to look like a much less logical policy response.

THE DIFFICULTY OF ASSESSING OUTCOMES

In a similar vein, proposed policy departures are frequently judged in light of whether the current policies are considered broadly successful by policy makers and participants in the political process. In practice, determining the success or failure of a policy is often much easier said than done.[24] Why? First, there is not always an agreed-upon standard for what constitutes "success." Perhaps to enact the policy, a broad political coalition reached agreement on the policy itself but not on the goals associated with it, which were left deliberately vague. Even without politically inspired ambiguity, the criteria for evaluation are frequently unclear. Is it any improvement in conditions at all? A certain level of improvement? An improvement that is proportionate to the cost? Merely mitigating a worsening situation? The Obama-era American Recovery and Reinvestment Act, or "stimulus" plan, was the source of great debate on these grounds. Obama argued that the stimulus "created or saved" three million jobs and was a success; critics considered it a failure because the unemployment rate continued rising and was higher with the stimulus than its supporters had claimed in early 2009 it would be if the stimulus did not pass.[25] Second, it is not always easy to collect accurate information about the results, or to draw accurate inferences from that data. Even if there is a common understanding about what outcome constitutes success, if you do not have adequate data on the outcome, it will be difficult to reach agreement. Other obstacles may interfere with assessment, including biases based on differing time horizons, local effects that are improperly generalized, or a particular cultural lens. Not least, political values are always part of the equation. The success or failure of a policy depends on whether the policy meets its goals, but "[s]ociety's goals, taken in total, are fundamentally a collective ethical problem and hence cannot be easily determined."[26] If a particular program reduces poverty or improves economic growth, but some people judge it to have done so in the process of violating fundamental American values of liberty or fairness, those people might well consider it a failure. The Reagan economic expansion in the 1980s was praised by some as a success of American liberty, while others condemned it for coming at the expense of economic equality.[27] As a result, differing interpretations of whether a policy succeeded or failed—and the degree to which it did so—is the norm in policy debates.

THE LAW OF UNANTICIPATED CONSEQUENCES

The importance of unanticipated consequences in social action was noted by sociologist Robert K. Merton in 1936.[28] Today, any good study of public policy makes a note of the importance of uncertainty in the policy-making process. Indeed, one of the most predictable features of policy making is that something unpredictable—or at any rate unpredicted by the policy makers—will result. In any political society as large and as complex as the United States, policy will affect individuals, groups, and institutions in some ways that are surprising. Sometimes those "unanticipated consequences" will be in addition to the consequences policy makers hoped to accomplish; sometimes they will be entirely in place of what policy makers had hoped. Sometimes the surprises are pleasant, sometimes they are neutral, but often they are unpleasant. The attempt to grapple with the negative unanticipated consequences of previous policy decisions is often part of the agenda for future policy. You cannot understand past policy development, nor should you try to advocate future policy departures, without being acutely aware of the law of unanticipated consequences.

For example, in an attempt to reduce the federal deficit, the Budget Enforcement Act of 1990 included a steep "luxury tax" on yachts and expensive automobiles. However, the tax discouraged buyers and led to a sharp decline in yacht sales and, ultimately, in employment by boat builders. Revenue from the tax was outweighed by lost revenue from decreased economic activity, and in 1993 the tax was repealed.[29] Similarly, while economists are divided on the question, there is evidence that large increases in the minimum wage, meant to help low-wage workers, have the effect of reducing employment and overall wages.[30]

IMPACT OF THE WORLD

Although this study will focus on domestic policy, we cannot ignore events abroad altogether. The reason is simple. Sometimes domestic policy is significantly affected by world events and international challenges to the United States. This can happen in several ways. Foreign crises can push domestic reform proposals off the national agenda, or can affect elections in ways that have important domestic policy implications. Events abroad can cause Americans to look at domestic issues in a different light (Nazi atrocities in World War II had that effect on American attitudes toward race[31]). And the US response can have a domestic as well as international component. The first major federal expenditure on K–12 education was a response to Soviet advances in the Space Race, and took the form of legislation called the National Defense Education Act. Indeed, historians and political scientists have long noted the transformational impact of war and international conflict on the domestic ordering of society, from politics to economics to social relationships to demographics.[32] The postwar baby boom, for example, had major consequences for American society and public policy.[33]

THE PLAN OF THIS BOOK

Each of these themes—inputs and outputs of public policy, shifting agendas, the importance of problem definition, the difficulty of assessing outcomes, the law of unanticipated consequences, and the impact of international affairs—will be considered in light of policy development since the New Deal. The organization of this study will rely on eras delineated by a presidential administration or series of presidential administrations. This is, of course, not the only way such a study could be structured. One could pick themes or policy areas and organize chapters that way. One could also simply give a chapter to each president, or organize around congressional rather than presidential policy eras. So why do it this way?

First, given how much new public policy is built on previous public policy efforts, a chronological structure makes sense. To understand the place of the Medicare prescription drug program of 2003, one has to understand the creation of Medicare in 1965. To understand Medicare, one has to understand the Social Security Act of 1935, Franklin Roosevelt's "Economic Bill of Rights," and Harry Truman's unsuccessful drive for national health insurance after World War II.

Second, since at least the New Deal, it has become the norm for Americans to expect the president to provide policy leadership. Nearly every president comes to office having pledged himself to a program, and the most dramatic public policy changes are usually connected to a president. However, presidents are far from the sole actors. Congress *is* important, and there have been long periods of congressional policy making that sometimes coincide with and sometimes conflict with what the president wants to do. So, this book is organized roughly into eras delineated by one or more presidents, recognizing that not every president is equally important to policy development, that sometimes extended periods of relative stability (or gridlock) separate short bursts of major policy change, and that the politics of the situation are always a critical input.

As a brief history of public policy since the New Deal, this study will not delve deeply into every policy area. But it will strive to provide both a solid foundation in the big picture of public policy and some useful frameworks for understanding public policy as you go forward as students and citizens.

1

The New Deal

★ ★ ★

Courtesy Everett Collection Inc./Alamy Stock Photo

On August 14, 1935, Franklin D. Roosevelt signed the Social Security
Act, launching the federal government's social welfare system.
The Act established the Social Security old-age pension system,
unemployment insurance, cash welfare for poor families,
and other programs.

THE NEW DEAL IS A GOOD place to start any study of modern American public policy. It established a new presumption of government activism, a new set of federal programs and bureaucratic structures, and a new relationship between citizens and the federal government. In many ways, the New Deal was a bloodless revolution that replaced a decentralized, limited government with a powerful central authority. In 1900, federal spending was equivalent to about 3 percent of the economy, and the post office was the most direct connection most Americans had to Washington. By 1950, federal spending approached 20 percent of GDP, and the federal government affected Americans through innovations including federal deposit insurance, unemployment benefits, public works, and old-age benefits. The political coalitions occasioned by the New Deal lasted for decades, and the policy debates stirred up in that era continue to drive much of the policy agenda even today. The New Deal's defenders have seen it as a timely intervention that rescued the nation from the worst of the Depression, strengthened the position of the "forgotten man" in American life, and laid the foundation for a more just economic order. Its critics see the New Deal as a policy failure that delayed recovery, undermined the Constitution, and led to an unhealthy dependency of the American people on government programs. Ideas, events, personalities, and politics combined to produce what was, outside of Civil War and Reconstruction, the biggest set of domestic policy changes in American history.

The identity of the event is obvious: the Great Depression. In September 1929, the US stock market suffered a dramatic decline, wiping out savings and driving scores of stock brokers and investors to suicide. The stock market crash was both the result of a weakening economy and connected to a financial crisis that dried up credit, grinding the economy to a halt. By 1932, industrial production had fallen 53 percent, business construction was down 84 percent, and about one in four Americans who wanted a job was unemployed. The banking system teetered, with 4,000 banks failing in 1933 alone. Tent cities of homeless Americans arose. About 1,500 colleges went broke; in 1932, schools in New York City were closed because the city could not afford to pay teachers and the Chicago public libraries were unable to purchase a single book. The Empire State Building, which opened in 1931, was able to rent out only one-third of its space.[1]

The Great Depression, as it came to be known, may have been the most severe economic shock to have ever jolted the nation, and economic discontent was clearly the fuel that fed the fire of the New Deal. Yet, by itself, the Depression is not an adequate explanation for the policy response of the New Deal. It was not the first such jolt the country had experienced. To the contrary, depressions (a term that denotes economic contraction combined with extreme deterioration of the financial system) had gripped the nation in 1837, 1873–1879, 1893–1896, 1907, and as recently as 1920–1921. In the depression of 1893, unemployment probably reached 20 percent, close to the Great Depression's peak of 25 percent. However, no policy response resembling the New Deal resulted.

A full explanation of the New Deal has to proceed into the territory of ideas, people, and politics. For one thing, the 1930s represented the culmination of a long period of development of ideas extolling an activist government. Those ideas were put forward by forces as diverse as the populists, the progressives, the socialists of Eugene V. Debs, and liberals of the 1920s, such as John Dewey.

The populists were a group of agrarian reformers in the late nineteenth century who organized politically to fight for regulation of banks and railroads and an inflated currency. Some populists even demanded government ownership of railroads and telegraphs.[2] The populists were defeated as "radicals" in the 1890s, but their commitment to interventionist government lived on.

Around 1900, the progressive movement arose. Where populists were usually rural, progressives were usually middle-class urban reformers. Much of their program had to do with making governmental processes less dependent on representative concepts of government and on political parties and more dependent on direct democracy or on unelected bureaucratic experts.[3] The New Deal would depend heavily on the progressives' concept of administration by experts. The progressives also had a broader theoretical perspective that was very influential among New Dealers. Progressive theorists such as Charles Merriam contended that the American founding was outdated, that limited government was no longer a viable model, and that the nation needed a "living Constitution" rather than a Constitution with fixed meaning. Merriam stressed that the revolutionary theory of natural rights was "discredited and repudiated" and that "the only limitations on governmental action are those dictated by experience or the needs of the time."[4]

In the view of progressives, public power (i.e., government) must serve as a counterweight to the growth of private economic power— all the more since they declared that property rights were not, as the founders had believed, a fundamental element of human rights but rather in tension with human rights.[5] However, there were important differences of opinion among progressives about how this vision should be realized. In the 1912 presidential campaign, Woodrow Wilson argued for breaking up concentrations of economic power and empowering those with less economic power; former president Theodore Roosevelt held that government should accept the consolidation of large concentrations of economic power as inevitable and then regulate them heavily.[6] This division, too, would reappear in the New Deal. For its part, Roosevelt's Progressive Party (or "Bull Moose" Party) endorsed social insurance for unemployment or old age, and Wilson's "War Democracy" during World War I offered a template for national economic planning by way of the War Industries Board.

Coinciding with the progressive movement was the rise of Eugene V. Debs' Socialist Party, which won 6 percent of the vote in 1912, appealing mostly to labor. Debs called for state ownership of factories, a position that is almost as radical today as it was then. He also demanded stronger protections for labor, such as the right to organize unions, a legal minimum wage and maximum to the number of hours that people could work, and provisions for workplace safety.[7] Many of these ideas would be adopted as part of the New Deal program in the 1930s.

During the 1920s, thinkers on the American left calling themselves "liberals" combined some of these themes, holding that principles of government should not be fixed but should constantly evolve. Before that time, the term "liberal" signified a political philosophy favoring limited government and free markets. Thinkers including John Dewey, on the other hand, held that "[n]o man and no mind was ever emancipated merely by being left alone. Removal of formal limitations is but a negative condition; positive freedom is not a state but an act which involves methods and instrumentalities for control of conditions."[8]

Not least, by the early 1930s, active state direction of the economy and a collectivist, rather than individualistic, ethos was ascendant abroad. In Great Britain, the economist John Maynard Keynes argued that laissez-faire, or free market, economics was no longer viable. In Keynes's view, government should take an active role in stimulating the economy through deficit spending during recessionary times.[9] Elsewhere, statism was taking a totalitarian turn. In Italy, the Fascist dictator Benito Mussolini came to power in 1922 and declared an end to the "night watchman" state. Mussolini's economic doctrine, known as "corporatism," rejected individualism in favor of a controlled economy directed by agreement of key groups in society—business, labor, and (especially) government. By 1932, Josef Stalin had imposed collectivized agriculture and central industrial planning in the Soviet Union. In Germany, Communists and National Socialists sought their own version of state economic control. Policy makers were clearly operating in a world in which free markets were passing out of fashion and state economic control in a variety of forms was gaining momentum. Defenders of the New Deal would later argue that it was a moderate alternative that saved the nation from totalitarianism; critics would see it as an Americanized version of the same collectivist disease afflicting the Old World.

As factors leading to policy making, ideas and events are most powerful when they magnify each other. The Great Depression and the ideas of interventionist government reinforced each other. Earlier depressions did not lead to an upsurge in government activism, because the intellectual environment was still strongly committed to ideas of limited government and property rights.

The New Deal was also made possible by the political circumstances of the time. From the election of Abraham Lincoln in 1860 until 1932, the Republican Party was the dominant organized political force in America. During that period, Republicans won 14 of 18 presidential elections. In that same period, Republicans held the majority in the US House of Representatives for 48 of 72 years and the Senate for 62 of 72 years. In the years after Woodrow Wilson left office in 1921, Democrats were deeply divided between their urban wing dominated by northern ethnic Catholics and their rural wing dominated by southern Protestants; in 1924, the Democratic National Convention took 103 ballots to pick a presidential nominee. Republicans had also been divided between their progressives and their conservative wing, but had maintained control nonetheless.

The Democratic presidential comeback of 1932 was anticipated (and helped along) by Democratic success in the preceding midterm elections. In the 1930 congressional elections, Democrats gained 52 House seats and 8 Senate seats. This was enough to give them a small partisan majority in the House by the time Congress convened, as well as a working majority in the Senate in combination with progressive Republicans and independents. Since they already controlled the Solid South, these gains came in the North, making the composition of the Democratic Party in Congress more liberal. In 1932, Democrats swept into the presidency with 57 percent of the vote for FDR and gained another 97 seats in the House and 12 in the Senate. This meant that Franklin Roosevelt began his presidency with the impetus of a crisis, with an apparent electoral mandate of his own, and with a very large partisan majority in Congress behind him.

This brings us to the people of the New Deal. Without a question, the dominant figure was Roosevelt himself.[10] Born into a wealthy New York family, FDR had served as Woodrow Wilson's assistant secretary of the navy, ran as the Democratic nominee for vice president in 1920, and was finishing his second term as governor of New York when he was nominated for president in 1932. In 1921, he was afflicted with polio, an experience that most biographers believe made him deeper and more tenacious. As governor, he gained a reputation for supporting an activist government response to the Depression at the state level. Roosevelt won the Democratic presidential nomination against foes who were formidable but represented only part of the Democratic formula for victory: 1928 Democratic nominee Al Smith, whose strength was in the northern urban wing, and House Speaker John Nance Garner of Texas, whose strength was in the rural wing. FDR was able to build an electoral coalition that included both wings, a fact that helped him when governing as much as it did when running for nomination and election.

In the general election, Roosevelt attacked incumbent president Herbert Hoover for economic mismanagement and ran on a vague and eclectic Democratic platform calling for federal relief programs but also demanding protection of states' rights and a 25 percent across-the-board cut in federal spending. At the same time, he was an articulate advocate for a more interventionist federal government and began laying the groundwork for major policy departures. In the "Commonwealth Club Address," he argued that limited government was no longer an adequate guide. Rather than openly reject the American founding, as had been done by many progressive theorists, Roosevelt appropriated it for his own ends. He argued that the nation must shift from a "negative" understanding of rights to a "positive" understanding that required government action. Hence the right to life meant also the right to a good living; the right to property meant the right to be made secure in your savings through government bank regulation.[11] In executing this rhetorical maneuver, Roosevelt either adapted the founders to a new time (the view of his admirers) or used a rhetoric of apparent fealty to the founders in order to cover over a new and opposite ideology (the view of his detractors). In office, Roosevelt would gradually expand on these themes until offering a full vision of positive rights in his 1944 State of the Union address.

Due to the Depression, it was highly likely that the Democratic presidential nominee was going to prevail against Hoover in the general election. The fact that Roosevelt was that Democrat proved extremely important to policy development, and not only because of his special skills and personality traits. By 1934, Al Smith had repudiated the New Deal as a betrayal of the Democratic Party's small-government Jeffersonian heritage; by 1940, John Nance Garner, who served as Roosevelt's vice president from 1933 to 1941, had likewise turned against his boss, and ran for president again as representative of a conservative Democratic backlash against the New Deal. Had either man been elected in 1932 instead of Roosevelt, the policy outcome might have been very different.

Hours before Franklin Roosevelt took office on March 4, 1933, Herbert Hoover remarked: "We are at the end of our rope. There is nothing more we can do."[12] Hoover was portrayed by Democratic candidates for decades after as a do-nothing president who let the Depression happen and cared little about the misery that Americans were enduring. Many historians have likewise portrayed him, in contrast to the activist FDR, as tied to an ideology of "rugged individualism" that prevented him from taking vigorous measures against the Depression. In actuality, Hoover owed more to the progressive wing of the Republican Party than to the conservative wing; conservatives like former president Calvin Coolidge mistrusted him. When the Depression began, Hoover attempted to maintain economic confidence through rhetorical pronouncements, and he put out of bounds a heavily centralized response. On the other hand, he encouraged business to keep wages high, a (mildly) interventionist policy that made it more difficult to regain economic equilibrium without high unemployment. He also signed the protectionist Smoot-Hawley Tariff, a significant jump in taxes levied on 900 imported goods, despite a letter signed by 1,028 economists urging him not to do so. This, too, was an activist policy, not one of neglect. In keeping with his principle of government actively coordinating a voluntary public response, Hoover prodded the private sector to establish a fund created by strong banks to shore up weak banks, while the new Federal Farm Board, created in the Agricultural Marketing Act, bought surplus agricultural products to prop up commodity prices. In the Reconstruction Finance Corporation, the federal government guaranteed loans to businesses threatened by bad economic conditions. Hoover also endorsed an impressive expansion of federal public works spending, products of which included the construction of the Bay Bridge and the Boulder Dam (later renamed the Hoover Dam). In 1932, under electoral pressure, Hoover even relented and signed a federal relief bill passed by the Democratic Congress after vetoing an earlier version. Many of these programs were voluntary and limited, and none of them solved the problems at which they were aimed. Viewed from a post–New Deal perspective, they were a relatively limited federal response to one of the greatest economic crises in American history. Looked at from the perspective of 1930, though, Hoover advocated a more active federal response to an economic downturn than had ever been proposed by any previous president.[13]

Among his other advantages, Roosevelt had a key advantage over Hoover and Republicans: he had a coherent account of the Depression that worked to undergird his new policy direction. In the view of Roosevelt and liberals more generally, the Depression was the result of unregulated speculation by investors and deeper structural deficiencies in the free-market economy. Most importantly, income inequality between the rich "plutocrats" and poor farmers and workers meant that there was not enough income at the bottom of the American economic pyramid to purchase the goods that were being turned out in mass production (the problem of "overproduction" or "underconsumption"). If unregulated capitalism caused the Depression, it was extended (in Roosevelt's interpretation) by the unwillingness of Hoover to use the full power of the federal government to address the crisis. If one accepted these propositions as true, the policy response was obvious, at least in broad outline. If an unregulated free market, income inequality, and government passivity caused and extended the Depression, then regulation, redistribution, and government activism could solve it.

Roosevelt's interpretation of the causes of the Depression are far from universally held today. One alternative school of thought, made famous by conservative economist Milton Friedman in his 1965 book *The Great Contraction*, points the finger at counterproductive monetary policy by the Federal Reserve Board. Friedman calculated that the Federal Reserve Board had taken actions that had reduced the nation's money supply by 27 percent in 14 years, producing massive deflation and the collapse of the financial system. In this view, it was not the free market that malfunctioned, but government control of the money supply; Hoover was more or less an irrelevant bystander.[14] Another interpretation is that the normal business cycle resulted in a recession in 1929, but that bad government policy turned the recession into a depression. That bad policy included contractionary monetary policy but also included Hoover interventions such as the high-wage policy, a 1932 tax increase that increased the top marginal tax rate from 25 percent to 63 percent, and, above all, the Smoot-Hawley Tariff. In this view, Hoover is to be criticized, but for being too much of an interventionist.[15] These critics compare Hoover's ineffective activist response to Warren Harding's response during the previous depression, which was to do nothing and allow the economy to reach its own equilibrium, from which point it quickly recovered.[16] Another understanding of the Great Depression points to factors mostly outside the realm of public policy altogether. This view emphasizes that economic growth in the 1920s was largely driven by the booming business in technological innovations such as the radio and (especially) mass-produced automobiles. However, by the end of the 1920s, most Americans had a radio and a car, and demand plummeted. Moreover, the farm sector was a drag on the economy throughout the 1920s.

Finally, some analysts pinpoint additional international factors, especially the international economic aftermath of the First World War. Here they note that the Depression was not just an American phenomenon, but a global downturn, so it makes sense to look to global explanations. The postwar economic structure rested on a shaky triangle. Germany was forced to pay war reparations to Britain and France; Britain and France had to pay back war loans made by the United States; and the United States invested in the German economy. When the global economy slowed, Germany stopped making reparations payments, the allies stopped paying back their war debts, and the United States stopped investing in Germany. The Smoot-Hawley tariff drove the final nail into international trade, and the whole international house of cards collapsed.[17]

Except for a sense among many observers that the Depression required an international response, most of these alternative explanations did not emerge until decades later, much too late to affect the debate over the New Deal. While the ineffectiveness of Hoover's response was immediately apparent, the degree to which it represented an unprecedented degree of government activism has not been a dominant theme. Hoover himself could no more argue that he had made the Depression worse through ineffective or counterproductive interventionism than he could concede Roosevelt's charge that he had made it worse by neglect. In the end, Hoover seemed to have been a well-meaning man bowled over by an event he could not fathom, and his party looked no better.

THE FIRST NEW DEAL

Altogether, when Franklin D. Roosevelt took the oath of office, the stage was set for a major shift in domestic policy. There was a "window of opportunity" for non-incremental change. Roosevelt's response took several forms, and is usually divided by historians into three stages: the First, Second, and Third New Deals. Roosevelt had as objectives the "three Rs": relief, recovery, and reform ...... immediate assistance to those hurt most by the Depression. *Recovery* meant putting the nation back on a path of economic growth and high employment. *Reform* meant making structural changes in the economy so as to minimize the probability of a future depression. In contrast, Hoover had concentrated almost wholly—though unsuccessfully—on recovery.

In what is now known as the First New Deal, Roosevelt addressed all three Rs.[18] His approach was clearly influenced by the progressives and other earlier advocates of interventionist government. Indeed, he formed a "Brains Trust" of intellectual advisors, most of whom had progressive backgrounds (the most prominent were Raymond Moley, Adolph A. Berle Jr., and Rexford Tugwell). In the First New Deal, Roosevelt was most consistent with the strand of 1912 progressivism represented by his distant cousin Theodore. FDR accepted large concentrations of economic power, moving to regulate them and bring them under some central direction.

In a flurry of legislative and executive activity that began the day after he was inaugurated, FDR and Congress moved to stabilize the economy. On March 5, the president claimed emergency powers to declare a "Bank Holiday," closing down banks until they could be certified safe by bank examiners; he followed this action a month and a half later by taking US currency off the gold standard, a move that allowed greater currency expansion. On March 9, Congress convened for the famous "Hundred Days Session" that saw the enactment of sweeping economic legislation. Among the key acts aimed at recovery or stabilization were the Emergency Banking Act, which extended Hoover's Reconstruction Finance Corporation and provided federal aid to private banks; the Agricultural Adjustment Act (AAA), which organized farmers to control production levels collectively with the aim of maintaining high commodity prices; and the National Industrial Recovery Act, which created the National

Recovery Administration (NRA). The National Industrial Recovery Act suspended antitrust legislation and aimed to use industrial "codes" to set production levels, control prices, and negotiate labor practices. Former industrial competitors would establish cartels that would agree on market shares and prices. In exchange for this power, business agreed to some labor demands, including higher wages, maximum hours, collective bargaining, and abolition of child labor. By the summer of 1933, 557 industrial codes were in effect throughout the economy. Thus, in two broad strokes, the industrial and agricultural components of the economy were suddenly directed from Washington. The theory behind both the AAA and the NIRA was that competition was harmful, because it caused producers to hold down wages and minimized their own profits. Instead, the First New Deal would aim for economic harmony under government tutelage, an American form of corporatism. In many respects, the recovery portion of the First New Deal differed from Hoover's recovery program not in direction but in extent; Roosevelt retained Hoover's RFC, his agricultural production controls, and his high wage policy, but put coercive teeth into what were once more voluntary programs.

Roosevelt did not see the international economic environment as a key variable for recovery. In 1933, an international economic conference widely seen as the last chance for world governments to cooperate on a recovery plan collapsed, in no small part due to Roosevelt's disinterest. The president was unwilling to anger domestic constituencies by aiding efforts at international currency stabilization, much less relieving foreign war debts. In short, his program aimed at "recovery in one country."[19] (In this respect, he varied from Hoover, who had allowed a one-year war debts moratorium in 1931.)

At the same time, Roosevelt went far beyond Hoover's policies in relief and reform. During the Hundred Days, Congress passed the Federal Emergency Relief Act, which created the Federal Emergency Relief Administration (FERA). FERA provided $500 million as direct aid to states to provide relief for the unemployed. As part of the NIRA, the Public Works Administration (PWA) was also created, run by the Department of the Interior, to fund big public works projects such as hospitals and dams. One of the hallmark programs of the New Deal was also established at this time through the Emergency Conservation Work Act: the Civilian Conservation Corps (CCC). The CCC originally put to work unemployed young men, then older skilled workers, in what was sometimes called "a peacetime army." It ultimately employed three million men and planted three billion trees between 1933 and 1942. In November, FDR also created by executive order the Civil Works Administration (CWA), largely aimed at building transportation infrastructure, schools, and hospitals, to give people jobs during the winter of 1933–1934. During that period, the

CWA employed around four million men on public works. Congress and the president also agreed on several programs aimed at providing credit aid to farmers and homeowners who were facing foreclosure. In the Hundred Days, these included the Home Owners Refinancing Act and the Farm Credit Act; added later were the Farm Mortgage Refinancing Act and Federal Farm Bankruptcy Act of 1934, which placed a moratorium on farm foreclosures.

Roosevelt's reform efforts sought to rebuild the financial system to minimize the possibility of a repetition of the rolling financial collapse of 1929–1933. In the Hundred Day session, Congress passed the Securities Act, providing for federal regulation of stocks and bonds, and the Banking Act of 1933, which created the Federal Deposit Insurance Corporation (FDIC). Banks would pay into a fund that would insure the savings of depositors up to $2,500 (some later) bank runs. Following up on the Securities Act, Congress went on to pass the Securities Exchange Act of 1934. This Act established the Securities Exchange Commission (SEC), whose task is to monitor stock traders to ensure that they were dealing honestly and with their clients' best interests in mind. These reforms satisfied the demand for a more regulated marketplace, especially in the financial sphere, arising from the dominant interpretation of the causes of the Depression.

One other major policy departure was more difficult to categorize. The Tennessee Valley Authority (TVA), established in 1933, made the federal government an electricity producer for the first time as hydroelectric dams were built along the Tennessee Valley, where electricity had not yet reached most people. The TVA also got into the business of selling fertilizer to farmers. It was hence a public works program, a rural electrification program, an agricultural support program, and an experiment in regional economic planning all at once. Perhaps more than any other piece of the New Deal in this period, the TVA drew accusations of socialism.[20]

During the first year of the Roosevelt administration, one other issue was active. While the nation was grappling with the Depression, it was also deciding what to do about Prohibition. Roosevelt had run on a platform of repealing Prohibition, and the issue had received much attention during the campaign. By December 1933, the Twenty-First Amendment repealing Prohibition had been ratified, an example of the unanticipated negative consequences of policy leading to a rethinking.

As 1933 turned into 1934, the scorecard on the New Deal was mixed. The banking crisis had subsided, the economic free fall had been arrested, and national morale had improved. Stabilization had largely been achieved and significant relief had been provided, but there were few signs of genuine recovery. The international dimension of the crisis had not been addressed, and the high wage/high price strategy at the heart of the NRA and AAA amounted, in the words of one analyst, to "fighting scarcity with more scarcity."[21] The AAA forced farmers to slaughter hogs to keep prices up when millions of Americans were hungry. Labor objected that it was too limited by the NRA codes, small business complained that the codes favored big business, and big business saw itself as too hamstrung by regulation. At the same time, Wilsonian progressives complained that the NRA represented the end of antitrust efforts, and some Jeffersonian Democrats—Al Smith among them—grew worried that their party had veered too far from its small government traditions. With the 1934 elections in view, business and the Jeffersonians combined forces to form the Liberty League, an organization devoted to curtailing the New Deal by defeating pro–New Deal Democratic congressional candidates.

With unemployment still extremely high, others began to speak out against Roosevelt in a more demagogic tone. The mildest of these was Dr. Charles Townsend, who put forward what became known as the Townsend Plan: send a monthly $200 check to every American over 60 years of age, on the condition that the recipient had to spend it all. By 1935, 20 million Americans had signed a petition urging adoption of the Townsend Plan, which was (as Roosevelt and others knew) flatly impossible financially. Another was Father Charles Coughlin, the "Radio Priest," whose radio show was sometimes heard by as many as 10 million Americans. Coughlin started as a supporter of Roosevelt, but turned against him. In Coughlin's view, the Depression could be blamed on a conspiracy of Jews and bankers, and FDR had not done enough to fight them. Perhaps most consequential was Huey Long, governor of Louisiana. Long, who organized the state police into his personal paramilitary unit, was a fiery but folksy orator who expressed some admiration for Benito Mussolini and promised a program to "Share Our Wealth." His proposal consisted of liquidating all personal fortunes and redistributing the money in order to guarantee every American a $5,000 lump sum and a $2,500 annual income. Long also developed a substantial following.[22]

In this environment, the 1934 midterm elections turned into a referendum on the president. Vice President John Nance Garner predicted that Democrats would lose 37 seats in the House of Representatives in the midterms, while other observers believed losses would be higher.[23] In the end, Democrats won a slightly smaller percentage of House votes nationally in 1934 than they had in 1932, but because of the way votes were distributed, they gained nine seats in the House. They also gained nine seats in the Senate. The 1934 elections were the only midterm elections between 1862 and 1998 in which the president's party gained net seats in the House.

This political fact was hugely important, and drove policy in two ways. First, Roosevelt was widely perceived to have received an endorsement from the electorate; his leverage was enhanced, while the Liberty League was discredited and unable to influence policy development. Second, the Democratic congressional gains were mostly among liberal Democrats, and by some calculations there were now 35 House Democrats noticeably to the left of Roosevelt.[24] The campaign itself had irreparably breached the early accommodation between Roosevelt and business. This outcome both allowed Roosevelt to move policy to the left and put him under considerable pressure to do so.

THE SECOND NEW DEAL

These economic and political circumstances   after 1934 in a new direction. The result was the Second New Deal, a policy turn characterized by rhetorical hostility to business and wealth accompanied by an attempt to break up concentrations of wealth and equalize economic power among varying elements in society.[25] The Second New Deal represented a shift from Theodore Roosevelt's progressivism to Woodrow Wilson's. The search for a new approach was also necessary after the Supreme Court found both the National Industrial Recovery Act and the Agricultural Adjustment Act unconstitutional (in *Schechter v. U.S.* 1935 and *U.S. v. Butler* 1936). Congress, the court found, had overstepped its authority to regulate interstate commerce. Even had the court allowed the NIRA to stand, it was unlikely to be reauthorized by Congress due to its ineffectiveness and unpopularity.[26]

As the recovery programs of the First New Deal fell away, Roosevelt focused less on direct policy promotion of recovery. Instead, he redoubled efforts at relief and reform. Part of this strategy included a big new public works program, the Works Progress Administration (WPA), which was formed in the Emergency Relief Act of 1935. The WPA cost a previously unprecedented sum of $5 billion. Although it was focused on construction projects, it also offered federal jobs programs for actors, writers, musicians, and artists, and included a National Youth Administration that developed public works jobs for high school and college aged people. Where the Public Works Administration had spent money cautiously under the direction of Interior Secretary Harold Ickes, the WPA, headed by Harry Hopkins, spent with reckless abandon and gained a reputation for partisan politics. Other relief efforts were also notable. The Resettlement Administration was formed to relocate destitute farmers, in some cases creating entirely new planned communities (such as Greenbelt, Maryland). The Rural Electrification Act offered low-interest loans for rural electrification projects.

However, the two biggest policy departures in the second New Deal—and perhaps in the whole New Deal period—were reforms that fundamentally changed the American economy and the relationship of citizens to the federal government.

The first was passage of the Social Security Act in August 1935. Some form of social insurance against unemployment, poverty, and old age had long been a part of the policy debate. The first voluntary government social insurance scheme came in France in 1840. In 1889, Bismarck's Germany adopted mandatory government social insurance, a policy that was common in Europe by 1935. America had begun backing into such a system through pensions for Civil War veterans and their widows, which represented more than one-third of the federal budget in 1894. Teddy Roosevelt's Progressive Party endorsed social insurance in 1912. By 1929, six states had such programs, and Herbert Hoover proposed a $50 per month federal pension for retirees, though the idea was withdrawn from consideration after the crash. By 1935, pushed by the Depression and widespread victories by liberal Democrats at the state level, 30 states had such a program. However, these programs were typically quite limited. Nearly 9 of every 10 dollars in pensions were spent in only three states: California, New York, and Massachusetts.

In June 1934, FDR named a Committee on Economic Security, chaired by Labor Secretary Frances Perkins—the first female cabinet secretary—which drafted a proposal. Roosevelt forwarded the proposal to Congress in January 1935, and by August it had been enacted. A number of key issues had to be sorted out, especially in regard to old age pensions. Would the program be welfare paid from the general fund or an insurance program funded by a dedicated tax? Would everyone receive the same benefits, or would benefits be tied to work?

When the Social Security Act of 1935 was completed, it included the following pieces:

> Title I provided for aid to states to pay for welfare programs for the aged poor.
>
> Title II established a system of old-age pensions. A dedicated tax on wages and salaries (FICA) would be imposed at a rate of 1 percent for workers matched by 1 percent for their employers. The tax would begin in 1937, and would apply to the first $3,000 of income. Upon reaching 65 years of age, workers could retire and receive benefits ranging from $10 a month to $85 a month, depending on how much money was paid in. Benefits would start being paid out in 1942 (this was soon revised to 1940). Those retiring between 1937 and 1940 would receive a modest lump sum payment from the federal government.

Another title established a system of unemployment insurance; workers and employers would pay into a fund, from which workers would be paid a benefit if they became unemployed. Assistance programs were also created to provide security to various categories of the needy: Aid to Dependent Children (which later became Aid to Families with Dependent Children) was funded with the states to aid destitute mothers and children (usually widows or abandoned wives). Programs for the blind, the handicapped, and maternal and child health were also created.

Though the bill faced some difficulty in committee, on the floor of the House it passed 372–33 and on the floor of the Senate it passed 77–6. It has served as the core of the American welfare state ever since.

The second major structural reform of the Second New Deal was passage of the National Labor Relations Act, otherwise known as the Wagner Act (after its main sponsor, Senator Robert Wagner of New York). The National Industrial Recovery Act of 1933 had included a number of labor protections, but these had been nullified when the Supreme Court overturned the NIRA. To fill the gap, the Wagner Act guaranteed the right of unions to organize and to engage in collective bargaining. The National Labor Relations Board, which had been created in 1934, assumed the task of enforcing these rules. FDR approached the Wagner Act cautiously, endorsing it rather late in the legislative process. Nevertheless, his support was important to passage and had important political consequences, helping cement the ties of organized labor to the Democratic Party.

Between the two key reform acts—the Social Security Act and the Wagner Act—Roosevelt had moved to restructure the American economy to shift economic power both downward and upward. Social Security would establish an economic floor and the Wagner Act would make it possible for unions to negotiate better wages. The result, Roosevelt hoped, would be an end to "underconsumption" and (in the case of social insurance) the creation of a set of "automatic stabilizers" that would prevent a weak economy from entering a downward spiral. At the same time, the federal government's power over the economy was significantly expanded.

Most other key policies enacted in the Second New Deal were consistent with this approach. One was the Revenue Act of 1935, otherwise known as the Wealth Tax Act. Responding to the pressure coming from Huey Long, Roosevelt endorsed a big tax increase on the wealthy. The Act increased the estate and gift taxes, created a new graduated corporate income tax, and created an individual income tax rate of 75 percent on incomes over $5 million. In some ways, the Wealth Tax Act was theater, aimed at drawing away Long's audience with a largely symbolic strike against the rich. It directly affected relatively few people, brought in little revenue, and was not, as advertised, a tax on accumulated wealth but rather a tax on yearly income that left accumulated wealth largely undisturbed.

After the failure of NRA corporatism, federal anti-trust efforts were revived by the Federal Anti-Price Discrimination Act of 1935 (Robinson-Patman Act), which outlawed discriminatory pricing strategies used to undercut competition. The Public Utility Holding Company Act of 1935 aimed to break up the large holding companies that controlled American utility companies. The Banking Act of 1935 sought to break up private economic power by making the Federal Reserve System more centralized. Not least, the Walsh-Healy Act of 1936 set minimum labor standards for wages and hours in federal contracts, the opening wedge of a drive to impose such standards throughout the economy.

While Roosevelt did not openly embrace Keynesianism—and a face-to-face meeting with John Maynard Keynes was reportedly unproductive—Keynes's ideas of stimulating the economy by "priming the pump" and encouraging consumption at the bottom were carried out piecemeal. In 1935 and 1936, Roosevelt and Congress succeeded in dramatically changing the policy baseline. They had been given a "window of opportunity," and they had climbed through it with one bill after another. In so doing, they had also cut the ground out from under demagogues to their left.

Even then, it is important to note that Roosevelt did not get all that he wanted. The balancing mechanisms of the American system were never completely suspended. Social Security was considered a fraud by some on the left due to its connection to work and its relatively low benefits. Despite giant Democratic majorities, Congress did not give the White House the utilities "death penalty" or the degree of control it wanted over the Federal Reserve Board.

After nearly four years in office, Franklin Roosevelt had to face the voters. His opponent was Alf Landon, Republican governor of Kansas. Huey Long, much feared by Roosevelt, was not a factor in the election, having first been emasculated by Roosevelt's program and then assassinated by (it was proven much later) his own bodyguards. Landon ran a campaign calling for a balanced budget and warning against one-man rule; FDR responded by pointing to the New Deal's stabilization of the economy, its alleviation of misery, and its promises of economic security. Landon won Maine and Vermont; Roosevelt won everything else. In all, it was one of the greatest landslides in American history: 61 percent of the popular vote, 98 percent of the electoral vote, and an additional Democratic gain of 12 in the House and 5 in the Senate. This meant that Democrats had made gains in four consecutive congressional elections. Republicans had been reduced to a total of 16 Senators and 88 Representatives.

THE THIRD NEW DEAL

At the pinnacle of his success, Roosevelt had visions of extending the New Deal much farther. His hopes for a Third New Deal included seven more local versions of the Tennessee Valley Authority and more extensive national economic planning. In the end, he got much less than he had hoped. Why that was the case is an instructive lesson in the power of incrementalism.[27]

What he did get was not negligible. Perhaps most important, Congress passed the Fair Labor Standards Act of 1938. The Act expanded on the Walsh-Healy Act of two years before, applying a minimum wage and maximum hours nationally. (Some farm laborers and workers at small businesses remained exempt.) Congress also provided aid to tenant farmers, who had been left out of most prior agricultural acts; repassed a modified version of the AAA; and passed the National Housing Act of 1937, which committed the federal government to funding public housing for the first time. Then, the New Deal essentially ran out of steam.

Why? A confluence of personalities, events, and politics. First, FDR himself overreached. Flush with victory and enjoying a huge partisan majority in Congress, he asserted himself in ways that caused many Americans, including many Democrats, to fear that he wanted too much power. Frustrated with the Supreme Court's unwillingness to approve key elements of the New Deal, within weeks of his second inauguration Roosevelt proposed expanding the size of the Court. Ostensibly to reduce the workload on older justices, his proposal would have allowed him to appoint six new justices, swinging the Court to a pro–New Deal stance. The public reaction to this "court-packing" scheme was strongly negative, as critics assailed Roosevelt for threatening judicial independence, separation of powers, and the Constitution itself. The political environment depends on the national mood, not just the partisan balance in government. Congress never approved the plan. Roosevelt got his way practically, when the Court reversed course and upheld the National Labor Relations Act and the Social Security Act in separate 1937 cases. Nevertheless, FDR suffered political damage, and congressional skeptics of the New Deal were emboldened.

The president also provoked resistance when he decided, against custom, to intervene heavily in the 1938 Democratic party congressional primary elections. In several races, moderate or conservative Democratic opponents of the New Deal faced pro–New Deal challengers who had the open support of the president. Critics accused Roosevelt of seeking a party "purge," a particularly loaded term in 1938; in the Soviet Union at that moment, Stalin's purges were claiming the lives of hundreds of thousands of people. Between court packing and the purge, Roosevelt appeared to many to be dangerously power hungry and in need of checking.[28]

Events outside of his easy control also worked against Roosevelt. After having openly embraced the cause of organized labor, the president was embarrassed when the Congress of Industrial Organizations (CIO) began a series of sometimes-violent sit-down strikes in 1937. The public quickly turned against the strikers, and some blamed Roosevelt for labor's new aggressiveness. More important than the CIO strikes, though, was the onset of the "Roosevelt Recession," a recession inside the depression that wiped away most of the halting economic gains that had been made since 1933. The recession of 1937–1938 featured the third steepest industrial decline in US history; unemployment, which reached a low of 14.3 percent in 1937, was back up to 19 percent in 1938. As with the Great Depression itself, economists and historians debate the causes of the Roosevelt Recession. Liberals blame FDR's 1937 cutback in federal spending, while conservatives argue that the downturn was the result of his anti-business rhetoric and policies, the wearing off of the temporary spending stimulus, and the onset of Social Security and other taxes. (As a percentage of GDP, revenue in 1937 went up more than twice as much as spending declined.) Whatever the cause, the effect was to call Roosevelt's leadership into question.

Altogether, by 1938, the public had turned against further expansion of government power. A Gallup poll showed two-thirds of Americans saying that they wanted "a more conservative direction" in public policy.[29] The political result was catastrophic for any hopes of extending the New Deal. In the midterm elections of 1938, Democrats lost 81 seats in the House and 6 in the Senate—almost all of them northern, New Deal Democrats. On paper, FDR's party retained large majorities in both houses, but in reality, the revived Republicans in combination with emboldened conservative Democrats controlled Congress most of the time. This "conservative coalition" was a dominant feature of Washington for at least the next two decades.

As a result, 1939 was the first year since he took office when Roosevelt did not propose new reform legislation to Congress. Some New Deal programs were trimmed, congressional investigations harassed the administration for the first time, and it was widely assumed that FDR would, like all presidents before him, seek no third term.[30] As events abroad grew more threatening, Roosevelt devoted more attention to the world. Finally, in May 1940, Germany invaded France. Its military machine then subjugated France in six weeks, something it had not been able to do in four years of World War I. Choosing not to change horses in midstream, Democrats renominated Roosevelt and Americans reelected him, albeit with a shrunken majority. Absent the abrupt collapse of France, FDR might very well have been a two-term president whose final impression was of a failed recovery.

THE NEW DEAL AT WAR

The approach and arrival of war completely suspended the New Deal ardor for domestic reform. FDR himself declared that he had turned from "Dr. New Deal" into "Dr. Win-the-War." The WPA, CCC, NYA, and Federal Writers Project were all ended, and all energy was directed to the war effort. At the same time, however, war produced greater centralization and national economic planning than ever before, including wage and price controls, rationing of consumer goods, and central allocation of economic resources. These policies were devised and executed by a whole new set of bureaucracies, including the Supply and Priorities Allocation Board, the Office of Price Administration, the War Manpower Commission, the National War Labor Board, and the Office of War Mobilization. In this sense, many New Dealers saw the Second World War as a testing ground for the planned economy that they preferred. Some also saw it as vindication of Keynesian economics. As a result of the war, federal spending skyrocketed by a factor of 10 and the number of federal civilian employees quadrupled. From 1939 to 1944, gross national product (GNP), a key measure of the size of the economy, grew from $88.6 billion to $198.7 billion, while a total of 17 million jobs were created during the war.[32]

Moreover, the war saw the development of what many call the "national security state." The failure of appeasement and isolationism to stem Axis aggression, culminating in the terrible shock of Pearl Harbor, resulted in a new willingness by Americans to maintain a permanent security structure and a long-term military and diplomatic engagement with the rest of the world. The primary effects of this change were in foreign and security policy, but it had important domestic implications that would play themselves out in the decades after the war.

One of those implications was budgetary. In 1935, at the time of the adoption of the Wealth Tax, only 5 percent of Americans paid income tax. Under the fiscal pressures of war, the Revenue Act of 1942 created a new 5 percent tax rate starting at only $624 income; by the end of the war, three quarters of Americans were paying income tax. To help Americans cope with the demands of the income tax, the federal government adopted income tax withholding, or the practice of automatically deducting some income tax from each paycheck rather than, as before, expecting taxpayers to pay the full amount due at the time tax forms were filed. These innovations—a much broader income tax that touched most

Americans and a withholding system that made possible higher rates—never went away when war ended and financed much of the subsequent expansion of domestic government.[33]

There were at least three other significant long-term effects of war on domestic public policy. First, wage and price controls led business and labor to seek alternative ways of compensating workers. This desire led the Internal Revenue Service to declare that employer-provided health insurance could be tax deductible. Driven by the tax deductibility of employer-provided insurance, the health care system that emerged was one in which most Americans received insurance through their employer, rather than as individuals (as most Americans purchase automobile or homeowners insurance), and in which Americans made most health care decisions with no clear idea of the costs involved because costs were covered by third-party insurers.[34]

Second, World War II clearly had a catalytic effect on civil rights in America. The bravery of black servicemen forced greater introspection by white Americans, as did the horrifying consequences of the theories of racial superiority espoused by the National Socialists in Germany. Prior to the war, Franklin Roosevelt had been mostly quiet about civil rights, though First Lady Eleanor Roosevelt stirred some controversy by promoting black rights. Indeed, one unsavory aspect of the New Deal was that it rested on an alliance between Roosevelt and segregationist southern Democrats. However, as war loomed, FDR issued an executive order creating the Fair Employment Practice Committee to stop racial discrimination in defense-related employment. Blacks themselves sensed growing power, and racial tensions grew. Black organizations threatened to march on Washington in 1941, only to pull back; in 1943, race riots broke out in Detroit between white residents and blacks who had arrived to work in the defense plants springing up around the city. More substantial action on civil rights—and deeper tensions—would come in the future, but the Second World War can be seen as the starting point of the ultimately successful drive for civil rights.[35]

Third, the war produced one of the most notable demographic shifts in American history. When US servicemen began returning home after the war, the result was the "baby boom"—a demographic bulge of Americans born between 1946 and 1966. By the early 1950s, the bulge was forcing Americans to rethink public policy toward schools. Since then, it has affected nearly every area of public policy.[36]

Not least, World War II kept the New Deal flame flickering by keeping Franklin Roosevelt in office. Rather than retiring as the architect of a failed economic recovery, Roosevelt died on the verge of victory in the biggest war in human history. Ten months before winning his fourth consecutive election as president of the United States, FDR laid out his hopes for a liberal resurgence after the war. In his 1944 State of the Union message, he contended that the nation should commit itself to an "Economic Bill of Rights" that would parallel the political Bill of Rights found in the Constitution. "We have come to a clear realization of the fact," Roosevelt told a national radio audience, "that true individual freedom cannot exist without economic security and independence." Among these rights were, according to FDR,

> The right to a useful and remunerative job in the industries or shops or farms or mines of the Nation;
>
> The right to earn enough to provide adequate food and clothing and recreation;
>
> The right of every farmer to raise and sell his products at a return which will give him and his family a decent living;
>
> The right of every businessman, large and small, to trade in an atmosphere of freedom from unfair competition and domination by monopolies at home or abroad;
>
> The right of every family to a decent home;
>
> The right to adequate medical care and the opportunity to achieve and enjoy good health;
>
> The right to adequate protection from the economic fears of old age, sickness, accident, and unemployment;
>
> The right to a good education.

"All of these rights spell security," Roosevelt contended. "And after this war is won we must be prepared to move forward, in the implementation of these rights, to new goals of human happiness and well-being."[37] Roosevelt had fleshed out more fully the theory of positive economic rights that he had outlined in his 1932 Commonwealth Club address. Roosevelt's "Economic Bill of Rights" would become a veritable checklist for future Democratic presidents and congresses intent on completing Roosevelt's work.

THE NEW DEAL, PUBLIC POLICY, AND POLITICAL INSTITUTIONS

The New Deal also produced outcomes that were institutional in character, or what Theodore Lowi would call "constitutive" policy. These were deep changes in the way American government operated, and they were closely intertwined with the policy debates. Altogether, Roosevelt and the New Dealers hoped to build the institutional capacity for an activist federal government that would plan and take responsibility for economic conditions.

One important institutional output was the strengthening of the presidency. In many respects, Franklin Roosevelt can be considered the first modern president.[38] He set the precedent of coming into office with an ambitious agenda demanding legislative action in the "First Hundred Days." (Of course, this is also a problem for presidents, few of whom are able to inspire Congress to act so decisively in the absence of a depression.) Roosevelt's aggressive posture with Congress continued after the Hundred Days, as he regularly maintained a list of "must pass" bills and ultimately set a record for the number of vetoes (635). He changed expectations in other ways, too, most notably his use of direct communication with Americans (such as the "fireside chats" on radio) and by assuming responsibility for national economic conditions. There were limits to this expansion of presidential power, which sometimes provoked a backlash. Nevertheless, it is clear that Franklin Roosevelt cast a long shadow over the presidency.

Not only did Roosevelt strengthen the office of the president; he strengthened the executive branch as a whole. The key moment came in 1939, when the Executive Office of the President (EOP) was created. The EOP guaranteed the president a large and loyal staff that was independent of the permanent bureaucracies of the cabinet departments. More generally, FDR announced "the age of enlightened administration," and realized much of the progressives' desire for government by a vast, powerful, and insulated (critics said unaccountable) bureaucracy. The New Deal also accomplished a significant change in the federal structure of American government. Prior to the 1930s, the federal government was generally assumed to be a government of limited and enumerated powers, while the states were the holders of substantial residual powers of government. Accordingly, in peacetime, total spending by state and local governments was about twice as big as the federal budget. Moreover, it was assumed that there was and should be a fairly clear line of division between the responsibilities of each level of government (what is sometimes called "dual federalism" or "layer-cake federalism"). The New Deal changed this relationship substantially, first by asserting that the federal government should be the activist leader of policy and next by creating a range of programs that involved a mixing of federal and state responsibilities. For example, the Aid to Dependent Children welfare program was federally funded, but states determined some benefit levels and administered the program locally. As this model was implemented in more and more programs, it gradually produced what some have called "cooperative federalism" or "marble cake federalism."[39]

More broadly, the New Deal represented a practical redefinition, without formal amendment, of the Constitution. In order to accomplish this redefinition, Roosevelt had to make the public argument for "positive rights" that were different from the original natural rights basis of the Constitution without openly seeming to repudiate it. He also had to change the attitude of Congress toward its constitutional duties. In 1935, during the debate over the Bituminous Coal Act, Roosevelt advanced the argument, never before heard from a president, that Congress should not concern itself with the constitutionality of the act but only with its desirability from a policy standpoint. Thus began a revolution in the way Congress viewed constitutional questions. Finally, FDR had to bypass the judiciary or persuade it to defer to his new view. This proved the most difficult, but by the end of 1937, this too was accomplished.

NEW DEAL: SUMMARY AND ASSESSMENT

The New Deal aimed for a combination of relief, ...d reform. In total, it produced the biggest change in federal public policy between the Civil War and the present.

Economic policy

Under Franklin Roosevelt, the federal government became much more active in spending, taxing, and regulating. From 1930 to 1940 federal spending as proportion of the economy tripled, growing from 3.5 percent of GDP to 10.4 percent.[40] Prior to 1939, when spending for defense preparation began to grow, almost all of this increase took place in domestic spending. A corporatist policy in the form of the National Industrial Recovery Act gave way to a policy aimed at breaking up concentrations of (private) economic power. While Franklin Roosevelt did not formally embrace Keynesianism, his policies generally reflected its interventionist assumptions. Pages in the *Federal Register*, compiling proposed regulations, enacted regulations, and executive orders, grew steadily from 2,620 in volume 1 (1936) to 6,877 in 1941. Regulation of the financial sector sought to protect people's savings and prevent a future depression. During the war years of 1942–1945, the *Federal Register* more than doubled in size, owing to wartime economic regulation.

Social welfare

The New Deal saw the creation of the national welfare state, most notably through the Social Security Act. Many other measures including public works jobs programs, rural electrification, and mortgage assistance programs could be considered social welfare programs. Moreover, in his 1944 State of the Union address, Franklin Roosevelt laid out a blueprint for a much more extensive welfare state. In addition to what government began doing, the New Deal was notable for what it required the private sector to do. The National Labor Relations Act protected union organizing and collective bargaining; the Fair Labor Standards Act established nationwide maximum hours/minimum wages rules. Theodore Lowi's distributive, redistributive, and regulatory policies overlapped and intertwined. Redistribution became a major goal of policy for the first time.

Civil rights
Though little progress toward civil rights was made in the 1930s, with the approach of war, Roosevelt established the Fair Employment Practice Committee to enforce non-discrimination in war industries. The war itself also changed the way many Americans looked at race.

Education
Although federal power grew significantly in many areas, education was not one of them. Traditions of local control of education remained strong. However, FDR put education on the long-term federal policy agenda by adding "good education" to his proposed "economic bill of rights."

Environment
In the Depression, economic development had priority over environmental protection; once war came, victory against the Axis powers had priority. And there was no large environmentalist movement pressuring lawmakers. However, many New Dealers looked back to progressive-era conservation as an important policy goal. This orientation manifested itself in the Civilian Conservation Corps, but the CCC was as much a depression-fighting instrument as it was an effort at conservation.

Moral/cultural issues
Once Prohibition was repealed in the first year of the New Deal, the "police power" over moral issues reverted to state and local governments, whose policies were undergirded by a broad cultural consensus on moral issues.

Federalism
Along with the growth of executive power, the reformulation of intergovernmental relations was the major instance of constitutive policy. By expanding the economic responsibilities of the federal government, the New Deal changed the nature of the federal system in fundamental ways. Constitutional barriers to federal aggrandizement—including attention to the limits placed by the enumeration of powers—were lowered, and the federal government started providing large sums in grants to state and local governments. From 1932 to 1940, the federal government's share of total government spending rose from 32.4 to 45 percent, while the

local government share fell from 51.3 percent to 37.6 percent (the state share remained roughly even, at a bit more than 16 percent).[41] The nation took a major step toward "cooperative federalism" or "marble-cake federalism." Federal involvement became increasingly intertwined with state and local responsibilities.

As a whole, the New Deal was the product of a process that looks quite a bit like the change frameworks of **punctuated equilibrium** or **multiple streams**. It was made possible by a combination of **inputs** working together: a traumatic national **event** (the Great Depression); a set of **ideas** from populists, progressives, socialists, and liberals, synthesized by Franklin Roosevelt, advancing a new conception of government and rights; a **political environment** featuring a... ...ized Democratic majority at all levels of government supported by the labor movement; and people, along with the leadership of Roosevelt, with his particular personality, experience, and political gifts. Other individuals such as Eleanor Roosevelt, Harold Ickes, Harry Hopkins, Frances Perkins, the Brains Trust, and even Huey Long and Charles Townsend also played an important part in the outcome. From 1937 on, the Supreme Court drifted into the background and ceased to effectively challenge the New Deal. In most areas of policy, the "**baseline**" consisted of a blank slate—a long tradition of federal non-intervention, meaning few existing programs to constrain policy makers. When some key inputs changed, domestic reform ran up against the roadblock of the "Roosevelt recession," the 1938 elections, and the approach of war.

Although the New Deal turned out to be a genuine departure from the past, matching the framework of punctuated equilibrium or multiple streams better than that of incrementalism, not even the New Deal completely escaped the gravity of path dependence: The high-wage recovery strategy of the New Deal in 1933–1935 clearly borrowed heavily from Hoover's strategy, and Hoover's Reconstruction Finance Corporation continued giving loans to promote stabilization and recovery until it was disbanded in 1957. Later stages of the New Deal also built on earlier stages. The Wagner Act built on labor provisions in the National Industrial Recovery Act; the Fair Labor Standards Act built on the Walsh-Healy Act, which itself borrowed other provisions from the NIRA.

Though Roosevelt deliberately sought "recovery in one country," **international events** ended up having a large impact on the New Deal and on domestic public policy more generally. The international trend against free-market, limited-government liberalism was part of the intellectual environment. War ended domestic reform efforts but also bolstered national economic planning, gave a long-term boost to civil rights, and even inadvertently reshaped the American health care system. War also ensured that FDR would be reelected in 1940 and 1944.

The **policy agenda** from 1933 to 1939, though filled with an explosion of proposed programs and an "alphabet soup" of new agencies, was uncluttered in another respect. No issue came close to dealing with the Depression as a topic of public concern, especially after Prohibition was disposed of by the Twenty-First Amendment.

The ability of Roosevelt and liberals to win the battle for **defining the problem**—in this case, the causes of the Depression—aided them considerably in their attempt to change public policy. Without a compelling alternative to their story of the Depression as a result of unregulated capitalism, a majority of Americans were willing to support policies that promised to regulate it and redistribute its fruits. The New Dealers' ability to reformulate the Constitution and national political values also gave them an advantage against adversaries who claimed, not implausibly, that they were undoing the Constitution with their policies rather than fortifying it.

The New Deal demonstrates how complicated it can be to **assess success**. Should the New Deal be considered a success? Politically, the answer is clear. Roosevelt is the only president in American history to win four terms. The Democratic coalition he put together with his policies—often called the New Deal Coalition—dominated American politics for nearly four decades.

As a policy matter, the answer is not as clear. Roosevelt's supporters argue that his actions stabilized the economy, preventing the nation from reaching the "end of our rope," as Hoover put it on FDR's inauguration day. He restored Americans' confidence in our institutions, in this view, and more generally restored the nation's morale. More tangibly, the New Deal mitigated the suffering of millions of unemployed and impoverished people, and established structures that provided an economic safety net for individuals and automatic stabilizers that have prevented any repetition of the severe downward economic spiral of 1929–1933. As historian Alonzo L. Hamby argues, in the end, the New Deal safeguarded American democracy through a time in the world when the survival of democracy could not be taken for granted.[42]

Critics argue that the New Deal was a failure. Its most important task was recovery, and this it clearly failed to achieve. The unemployment rate in 1939 was still 19 percent and was only that low because of artificial short-term government jobs. With much less interventionist policies, Great Britain had escaped the Depression by 1935. More broadly, critics of the New Deal worry that it began the process of creating an "entitlement mentality" among Americans, which has led over time to a mass dependence of Americans on the largesse of government; that it has led the nation into massive and unsustainable government debt; and that it did violence to the Constitution and valuable norms of limited government that cannot be compensated by greater feelings of economic security.

Indeed, critics of the New Deal frequently focus on the **unanticipated negative consequences** of Roosevelt's program. Amity Shlaes and Jim Powell, for example, argue that the failure of the New Deal to end the Depression was not incidental but was a direct consequence of the policies themselves, which raised taxes, controlled business, and exuded hostility to entrepreneurs in ways that made it much more difficult for private business to recover. The strategy of fighting Depression with high wages and high prices—which was both Hoover's and Roosevelt's strategy—also meant that money was going into one pocket of workers and farmers and going out the other.[43]

This debate is still going on, and still demonstrating its relevance through a variety of issues, including the usefulness of Barack Obama's 2009 fiscal stimulus package. The debate can never be fully resolved, since it depends in part on different values placed on liberty and equality, opportunity and security, constitutional faithfulness and constitutional innovation.

2

The Truman-Eisenhower Equilibrium

★ ★ ★

Civil rights grew in prominence as an issue. In 1957, President Eisenhower sent federal troops to enforce a federal court order to desegregate Central High School in Little Rock, Arkansas.

AFTER THE BURST OF POLICY MAKING in the New Deal, the United States entered a period characterized by incrementalism and consolidation. The core of the New Deal was preserved but not expanded as liberals had hoped. The inputs were not right for anything more dramatic, and the most consistent influence was international affairs, which dominated the national agenda and even drove the few domestic policy innovations that occurred.

When Franklin Roosevelt died in April 1945, the end of World War II was four weeks away in Europe and four months away in the Pacific. The new president, Harry S. Truman, had been vice president for less than three months. Truman was Roosevelt's third vice president, following two terms by the relatively conservative John Nance Garner and one term by Henry Wallace, the liberal carrier of the New Deal torch within the administration. That Truman rather than Wallace rose to the presidency upon Roosevelt's death made an enormous difference to the approach of the administration to both domestic and foreign policy.

During World War II, two contrary tendencies were apparent in regard to domestic policy. On one hand, the war years represented an end to liberal reform, underscored by control of Congress by a conservative (though not Republican) majority. On the other hand, some liberals were invigorated by the opportunities of national economic planning made evident during the war. Roosevelt himself, in his 1944 State of the Union address, had established a list of "economic rights" to things like income, health care, housing, and good education in hopes that the nation would act on those priorities when the war ended. The question of American politics in 1945 was which tendency would predominate. For most of the next 16 years, the answer was closer to the former than to the latter. The Truman presidency and the Eisenhower presidency that followed should be seen mostly as a period of consolidation and equilibrium.

The politics of the time featured an underlying Democratic partisan majority in the electorate, built on the New Deal coalition. However, both parties were split into identifiable wings which limited their effectiveness, and whatever the partisan balance may have been, the end result was an ideological stalemate. The "conservative coalition" remained in control of Congress most of the time, through several shifts in party control.

Truman and Eisenhower were both very different from Roosevelt. Both midwesterners, Truman (from Missouri) and Eisenhower (from Kansas) were plain-spoken men with several admirable qualities but largely unable to inspire through their words. Truman had been a US Senator from Missouri, and before that had risen through the Pendergast political machine of Kansas City, causing many Americans to view him as a hackneyed politician. Even many Democrats saw Truman as an unworthy successor to the articulate and debonair Roosevelt. Politically, he was moderately liberal—too liberal for many southern conservatives, not enough for fiery New Dealers like Wallace.[1] Eisenhower was a lifelong soldier who had risen to command allied forces in Europe in the fight against National Socialist Germany. He was, by all accounts, a master of organization and internal diplomacy, but he had, in keeping with army tradition, been completely apolitical. He was temperamentally conservative but had no strongly developed ideology, and his ties with the Republican Party were minimal; indeed, one of the reasons Republicans nominated him in 1952 was because he was relatively untainted by the damaged Republican "brand." He ended up being moderately conservative—not conservative enough for the conservative wing of the party, too much for the eastern liberals such as New York Governor Nelson Rockefeller.[2]

Not least, external events worked to limit the focus on domestic policy change. Truman contended with the opening stages of the Cold War, including the Soviet repression of Eastern Europe, the communist coup in Czechoslovakia, the Soviet blockade of Berlin, Soviet pressure on Iran, Greece, and Turkey, Soviet development of the atomic bomb, the communist revolution in China, and the Korean War. Foreign issues intruding on the national agenda in the Eisenhower years included the ongoing Korean War, the rise of the anti-Western leaders Mohammed Mossadegh in Iran and Jacobo Arbenz in Guatemala, uprisings against Soviet rule in East Berlin in 1953, the collapse of French power in Indochina, the Hungarian revolution and closing of the Suez Canal by Egypt's Abdel Gamal Nasser in 1956, launching of the Sputnik satellite by the USSR in 1957, another Berlin crisis and confrontation with communist China in the Straits of Formosa in 1958, Cuban revolution and takeover by Fidel Castro in 1959, and loss of a U-2 reconnaissance plane and pilot over the Soviet Union in 1960. It is little wonder that foreign affairs crowded out domestic policy questions during much of this period.

THE TRUMAN PRESIDENCY

The first thing to notice about domestic policy in the Truman years is that, in comparison to the New Deal era, policy makers faced a broader range of significant issues.[3] Where Roosevelt and Congress had only to concentrate on issues of Depression and economic scarcity, Truman faced at least three distinct (though related) economic issues and several other major concerns. The first economic issue was military demobilization. The United States went from 12 million men under arms in 1945 to 1.5 million in 1947. The task of reintegrating those veterans into the national economy and placing the US economy back on a peacetime footing, instead of maximum industrial mobilization and regulation for war, was an urgent one. A second, related, task was how to keep the country from slipping back into Depression once the war was done. By 1945, prosperity and full employment had returned, but Americans understood that this change in economic fortune had resulted from war mobilization. Many feared that, absent the stimulus of the war, return to depression was likely. At the same time, though, Americans began to experience a phenomenon not seen in nearly three decades: inflation, which reached double digits in 1947. Rising prices affected everyone, stirring a political and policy backlash and serving as a third key economic problem facing policy makers.

Other issues also came to the foreground. Civil rights grew as an issue, as blacks who had fought in the battles of World War II returned home and were less inclined to accept second-class citizenship. Many whites, too, had second thoughts about segregation when they reflected on the racial theories of the Nazis.[4] Clashes between organized labor and business put labor issues near the top of the agenda: the year 1946 saw 4,985 strikes nationwide, costing 116 million days of man labor.[5] And, heavily influenced by events abroad, internal security against communist espionage and subversion became a key policy concern.

Demobilization was actually anticipated by federal legislation in 1944, though Truman's administration had to execute it. Two measures were particularly important. The "GI Bill" provided federal assistance to veterans who wanted to go to college and was responsible for massively expanding the number of Americans enrolled in college. In 1940, there were a grand total of 1.5 million Americans attending college; by 1947, there were 1.2 million veterans in college. The other major demobilization bill was the "VA Bill" (named after the Veterans Administration). This legislation offered subsidized loans to veterans to help them buy houses. These popular programs were seen as repaying the nation's debt to those who had served. At the same time, since there were so many veterans, the programs considerably extended the reach of the federal government into higher education and housing, and served as the prototype for later federal programs with an even broader reach.

As a follow-on to the New Deal, Truman proposed a legislative program he called the "Fair Deal." In September 1945, he proposed a 21-point program, including an increased minimum wage, more generous unemployment insurance, housing assistance, increased farm aid, aid to small businesses, expanded public works, tax reform, and making permanent the Fair Employment Practice Committee, among other things.[6] However, little of the 21 point program passed before the 1946 elections, which resulted in the first switch in the party majority in the House since 1930 or the Senate since 1932. Unimpressed with Truman and angry at inflation, continuing wartime economic regimentation, aggressive use of executive power, and labor unrest, voters turned sharply toward Republicans. The GOP gained 55 seats in the House and 12 in the Senate, as well as enough governorships to have the majority in the nation.[7]

The backlash against Truman was so thorough that some prominent Democrats suggested that he should appoint a Republican Secretary of State and then resign. (In 1946, this maneuver would have made the Secretary of State the next president.) Many viewed him as politically doomed. In this environment, the Republican Congress sought to make a course correction.[8] In domestic policy, there were at least three major policy shifts that resulted. Congress ended many of the wartime economic controls and pushed Truman to end the rest through executive order. Congress also passed a significant tax cut over Truman's veto, following up on a tax cut passed by the previous Congress. Finally, Congress passed (again over Truman's veto) the Taft-Hartley Act, which modified the Wagner Act's approach to labor. The Taft-Hartley Act preserved the right to collective bargaining but responded to complaints by business that the Wagner Act had specified unfair practices that business could not use but no unfair practices that labor could not use. Taft-Hartley specified unfair practices by labor that were also prohibited, including use of secondary boycotts (picketing a neutral company because it does business with a company engaged in a labor dispute) and jurisdictional strikes (for example, strikes by unions protesting the assignment of work to members of another union). It also allowed states to choose to be a "right to work" state, meaning that they could adopt laws that guaranteed that workers could not be forced to join a union as a condition of retaining their jobs. The legislation also banned communists as union leaders, prevented unions from using mandatory union dues for political campaigns, and allowed the president to order a "cooling off period" for nationally disruptive strikes, during which time workers would have to return to work while negotiations continued.

In all, organized labor detested the Taft-Hartley Act and has consistently demanded repeal of some of its provisions (especially the state right-to-work option). However, many Americans viewed it as a necessary restoration of some balance between labor unions, business, and individual workers, and it has retained broad enough support to survive intact since 1947.

The Eightieth Congress also initiated an institutional change with far-reaching impact. In response to perceptions that Franklin Roosevelt had built up too much personal power during his multiple terms as president, two-thirds of each house of Congress forwarded to the states a proposed constitutional amendment limiting the president to two terms. By February 27, 1951, the amendment had been ratified by three-fourths of the states and became the Twenty-Second Amendment to the Constitution. It is widely acknowledged by students of the presidency that the Twenty-Second Amendment has had the effect of constraining presidential leverage in a president's second term, when allies and adversaries alike know with certainty that the president is a "lame duck" who cannot be reelected.[9] Ironically, the two presidents who were the most plausible beneficiaries of a third term since 1952 were both Republicans—Dwight D. Eisenhower and Ronald Reagan.

These measures were significant policy changes (or, in the case of the Twenty-Second Amendment, a significant institutional change), but they were nonetheless incremental rather than radical. Taft-Hartley, for example, modified the Wagner Act in a more conservative direction. Although Republicans sponsored the key policy measures of the Eightieth Congress, without considerable support from Democrats, they would have been unable to override presidential vetoes or secure adoption of a constitutional amendment, which requires approval of three-fourths of the states.

Although the Republican Congress clashed with Truman on domestic policy, the two worked together on foreign policy, which occupied a great deal of their attention. It was in this period that the foundation was laid for the bipartisan policy of containment of Soviet communism, such as the Marshall Plan, aid to Greece and Turkey, and the National Security Act of 1947. Obtaining passage of the Marshall Plan alone was a difficult legislative challenge and a major commitment of policy-making resources that were diverted from domestic issues.

As the 1948 election loomed, Truman was in trouble. Democrats were split three ways: Truman represented the center of the Democratic Party, Henry Wallace ran a third-party campaign as the candidate of the Progressive Party, representing the far left of the Democratic Party (as well as many radicals and communists), and Strom Thurmond represented hard-core southern segregationists as the nominee of the States Rights (or Dixiecrat) Party. But Truman was able to exploit the long-standing Republican divisions between their conservative congressional party and their more liberal presidential wing, represented by nominee Thomas Dewey, governor of New York (and FDR's opponent in 1944). In his nomination acceptance speech at the Democratic national convention, Truman called a special session of Congress to consider some of the more liberal proposals contained in the Republican platform, knowing the more conservative Congress would not act. He then lambasted the "Do-nothing Eightieth Congress," a label that stuck despite that Congress's significant legislative achievements. Moreover, in retrospect it is clear that the New Deal coalition was still fundamentally stable; voters in 1946 had wanted to moderate the New Deal, not overthrow it. Truman ran an aggressive campaign, while Dewey was cautious and defensive. In the end, Truman won, and Democrats swept back into control of Congress, briefly giving him a more favorable environment for domestic policy making.[10]

In 1950, the Korean War began and the conservative coalition reasserted itself in the midterm elections as Republicans gained 29 seats in the House, closing any opportunity for significant domestic policy change. The Korean War, which began in June and seemed almost won in

November, became much harder when communist China intervened with hundreds of thousands of troops. The next two and a half years featured a costly stalemate fought back and forth over the thirty-eighth parallel, a war that could not help but be the president's first priority. Truman, who had initially committed US troops to the defense of South Korea without approval of Congress, lost support as the war dragged on. In 1952, Truman considered running for reelection, but decided against it in the face of deep unpopularity.

Overall, the Fair Deal fell well short of Truman's hopes. Though he is today widely praised for foresight and courage in his foreign policy, his domestic policy accomplishments were minimal. He failed to convince Congress to approve national health insurance, federal aid to education, or the "Brannan Plan" for agriculture, which aimed to simply transfer income directly to farmers rather than relying on manipulation of the market to boost prices. Items that were passed were usually moderated considerably. Truman was no Roosevelt, partly because he was a different man and partly because his circumstances were different.

Despite general disappointment, the Fair Deal agenda was not completely thwarted. During moments of greater opportunity—before the 1946 elections, and between the 1948 and 1950 elections—some important domestic legislation was passed. These included:

- The Employment Act of 1946, which was originally titled the "Full Employment Act." The original version contained a "right to a job," which was removed as the legislation was moderated. In the end, the Act created the Council of Economic Advisors, a panel of three economists whose job is to advise the president. It also assigned legal responsibility to the president for maintaining employment growth and price stability, codifying the new expectation of presidential economic leadership spawned by FDR. This expectation has, ever since, been a double-edged sword for presidents, putting them in a stronger position to claim credit when the economy does well—and virtually assuring that they will be blamed when the economy goes awry. At the same time, the Act did not actually give the president any greater tools to control economic policy. Spending and taxing decisions remained in Congress, though the president could make proposals, and monetary policy remained in the hands of the Federal Reserve Board.
- The Housing Act of 1949. This legislation authorized the first federal urban renewal projects and provided federal subsidies for low- and medium-income housing. Major expenditures for public housing programs, however, were nixed by Congress.

- The Fair Labor Standards Act Amendments of 1949, which nearly doubled the minimum wage (from 40 cents to 75 cents an hour).
- The Social Security Act Amendments of 1950, which increased Social Security benefits (in some cases, by roughly doubling them) and added coverage to about 10 million workers. As a result of these amendments, for the first time since the passage of the Social Security Act, more people were receiving Title II old-age pensions than Title I old-age welfare assistance, and for the first time, the pension benefits were generally higher than the welfare payments. During debate over these amendments, a version of the Townsend Plan was once again brought forward in Congress as an alternative and was defeated, for the last time.

Perhaps the most significant domestic policy departure during the Truman years, however, was driven by executive orders and presidential leadership. Truman, from the former slave state of Missouri, was the first president since Reconstruction to fully embrace a civil rights agenda. Though he proposed civil rights legislation to Congress, it did not pass. In 1948, Truman issued a momentous executive order banning employment discrimination in the federal government and desegregating the US armed forces. He also took the step of authorizing the Justice Department to support blacks suing in civil rights cases. Truman's civil rights stand was a defining mark of his domestic presidency, and his support of a pro-civil rights plank in the 1948 Democratic platform precipitated the bolt by Thurmond and the Dixiecrats. In comparison with later civil rights measures, Truman's were modest, but they expanded considerably on the steps taken by FDR during the war.[11]

There were both continuities and discontinuities between Roosevelt and Truman. On one hand, Truman tried to fulfill FDR's ambitions as outlined in the 1944 "Economic Bill of Rights," including seeking (unsuccessfully or only partly successfully) to establish a right to a job, to health care, to housing, and to good education. Like Roosevelt, Truman's primary domestic focus was economic. And he met the expectation established by Roosevelt that presidents would exert economic leadership.

On the other hand, Truman was generally more conservative than Roosevelt on a number of issues. He took a more balanced approach toward labor: he vetoed Taft-Hartley, but he also seized the coal mines in 1946 and steel mills in 1952 to shut down strikes that he saw as against the national interest. He drove the Henry Wallace hard left out of the Democratic Party and built a new consensus of anti-communist liberalism. Truman was more concerned than FDR with balancing the budget. At the same time, though he and Roosevelt doubtless shared views on civil rights, Truman's actions as chief executive were bolder.

THE EISENHOWER PRESIDENCY

Like Truman's Democrats, Eisenhower's Republicans were divided. One side of the party traced its lineage back to the progressive Republicans. With their base in the northeast, they believed in a strong president and believed that Republicans should accommodate the New Deal. Abroad, these Republicans were internationalists and looked first to relations with Europe. The other side of the party traced its heritage back to the stand-pat wing that fought the progressives. These Republicans feared executive power and wanted to cut back the New Deal. They found their greatest strength in the Midwest, had isolationist leanings, and were most concerned with relations with Asia. The Eastern wing had dominated Republican presidential politics for decades, and had most recently succeeded in nominating Dewey in 1944 and 1948. Eisenhower was its candidate in 1952. The Midwestern wing had long dominated the Republican contingent in Congress, and tried unsuccessfully to nominate Senator Robert Taft of Ohio in 1952.[12]

With the backing of the Eastern Republicans, Eisenhower promised to fashion a "Modern Republicanism."[13] This meant that Eisenhower spent much of his presidency working to find an intermediate position between congressional Republicans and Democrats. He was reportedly not disturbed when Republicans lost control of Congress in 1954, and many thought he found it easier to work with Democratic Senate leader Lyndon Johnson than with his own party. Forty years later, Bill Clinton would try to "triangulate" between his party and the opposition, but Eisenhower pioneered the technique. For most of his presidency, the partisan stalemate remained a feature of American politics. Republicans gained a small majority in both houses of Congress when Ike was elected in 1952, then Democrats regained a small majority in the 1954 midterm elections and held it in 1956, when Eisenhower was handily reelected. The 1956 election represented the first time in American history that a president was reelected but the opposition party won a majority in Congress. Not until the 1958 midterm elections did the partisan stalemate in Congress show signs of breaking decisively in favor of the Democrats.

Domestic policy in the 1950s mostly reflected this political stalemate.[14] The Eisenhower years saw no significant curtailment of the New Deal's programs, and no real attempt to intellectually challenge its premises. At the same time, no large new welfare or entitlement programs were instituted. The result, on balance, was a consolidation of the New Deal, as it survived intact eight years of a Republican administration. Eisenhower described this balance in a letter to his brother Edgar. "I believe this country is following a dangerous trend when it permits too great a degree of centralization of governmental functions," the president began.

However, "[s]hould any political party attempt to abolish social security, unemployment insurance, and eliminate labor laws and farm programs, you would not hear of that party again in our political history."[15]

Eisenhower succeeded in winning some marginal tax and spending cuts, and, like Truman, made a fairly consistent effort to balance the budget, though a big proposed spending increase in 1957 brought howls of protest from Treasury Secretary George M. Humphrey. Eisenhower also cut the federal workforce by 10 percent and supported a tight-money, anti-inflationary policy by the Federal Reserve.[16] He also showed considerable deference to big business. Policy toward labor unions remained a topic high on the national agenda. Senate hearings in 1957–1960 showed evidence of union corruption, and there was a big fight over state right to work laws in 1958, when a number of states had right-to-work initiatives on the ballot (most lost). The Landrum-Griffin Act of 1959, supported by Eisenhower, was a piece of congressional legislation that attempted to guarantee free union elections.

Like Truman, Eisenhower was largely preoccupied with foreign policy issues. Several of these crises, if mishandled, could have led to general war. Like Truman, Ike received bipartisan support for his policies abroad. Again, this era saw numerous examples of interplay between foreign and domestic policy. For example, Eisenhower's domestic priority on limited spending and a balanced budget affected US foreign policy. In an attempt to restrain the burden of armaments on the US economy, Eisenhower announced the strategy of "massive retaliation." Massive retaliation meant that the United States would respond to a Soviet conventional invasion of Europe with nuclear retaliation against the USSR. It was Eisenhower's hope that reliance on this strategy would allow the United States to limit its defense budget by requiring fewer relatively expensive conventional forces.[17]

Just as domestic considerations affected national security policy, national security issues affected domestic policy in a number of key areas. For example, Eisenhower continued and expanded Truman's civil rights thrust, desegregating the District of Columbia, sending federal troops to Little Rock, Arkansas, in 1957 to enforce the Supreme Court's 1954 *Brown v. Board of Education of Topeka, Kansas* ruling requiring public schools to desegregate. He also supported the Civil Rights Acts of 1957 and 1960, which were enacted by Congress over stiff opposition by segregationist Democrats. The Acts established the Civil Rights division of the Justice Department and took steps to try to ensure the right to vote. Eisenhower also acted to implement Truman's executive order desegregating the military.[18] One of Eisenhower's motivations—and, later, John F. Kennedy's—was to bring American practice more in line with American ideals as part of the Cold War competition with the Soviet Union. The late 1950s and 1960s saw many new countries created in the Third

World as European powers gave up their overseas colonies. These countries became a key battleground of the Cold War, and Eisenhower and many other Americans realized that an America that tolerated segregation would not be an attractive model for Africans or Asians deciding which way to tilt as they became independent.

The federal government extended its reach into other areas of domestic policy as a consequence of the Cold War. For example, in response to the shock of Sputnik and fear that the United States was losing the "Space Race," Congress passed the National Defense Education Act (NDEA). The NDEA provided federal funds to secondary education to bolster science and mathematics instruction, where the United States was feared to be lagging behind the Soviets. Even before NDEA, the federal government had begun approving "impact aid" to local school districts affected by the presence of military bases. Thus, defense became the hook through which Washington finally began to make K–12 education a federal concern, just as the GI Bill was the avenue through which higher education first became one.[19] Similarly, when the Eisenhower administration proposed a national system of federal highways, the need to transport troops and supplies in wartime was a crucial justification. The interstate highway system—perhaps Eisenhower's chief domestic accomplishment—came by way of the National Defense Highway Act.

Inextricably linked with the Cold War, a mostly new domestic policy question that consumed the nation's attention during the Truman presidency and early Eisenhower presidency was the issue of internal security. Abroad, both the Nazis and Communists had proven themselves adept at using internal subversion to weaken and bring down their enemies. In the 1930s there had been a large and active Communist Party of the United States (CPUSA), and the CPUSA was understood by most Americans (correctly, it turned out) to be little more than an arm of the Soviet Union. (On more than one occasion, the general secretary of the CPUSA was replaced on orders from Moscow.) When relations with the Soviets turned sour again soon after World War II, many Americans were afraid that communist subversion and espionage might threaten the nation. These fears were fueled when it became known that some high positions in the Roosevelt administration had been held by Soviet agents. In a dramatic case, Alger Hiss, assistant to the Secretary of State, was convicted of perjury for lying about his role in Soviet espionage; he only escaped conviction for espionage itself because the statute of limitations had run out. The Hiss case catapulted to public attention Richard Nixon, the California congressman whose questioning in a House committee hearing caught Hiss in a lie.

Although Truman stubbornly stood by Hiss, public worries pushed him to institute a loyalty program within the federal government that resulted in 308 dismissals and about 5,000 resignations. Nationally, state and local governments and private groups contributed to the anti-communist drive. State legislatures investigated communism at state universities while the Hollywood "blacklist" was largely constructed by the Association of Motion Picture Producers and the American Legion.

The issue of communist infiltration of government was important enough that Eisenhower was elected on a campaign attacking the Democrats for "corruption, communism, and Korea," and he continued and even intensified the internal security efforts of the federal government. At the same time, he ultimately took a stand against Senator Joseph McCarthy, who had gained considerable notoriety accusing varying government entities of harboring secret communists. Although for many Americans McCarthy became the nefarious symbol of the internal security drive, he was in truth a sideshow. The committee he chaired (the Senate Permanent Subcommittee on Investigations) had only a peripheral role in internal security policy; the key congressional committees were the House Un-American Activities Committee (HUAC) and Senate Internal Security Subcommittee. In late 1953, McCarthy crossed a line, attacking the army itself. He was censured by the Senate, with the quiet approval of Eisenhower, and his power was broken. Although internal security remained a concern after McCarthy's fall, it was gradually supplanted by other issues.

Thus, for most of the Truman-Eisenhower period, events abroad and the implications that those events had for domestic policy were the chief focus of the nation. Neither political party and neither ideological coalition had a strong enough majority to impose dramatic shifts in policy. Truman tacked a bit left of center, Eisenhower a bit right of center. Neither the politics of the moment nor the individual policy makers were right for anything but incrementalism. Labor policy shifted a bit to the right compared to the baseline established by the Wagner Act; Social Security, the minimum wage, and housing policy shifted a bit to the left compared with the New Deal baseline. The Employment Act made explicit what Roosevelt had already established—the president would be held accountable for the economy—and added an institutional infrastructure (though few additional powers) to help him succeed. Yet the "rights" to a job, health care, or housing envisioned in the Economic Bill of Rights were not enacted.

Civil rights was, in some ways, an exception to the predominance of incrementalism. It was a fresh issue (if not entirely new), brought to the fore at Truman's decision and kept there by the Supreme Court and Eisenhower's decision to send troops to Little Rock. Yet, even here, the steps themselves were a modest beginning. By 1960, six years after *Brown v. Board*, most southern schools had not yet desegregated. This is not to say that limited federal aid to K–12 education, creation of the interstate highway system, or veterans housing and college benefits were unimportant—quite the contrary. But they were the exceptions, not the rule, in the late 1940s and 1950s.

That was about to change. In the midterm elections of 1958, Democrats finally broke out of the close partisan balance in which the parties had been locked throughout the decade. After six years in the White House, Eisenhower was in ill health, having suffered two heart attacks, and was politically weakened by intraparty fights occasioned by his attempt to nurture "Modern Republicanism." Unions were mobilized to fight right-to-work initiatives in six states, including California and Ohio, and brought out their voters in droves. Most importantly, the nation was in a sharp recession in 1958, the worst slowdown since the Depression. Unemployment rose from 4.1 percent in 1956 to 6.8 percent in 1958, the highest level since 1941. Although the recession proved relatively short-lived, it brought back memories of Hoover and Republican economic mismanagement.

In this environment, the midterm elections gave Democrats gains of 49 seats in the House and a whopping 16 in the Senate, the biggest Senate turnover in the twentieth century. Almost all of the gains added strength to the northern, liberal wing of the Democratic Party, and many of the new members were beholden to the AFL-CIO. Underscoring their new influence, liberal House Democrats formed the Democratic Study Group to organize their efforts.[20]

Despite their new large majorities in Congress, Democrats were not able to take the legislative offensive in Eisenhower's last two years. The Landrum-Griffin Act regulating union elections was enacted during this period, and Eisenhower continued holding the upper hand on budget questions. However, Democrats grew more confident and began laying the rhetorical groundwork for a new round of liberal activism. After two decades of dominance, the conservative coalition in Congress was greatly weakened; the 1958 elections went a long way to creating the legislative majorities that would undergird the Great Society, creating a liberal House that lasted until 1966 (or perhaps, with momentary exceptions, until 1994). The cautious domestic policy consensus of the 1950s was about to give way to a new burst of non-incremental policy making.

THE TRUMAN-EISENHOWER EQUILIBRIUM: SUMMARY AND ASSESSMENT

For the most part, the Truman-Eisenhower years represented a period of incrementalism and consolidation of the New Deal.

Economic policy

The overall fiscal picture remained stable, as real federal spending actually shrank slightly from 1946 to 1960; the budget was balanced in seven of 15 years between 1946 and 1960, and there was a deficit equal to less than 1 percent of GDP in another four years. Overall regulatory activity also remained relatively stable. There were 14,736 pages in the Federal Register in 1946 and 14,479 in 1960. However, non-defense spending grew by 126 percent in real dollars and from 4.3 percent of GDP to 8.2 percent. The equilibrium of economic policy represented a compromise consensus: a "domesticated" Keynesianism in which unintentional deficits were tolerated in downturns but deficits were otherwise combatted.[21]

Social welfare
There were important incremental expansions of Social Security and the federal minimum wage, but no large new social welfare programs. Federal payments to individuals grew from 2.6 percent of GDP in 1946 to 4.5 percent in 1960, driven largely by the maturation and expansion of Social Security retirement programs. Truman's proposal for national health insurance failed, though public housing advanced.

Civil rights
Progress on the civil rights front gained momentum incrementally, as all three branches contributed. Truman ordered desegregation of the armed forces and unsuccessfully proposed a civil rights package to Congress. The Supreme Court ordered desegregation of schools, which had limited tangible effect immediately but laid a legal groundwork for significant change. Congress passed and Eisenhower signed the Civil Rights Acts of 1957 and 1960, and Ike sent troops to Little Rock to enforce desegregation orders.

Education
Once servicemen began returning home from World War II, higher education received a boost from the GI Bill. Truman's proposal for large-scale aid to K–12 education failed in Congress, but the Soviet Union's Sputnik launch led to enactment of the National Defense Education Act.

Environment
Although routine federal conservation programs continued, there were no big new departures in environmental policy.

Moral/cultural issues
The moral consensus of American society remained stable, at least on the surface, and there was no significant change in policy.

Federalism
Eisenhower and Republicans in Congress expressed a desire to restore some power to states, but little was done to shift this area of policy. The trajectory of federalism in the New Deal—toward "cooperative

federalism" or "marble cake federalism"—continued. An example was the interstate highway system, maintenance of which was to be shared by federal and state governments.

In terms of **inputs**, the dominant ideas revolved around the New Deal—the question was how fast or far to take those ideas. Truman wanted to fulfill Roosevelt's "Economic Bill of Rights," while Eisenhower hoped to moderate it. The events that dominated the time were predominantly foreign: the end of World War II, the rise of the Cold War, the Korean War, and the myriad of crises in the late 1940s and 1950s. Indeed, **international affairs** and national security played an outsized role here, not only by monopolizing public attention and the time and energy of policy makers, but by driving a number of key domestic policy departures, including internal security policy, K–12 and higher education policy, civil rights, housing policy (GI Bill), and transportation policy (interstate highways). Adding to an environment with no new driving ideas and most energy focused abroad, the politics of the era was made for domestic gridlock manifested in a close partisan balance and powerful cross-cutting coalitions in Congress. Given stable ideas, politics, and domestic events, the analytical frameworks that explain big policy change would not expect it.

Moreover, unlike FDR, who faced few constraints due to **path dependency**, policy makers in the Truman-Eisenhower era were constrained by the New Deal. Eisenhower's letter to his brother Edgar made note of that reality, and his policies were consistent with his observations. Most of the key policy changes of the Truman years used previous policy as a starting point, including the Social Security Amendments of 1950 and the minimum wage increase. Even the Taft-Hartley Act, which took labor policy in a different direction, was a modification of the Wagner Act and did not alter the Wagner Act's fundamental contribution, which was the protection of collective bargaining rights.

The end of Depression and of global war launched a new era with a broader **policy agenda**. Items included inflation, military demobilization and wartime controls, economic growth, labor disputes, civil rights, and a variety of domestic issues related to America's new role in the world.

In the broadest sense, control over **problem definition** played a smaller role than in the New Deal, perhaps because the domestic problems themselves were on a smaller scale. Nevertheless, it was an important factor in specific cases. A bipartisan coalition supported Taft-Hartley because proponents succeeded in arguing that labor radicalism was a problem, and that it was traceable to an unbalanced approach in the Wagner Act. Civil rights began to advance because World War II shone a light on the fact that treatment of black citizens was a violation of fundamental American principles. In the late 1950s, Eisenhower and liberal Democrats fought over whether excessive federal spending was a problem—a battle eventually won by liberals, paving the way for the Great Society.

The policy period from 1945 to 1960 is also relatively free of heated disputes over **assessment**. However, the anti-communist internal security measures remain among the most contentious domestic issues of the century. Critics argue that, driven by a paranoid obsession, the anticommunist "witch hunts" inflicted severe damage to civil liberties.[22] There is no doubt that the innocent were swept up with the guilty, and that guilt by association was too often a tactic of investigators. Yet, it is also clear that there was a very real "communist problem" within the US government. Despite his life-long denials, there is overwhelming evidence that Alger Hiss was guilty.[23] Moreover, after the fall of the Soviet Union in 1991, Soviet files were made available to Western researchers, and some crucial FBI files were also opened. Researchers uncovered a series of messages from Soviet intelligence officers to the Soviet embassy in the United States that had been intercepted and decoded by the FBI. Code-named the Venona Cables, the messages showed that the US government had indeed been honeycombed with communist sympathizers engaging in espionage for the Soviets. These included Hiss, Laurence Duggan (head of the State Department's division of American Republics), and at least 4 others in the State Department; Assistant Secretary of the Treasury Harry Dexter White, along with at least 7 others in the Treasury Department; 15 to 20 in the Office of Strategic Services, including the senior aide to the head of the OSS; at least 6 each in wartime agencies, including the War Production Board, Office of the Coordinator of Inter-American Affairs, and Office of War Information; Presidential Administrative Assistant Lauchlin Currie; and several in the Manhattan Project and subsequent nuclear weapons development efforts.[24] The issue of internal security exemplifies the difficulty of assessing policy; some information crucial to assessing it was not even available to analysts until half a century later (Venona documents were not released until 1995).

Other policies would seem to be easier to assess. The interstate highway system, for example, has contributed considerably to American prosperity (and leisure). Even then, some critics can point to its **unanticipated consequences**: the promotion of an automobile culture that emptied major cities, grew the suburbs, and contributed to pollution, carbon emissions, and the homogenization of society. These go side by side with the facilitation of commerce and defense, which were the intended results.[25]

3

The New Frontier / Great Society

★ ★ ★

In 1964, President Lyndon Johnson opened his quest for a "Great Society" in a commencement address at the University of Michigan.

IF THE NEW DEAL DEMONSTRATED the usefulness of the concepts of "punctuated equilibrium" and "multiple streams" for understanding broad tendencies in public policy, the Great Society confirmed it. After the long equilibrium of the Truman and Eisenhower years, the mid-1960s saw the right combination of ideas, events, people, and politics to produce a new burst of domestic policy making. The era also amply demonstrated the importance of foreign policy issues to domestic policy making and the relevance of the law of unanticipated consequences.

One idea that helped drive domestic policy in the 1960s was the ongoing loyalty of liberal Democrats to Franklin Roosevelt's Economic Bill of Rights. This was especially true in areas of health care, housing, and education. To this degree, policy was not driven by a new idea as much as by an old idea getting a second wind. Similarly, John Maynard Keynes had contributed to the intellectual atmosphere around the New Deal, then had been "domesticated" in the budget-balancing Truman-Eisenhower era, but his ideas reappeared with vigor in the technocratic era to come. Neo-Keynesians came to believe macroeconomic policy could and should be calibrated in good times and bad to maximize growth and employment.

At the same time, the intellectual environment shifted in ways that influenced a new policy agenda. During the Depression, the agenda had focused on grappling with widespread economic scarcity—as FDR bemoaned in his second inaugural address, "one-third of a nation ill-housed, ill-clad, and ill-nourished." In the immediate postwar years, the economic challenge was to prevent a return of scarcity. By 1960, the question was how to maintain a growing prosperity for most Americans. To some thinkers, the question was also what to do with that prosperity. The ideas that most influenced the Great Society policy era were ideas put forward by people who sought to adapt liberalism to the new circumstance of widespread affluence.

Three examples were highly influential books written by John Kenneth Galbraith, Michael Harrington, and Rachel Carson. Galbraith argued in *The Affluent Society*, published in 1958, that the main problem facing America was a combination of excess affluence and lack of public purpose. The solution, Galbraith contended, was to expand the public sector at the expense of the private sector, directing the excess affluence to socially beneficial government projects.[1] Harrington, writing in 1962, contended in *The Other America: Poverty in the United States* that America's growing affluence had made the poor an "invisible minority." Harrington advocated government social reforms to address poverty. In one sense, Harrington's book sought to correct Galbraith's, by reminding people that the new affluence had bypassed what he estimated to be 40 to 50 million Americans who remained in poverty.[2] However, both agreed that affluence had increased and that increased government activism was the proper next step. Finally, Rachel Carson sparked the modern environmental movement with her 1962 book *Silent Spring*, which claimed that the anti-malaria pesticide DDT was contaminating the food chain and causing cancer among humans.[3] Her book caused Americans to consider the negative side effects of affluence, such as pollution, which previously had received little consideration.

Like the intellectual environment, the political environment moved in the direction of activist government. By the end of the 1960s, a number of dramatic political developments had shaken up the world of policy. Most obviously, liberal Democrats had gained the upper hand in their party. At the same time, the conservative movement took over the Republican Party. The South, which had tottered in 1928, 1948, and the 1950s, was lost to the Democratic Party as a reliable bloc at the presidential level. And the 1960s saw the growth of a variety of social and political movements that created great ferment. These included the mainstream civil rights movement and some radical spin-offs (such as the Black Panthers and Muslim black nationalists), beginnings of the modern environmental movement, feminist and gay rights movements, and the anti–Vietnam War movement. The hippie "counterculture" affected social mores (though it was also detested by many Americans), and the New Left, represented by Students for a Democratic Society (SDS), issued the Port Huron Statement in 1962 and became increasingly radicalized. These movements influenced the policy-making environment by introducing new issues and new forms of public pressure.

In partisan terms, the midterm elections of 1958 set the stage by breaking the partisan stalemate in Congress. While the bipartisan conservative coalition survived in weakened form, the 1960 election produced unified government by liberal Democrats as John F. Kennedy won one of the closest presidential elections in American history. The conventional tabulation of national popular votes showed Kennedy beating Vice President Richard M. Nixon by a 49.8 percent to 49.5 percent plurality (or about 118,000 votes). (Because of complications in the vote in Alabama, another plausible way of calculating shows Nixon with a small national plurality over Kennedy.[4]) Allegations of fraud in Illinois and Texas tainted Kennedy's narrow victory. In the congressional elections, Kennedy had no coattails; Democrats actually lost 2 seats in the Senate and 20 seats in the House, giving back about 2 out of 5 of the House seats they had gained in 1958. Nevertheless, Democrats held all the elected portions of the federal government.

Kennedy ran on an extensive platform of domestic policy change and promised to "get America moving again" after the recession of 1958 and another economic slowdown in 1960. In a critical campaign decision, he moved to contact the jailed civil rights leader Martin Luther King Jr., through his brother Robert F. Kennedy. Kennedy himself was the wealthy son of Joseph Kennedy, a politically active member of the Boston Irish community who had served as Franklin Roosevelt's first chairman of the Securities Exchange Commission and US Ambassador to Great Britain from 1938 to 1940. Though viewed by some as an intellectual lightweight and a playboy, JFK was also a dashing and articulate World War II navy veteran who had survived the sinking of his patrol and torpedo boat in the Pacific, with a painful chronic back injury to show for it. Before becoming president, he had served three terms in the US House and was then elected to the US Senate in 1952. He was generally a cautious liberal in domestic policy and was an anti-communist internationalist in foreign policy, having run to Nixon's right on Cuba and defense spending in 1960. Kennedy was both the first Roman Catholic and the youngest man ever elected president (Theodore Roosevelt was younger when he took office by succession upon the assassination of President McKinley).[5] As a candidate, Kennedy promised a program he called "The New Frontier," including government health care for the elderly, federal aid to education, and greater anti-poverty efforts. At the same time, it was clear that he had imbibed the growing intellectual spirit of the time. As he described it: "The new frontier of which I speak is not a set of promises—it is a set of challenges. It sums up not what I intend to offer the American people, but what I intend to ask of them. It appeals to their pride, not their pocketbook—it holds out the promise of more sacrifice instead of more security."[6] The contrast with Roosevelt, who promised to reduce scarcity and increase economic security, proved to be important.

Kennedy's running mate and the new vice president, Lyndon Johnson, was a tough and wily Washington insider. First elected to the House from Texas in 1934, Johnson was sent to the Senate in 1948 and became Democratic leader in the Senate after the 1952 elections. From 1954 until his election as vice president, LBJ served as Senate Majority Leader, working closely with President Eisenhower. Though he was elected to Congress as a New Deal Democrat, by 1960 Johnson was widely seen as moderately conservative. He had sought the Democratic presidential nomination in 1960, but fell short against Kennedy. Where Kennedy excelled at public speaking, Johnson was best known for his skill at operating in the corridors of the Capitol out of the glare of publicity.[7] Leading the House would be Sam Rayburn, the quiet but effective Speaker.[8]

There are two key starting points for understanding policy making in the New Frontier / Great Society. First, policy makers saw the relationship between maintaining prosperity and redistributing income through anti-poverty programs as crucial. Not only was there little sense that redistributionism might undercut prosperity, but they were widely considered complementary. Without continued prosperity, the anti-poverty drive could not be sustained economically or politically. Thus economic growth was not only an end of policy, but a means.

Second, the dominant policy makers in this era did not perceive any real limits to what federal activism could accomplish, and they made wide use of social science "experts" to formulate policy. Keynesianism, which served as a vague backdrop to the New Deal, came into its own in the 1960s, as Keynesian economists argued that they could calibrate the economy centrally by a constant adjustment of aggregate demand.[9] This meant that policy makers aimed high, but it also meant that they lacked humility about the capacities (or right) of government to engineer society and bring about positive change. They made little effort to imagine what might go wrong, and therefore frequently did not take into account the law of unanticipated consequences. Models of rational policy making tell us that policy makers should always seriously consider the option of not doing anything at all; in the heyday of the New Frontier / Great Society, that option was seldom on the table.

Despite these activist inclinations, as Kennedy settled into office, it became clear that his hopes for domestic policy change were not going to be realized quickly.[10] He balanced labor and business in 1962 by winning passage of a business investment tax cut and greater authority to negotiate free trade agreements, and forcing an end to a steel strike while pushing the steel industry to keep prices low. On the domestic front, not much else happened. For one thing, the shrinking of the Democratic congressional majority in 1960 and lack of a clear electoral mandate limited his leverage. Key southern Democrats like House Rules Committee chairman Howard W. Smith blocked movement of liberal legislation. As importantly, Kennedy's administration was overwhelmed with foreign crises from the very beginning. Indeed, Kennedy's stirring inaugural address, in which he promised that America would "pay any price, bear any burden, suffer any hardship, support any friend, and oppose any foe to assure the survival and the success of liberty,"[11] was devoted entirely to foreign affairs. His first year in office saw a major crisis in Cuba, as a US-supported invasion by Cuban exiles at the Bay of Pigs failed and Fidel Castro consolidated his communist regime, and a major crisis in Berlin, where the Soviets once again threatened. His second year in office featured growing danger in Cuba, culminating in the Cuban missile crisis of October and November 1962, which brought the world closer to nuclear war than any other incident in the Cold War. The next year saw a deteriorating situation in South Vietnam, where a US-supported government was facing increasing pressure from communist guerrillas aided by North Vietnam's communist dictatorship.

However, the missile crisis also contributed to ultimately breaking the domestic policy logjam by the way that it affected the 1962 midterm elections, which took place only days after the Soviets agreed to remove their missiles from Cuba. Normally, the president's party loses a significant number of seats in midterm elections, and some Republicans thought a 44-seat swing and GOP majority was not out of the question.[12] However, the atmosphere of crisis in early November 1962 and the president's management of the crisis served to limit Democratic losses to four seats in the House; Democrats actually picked up four seats in the Senate and won crucial gubernatorial elections. Commentators such as Tom Wicker of the *New York Times* declared that "Democrats have scored a remarkable midterm election success,"[13] and the president gained discernable momentum. Some analysts would point to the 1962 midterms as the point when the president's legislative agenda began to move forward.[14]

After a year of slow but clear progress on a number of bills, the biggest domestic event since the Great Depression radically changed the calculus. On November 22, 1963, President John F. Kennedy was assassinated. When Lyndon Johnson was sworn in as the thirty-sixth president of the United States, he inherited Kennedy's legislative program and a nation in deep mourning and determined to honor the slain president's memory. On November 27, 1963, Johnson delivered an address to a joint session of Congress saying "Let us continue" in the work begun by Kennedy.[15]

One key priority of the late president was a tax cut to get the economy moving again. A major tax cut had been proposed by Kennedy in 1962, but had encountered stiff resistance in Congress. The proposal itself was the culmination of a battle within the administration over whether to stimulate the economy with a big tax cut or a big spending increase. Advocating the tax cut was Walter Heller, chairman of the Council of Economic Advisors. On the other side was John Kenneth Galbraith, author of *The Affluent Society*, who argued for the spending option. Both Heller and Galbraith were Keynesians, and pushed their proposed solutions on Keynesian grounds. In the end, Kennedy went with Heller and Galbraith became ambassador to India, far away from policy disputes in the White House. His broad diagnosis of American life was influential, but that did not mean all his specific prescriptions were followed.

After the assassination, President Johnson redoubled efforts to secure passage of the tax cut. In February 1964 what became known as the "Kennedy Tax Cut," or the Revenue Act of 1964, was finally passed by Congress and signed into law. The Act cut the corporate tax rate from 52 percent to 48 percent, cut the top marginal income tax rate from 91 percent to 70 percent, reduced the bottom income tax rate from 20 percent to 14 percent, and included an across-the-board cut in income tax rates for everyone in between. As a percentage of the federal budget, the Kennedy tax cut was bigger than either the Reagan tax cut two decades later or the cumulative Bush tax cuts 40 years later.[16]

Economists widely agree that the Kennedy tax cuts contributed significantly to the subsequent prosperity of the 1960s. Years later, however, there continues to be a debate about the real character of those tax cuts. Some analysts point out that Kennedy and Johnson promoted the tax cuts on largely Keynesian grounds, as a measure that would put money in people's pockets to stimulate consumption. However, during the debate over the Reagan tax cuts and Bush tax cuts, many conservatives argued that the structure of the Kennedy tax cuts was more in keeping with a "supply-side" conservative approach: they were permanent and they cut taxes across the board for rich and poor alike. A pure Keynesian approach typically calls for temporary tax cuts targeted at lower income individuals, who are likely to spend most of it immediately.[17]

THE BIRTH OF THE GREAT SOCIETY

Lyndon Johnson was not willing to merely carry out the Kennedy program. He wanted a legacy of his own. In his 1964 State of the Union Address, Johnson announced that he was going to wage a "War on Poverty." Two months later, he proposed to Congress an Economic Opportunity Act that would put together the structures and programs he wanted to use as weapons in that war. Two months after that, he gave an important address at the University of Michigan in which he outlined his vision of America as a "Great Society," which became the moniker of his overall program. (Four decades before, liberal theorist John Dewey had also called for a "Great Society.") In his speech, he identified with the themes found in *The Affluent Society* and *The Other America*. "For half a century we called upon unbounded invention and untiring industry to create an order of plenty for all our people," the president began. "The challenge of the next half century is whether we have the wisdom to use that wealth to enrich and elevate our national life, and to advance the quality of American civilization ... [I]n your time we have the opportunity to move not only toward the rich society and the powerful society, but upward to the Great Society."

Johnson listed several goals necessary to achieve the Great Society: "abundance and liberty for all," "an end to poverty and racial injustice," making the American city a place where people will come "not only to live but to live the good life," preserving the beauty of the countryside, and improving education to free every young mind "to scan the farthest reaches of thought and imagination." While admittedly challenging, this effort could be successful, the president intimated, with a proper reliance on the right experts:

> We are going to assemble the best thought and the broadest knowledge from all over the world to find those answers for America. I intend to establish working groups to prepare a series of White House conferences and meetings—on the cities, on natural beauty, on the quality of education, and on other emerging challenges. And from these meetings and from this inspiration and from these studies we will begin to set our course toward the Great Society.

Johnson also made it clear that he viewed the challenges facing America—unlike the Great Depression—as primarily a set of moral rather than material challenges. Telling the Michigan graduates that "[y]ou can help build a society where the demands of morality, and the needs of the spirit, can be realized in the life of the Nation," the president invited them to prove that "our material progress is only a foundation on which we will build a richer life of mind and spirit." We are not, he concluded, "condemned to a soulless wealth."[18]

In one sense, Johnson was following in Franklin Roosevelt's footsteps, advocating a significant expansion of the power of the federal government guided by experts in the progressive tradition. In another sense, what Johnson was proposing assumed a competence of the federal government far beyond anything imagined by Roosevelt, whose program was aimed at building dams, giving jobs to unemployed people, and establishing a social safety net, but who did not emphasize the needs of the spirit.[19]

In the immediate aftermath of the Great Society speech, the administration and its allies in Congress began the final push toward passage of the civil rights legislation that Kennedy had introduced in June 1963. The civil rights bill had been the other key item highlighted by Johnson after Kennedy's death; it passed the House 290–130 in February, but was long delayed in the Senate. After finally overcoming a Senate filibuster, the Civil Rights Act of 1964 passed by a vote of 73–27. The Civil Rights Act was arguably Johnson's most important domestic policy accomplishment. While building on the civil rights acts of 1957 and 1960, the 1964 Act was much more aggressive in promoting civil rights. Key provisions included

- a prohibition on federal funds going to any government entity engaged in segregation;
- authorization for Justice Department attorneys to sue local school districts that were not desegregating in keeping with the Supreme Court's *Brown v. Board of Education* decision;
- a ban on employment discrimination on the basis of "race, color, sex, religion, or national origin" (To enforce this, an Equal Employment Opportunity Commission [EEOC] was created to handle job discrimination complaints. In 1963, Congress had already passed a requirement that women receive equal pay for equal work.);
- a ban on discrimination in public accommodations such as restaurants, hotels, and gas stations;
- a prohibition on racially discriminatory practices in elections, particularly literacy tests, which had frequently been used to disenfranchise black voters in the South; and
- the creation of the Community Relations Service for the purpose of fostering better relations between varying racial communities.

Provisions of the Act declared that it should not be construed as requiring either racial quotas in employment or college admissions or forced busing of students to achieve desegregation of schools. It was the first comprehensive federal civil rights legislation since an 1877 bill that had been ruled unconstitutional by the Supreme Court. Important in itself, the Civil Rights Act of 1964 was the starting point of a much broader civil rights agenda in the Johnson administration.

Parallel to the Civil Rights Act, the Economic Opportunity Act was winding its way through Congress. It was approved by the Senate in July 1964 and by the House in August. As a vehicle for coordinating and advancing Johnson's "War on Poverty," the legislation established the Office of Economic Opportunity (OEO) as a part of the Executive Office of the President. The OEO was to oversee the Job Corps, providing jobs for poor youths; 40 percent of the jobs were to be in conservation work, modeled after the New Deal's Civilian Conservation Corps (CCC). The OEO also managed VISTA (Volunteers in Service to America), the Legal Services Corporation (providing legal aid to poor people), loans to small businesses in impoverished areas, family health centers for the poor, and (starting in 1965) Head Start, a program providing federally funded preschool for poor families. The OEO was under a mandate to seek "maximum feasible participation" by the poor themselves in the design of the programs it was administering. The OEO enjoyed the advantage of close proximity to the president, but it also fostered political problems by seeming to bypass the big-city mayors whose help was essential to its success. Other poverty-fighting measures that Johnson promoted in 1964 in his "War on Poverty" included the Food Stamp Act of 1964 and the Housing Act of 1964. Food Stamps had started as a pilot program in 1961 to provide coupons for poor people who could use them to purchase food at cooperating stores, and the 1964 legislation extended and solidified the program. The Housing Act added public housing projects.

After attaining passage of the tax cut, the Civil Rights Act of 1964, and the Economic Opportunity Act, Johnson was nominated by Democrats to serve a full term as president with Hubert Humphrey as his vice president. He faced conservative Republican Senator Barry M. Goldwater of Arizona, nominated in a tough fight that represented the successful takeover of the Republican Party by the conservative movement. In early 1963, some newsmagazines had declared that President Kennedy might face a close election against Goldwater, but against Johnson in the aftermath of the assassination, Goldwater had no chance. Goldwater criticized big government and introduced what he called "the moral issue," the decay of traditional American morality. Johnson attacked Goldwater as an extremist, suggesting that the Arizonan would destroy Social Security or launch a nuclear war if elected. Johnson won 61 percent of the nationally aggregated popular vote to Goldwater's 39 percent, and 44 states to Goldwater's 6 (5 deep South states plus his home state). As importantly, LBJ's coattails added 38 seats to the Democratic majority in the House and two in the Senate. The Democratic victory was so complete at all levels that some commentators speculated that both conservatism and the Republican Party were fatally wounded.

Johnson, however, understood that the 1964 election opened a window of opportunity that was likely to remain open for only a limited period of time. There followed a flood of legislation that rivaled in its scope (while Johnson thought it surpassed) the New Deal itself.

THE GREAT SOCIETY IN FULL BLOOM

Possessing large majorities in both houses of Congress as well the legitimacy that came from being elected by a landslide in his own right, Johnson pushed hard for legislation on a number of overlapping fronts.[20]

New Deal-style middle-class entitlements

In 1965, LBJ finally secured passage of Medicare, a program to guarantee health care for elderly Americans, as an amendment to the Social Security Act. A Medicare payroll tax was added to Social Security tax, requiring a payment by employees and by employers. At age 65, workers would be eligible to pay subsidized premiums for a government-run health insurance program. Initially, the costs of the program were supposed to be covered 50 percent by payroll taxes and 50 percent by premiums, and Johnson promised that the average American worker would not pay more than $1 per month in additional payroll tax. The proposal had been quite controversial (the American Medical Association strongly opposed it as the leading edge of socialized medicine) and had been voted down by Congress under Kennedy. On the strength of the additional liberal votes gained in the 1964 congressional elections, Medicare became law.

The War on Poverty

Added to the Medicare bill at the last moment was a health care program for poor Americans. Medicaid was a means-tested entitlement program for Americans below a certain income level. It was designed to be a joint federal-state program, with both sides contributing to the cost. Within limits set by the federal government, states could set their own eligibility levels and the range of medical services that were covered. When Medicaid was enacted, Secretary of Health, Education, and Welfare John Gardner said, "We are heading toward a new kind of creative federalism."[21]

Continuing the drive against poverty, Johnson also won passage of regional aid targeted to Appalachia, one of the poorest areas of the

United States, and convinced Congress to provide rent supplements to the poor. He also won passage of a major federal education initiative aimed at funneling money toward school districts serving large populations of poor people. Proposals for federal aid to education had long been a lightning rod for criticism; education is nowhere to be found in the enumerated powers of Congress found in the Constitution, and it had overwhelmingly been a matter of policy reserved to the states and local school districts. Moreover, Catholics and Protestants clashed over whether federal aid should help parochial schools or only public schools. Some federal aid had gone to schools in the 1950s, but it had been tied to national defense and had been targeted to schools affected by military bases and (after Sputnik) to math and science instruction. The Elementary and Secondary Education Act (ESEA) of 1965 represented the first major federal aid to education that broke out of those bounds. Title I, the heart of ESEA, provided "compensatory education" funds based on the number of poor children being served; Title II funded educational materials, including textbooks; other titles gave federal money for education research and innovation, as well as building up state departments of education. To quell fears of federal domination, Title VI said that no federal official could "exercise supervision over the curriculum, administration, or personnel of any institution or school system or over the selection of any instructional materials." Johnson saw ESEA as a crucial part of his anti-poverty program.

After his election, Johnson also turned greater attention to the needs of the cities, which were intertwined with the needs of the poor. In 1965, at Johnson's suggestion, Congress created the federal Department of Housing and Urban Development (HUD) to manage federal housing programs and to focus on policy for the cities. As part of his urban efforts, Johnson launched the "Model Cities" program. The Demonstration Cities and Metropolitan Redevelopment Act of 1966 provided grants for cities to create a plan for urban renewal. Once the plan was approved by HUD, a second federal grant would fund up to 80 percent of the implementation of the plan. Most money was to be concentrated in areas of high poverty. Also in a bid to improve city life, the Department of Transportation was created in 1966 to (among other things) administer the urban mass transit projects funded by the federal government starting the same year.

One more measure of enormous long-term importance was not, strictly speaking, part of the War on Poverty, but it shared the War on Poverty's aim of reducing barriers faced by the poor and disadvantaged. The Immigration and Nationality Services Act of 1965 was the first major change in immigration law since 1924, when law made it difficult for non-European immigrants to gain entry into the United States (the

1924 Act created a "quota system" in which annual immigration from any nation could not exceed 2 percent of the number currently living in the United States). The 1965 Immigration Act replaced the nationality quotas with broader and more equal ceilings by hemisphere, eliminated the 1924 ban on Japanese immigration, and exempted from the limits immigration based on family reunification. It thus provided much greater openness for immigration by non-Europeans and has been a crucial reason for the changing demographic composition of the American people since 1965.[22]

Civil rights

Johnson and Congress followed up on the Civil Rights Act of 1964 with a number of other steps. Most important of these was the Voting Rights Act of 1965. The Civil Rights Act had contained a title banning literacy tests and otherwise aiming to guarantee blacks the right to vote, but many concluded that separate and stronger legislation was needed. The move for stronger voting rights laws picked up steam when peaceful marchers demanding equal voting rights were attacked by angry whites in Selma, Alabama, on March 7, 1965. The Act strengthened provisions against literacy tests and allowed the Attorney General to identify problematic counties that required special enforcement efforts, including the use of federal marshals to guarantee access to the polls. It also required some areas to obtain Justice Department approval if they wanted to change voting procedures or election districts. Finally, the Voting Rights Act directed the US Attorney General to challenge in court the use of the poll tax, which had been rendered illegal by the Twenty-Fourth Amendment to the Constitution in 1964. (By 1966, the US Supreme Court ruled against the poll tax in *Harper v. Virginia State Board of Elections*.)

Other strategies were used to extend civil rights. The ESEA prohibited federal education aid from going to schools that were not desegregating. The Fair Juries Act of 1968 banned all-white juries for black defendants in federal cases. On the third try, the Fair Housing Act was passed in 1968. The bill, which extended the Civil Rights Act's ban on discrimination to housing sales, lease, or rental, garnered the necessary votes only in the wake of Martin Luther King Jr.'s assassination and the race riots that followed. Not least, by executive order, LBJ established "affirmative action" (or racial preferences) for federal contracts, starting a debate over "reverse discrimination" that continues today.

Quality of life

Finally, in keeping with Johnson's concept of the "Great Society," an important strand of domestic policy in this period aimed at improving quality of life rather than material prosperity. This broad thrust included environmental regulations and conservation measures (building on the Clean Air Act of 1963), measures to aid the arts and humanities, and consumer and transportation safety measures.

Without belaboring the details of each piece of legislation, 1964 saw pesticide controls; water resources research; and the establishment of Medicine Bow National Forest, Ozark Scenic Riverway, Fire Island National Seashore, and other wilderness areas. In 1965, the Arts and Humanities Foundation was formed, as were the companion National Endowment for the Arts and National Endowment for the Humanities. Auto pollution and water pollution control standards were adopted, the Water Resources Council was created, and First Lady "Lady Bird" Johnson launched her signature program of highway beautification. The year 1966 saw measures promoting clean rivers, traffic safety, highway safety, tire safety, fish and wildlife preservation, and exchanges for scientific knowledge and cultural materials. In 1967, limits on industrial emissions from coal and steel were enacted, and the Public Broadcasting Corporation (which runs the Public Broadcasting System, or PBS) was created. In 1968, Johnson's last year in office, measures were passed promoting wholesome poultry, abatement of aircraft noise, and fire safety. Overall, an unprecedented amount of federal legislative energy was devoted to these sorts of quality-of-life issues.[23]

THE GREAT SOCIETY COMES TO A HALT

Despite (or perhaps because of) this cornucopia of legislation, the Great Society came to a screeching halt within two years. As Johnson had predicted, the window of opportunity slammed shut. However, no one, including Johnson, could have predicted in 1964 exactly why. Just as events such as the Cuban missile crisis and the assassination of President Kennedy launched the Great Society, unforeseen events helped pull it back down to earth.

Domestic disturbances proved to be an enormous distraction to policy makers, including Johnson. Destructive riots in Watts in 1965, Newark and Detroit in 1967, and Washington, DC, among many other places in 1968 created a sense of disorder. The overall crime rate increased by 111 percent between 1960 and 1970, and the violent crime rate increased by 120 percent. Drug usage ballooned. Assassinations of John F. Kennedy, Martin Luther King Jr., Robert F. Kennedy, and others (such as black nationalist leader Malcolm X) angered and unnerved millions. After 1965, campus disturbances became increasingly common, as radical students made demands and shut down major universities.

Growing concerns about disorder could be seen in the evolution of the legislative agenda. Anti-narcotics bills were passed in 1965, 1966, 1967, and 1968; in 1967, the presidentially appointed Kerner Commission concluded that "[o]ur nation is moving toward two societies, one black, one white—separate and unequal."[24] A federal gun control bill was passed in 1968; bills purporting to address crime generally and juvenile crime were commonplace. By the end of the Johnson administration, LBJ was portraying some of his anti-poverty program as an anti-crime program. Critics blamed the liberal administration and permissive courts for the disorder.

Some of the disorder apparent after 1964 was directly related to the Vietnam War. Inheriting a commitment from Kennedy to preserve the independence of South Vietnam against communist aggression, Johnson boosted troop totals in Vietnam from 23,000 in 1965 to 550,000 in 1968, but with what seemed to be a determination only to avoid defeat. The war became increasingly contentious and unpopular. There was no agreement among Americans on the best alternative: the left preferred withdrawal, the right a sharper escalation aimed at outright victory. But there was agreement that Johnson was not getting the job done. American war dead, which numbered 1,863 in 1965, surged to 6,143 in 1966, 11,153 in 1967, and 16,592 in 1968.[25] The war was also becoming increasingly costly in financial terms—ultimately totaling $111 billion (or $738 billion in 2011 dollars).[26]

Along with the breakdown of order at home and the unsatisfactory war abroad, Johnson lost the confidence of many Americans who feared that the Great Society represented an unprecedented centralization of power in Washington. To these Americans, Johnson's talk about "consensus" and avoiding a massive top-down Washington program was disingenuous.

As a result, LBJ's approval rating in the Gallup poll fell from 62 percent in December 1965 to 48 percent in November 1966 to 39 percent in mid-1967. In November 1966, the window of opportunity closed completely, as Republicans rebounded to gain 47 House seats, 3 Senate seats, and a number of important governorships (including California, where Ronald Reagan upset incumbent Democratic Governor Pat Brown). Johnson's favorable balance in Congress was gone, as was any sense of policy momentum.[27] The Fair Housing Act, Federal Juries Act, and a new Housing Act that gave more market-oriented incentives to builders were the only major pieces of legislation to make it through the post-midterm election gauntlet, and Johnson himself began proposing spending cuts in some domestic programs. What 1938 had been to the New Deal, 1966 was to the Great Society. What became obvious over time was that the Great Society also served as the death knell for the New Deal electoral coalition.

NEW FRONTIER / GREAT SOCIETY: SUMMARY AND ASSESSMENT

The Great Society was one of a handful of major eras of new domestic policy since 1932. This era of policy making saw major changes in every one of the seven areas of policy we are tracking, plus others.

Economic policy

The Great Society led to a significant growth in federal spending and regulation. From 1960 through 1968, spending grew from 17.2 percent of GDP to 19.8 percent of GDP, and by 61 percent in inflation-adjusted dollars. Keynesianism was the dominant approach, though policy makers also sought to boost economic growth through cuts in marginal income tax rates. Annual deficits in good times became the norm. Non-defense spending grew by another 90 percent in real terms, and from 8.2 percent of GDP to 10.7 percent. Pages in the *Federal Register* expanded from 14,479 to 20,072 in the same period.

Social welfare

Two large new health care programs were created—Medicare for the elderly and Medicaid for the poor. More broadly, Lyndon Johnson declared a "War on Poverty" that included creation of the Office of Economic Opportunity, several new programs under the OEO, Food Stamps, aid to poor regions such as Appalachia, an expansion of AFDC, urban renewal, and an expansion of public housing. Social program payments to individuals rose from 4.5 percent to 5.6 percent, and the stage was set for much larger increases in the future.

Civil rights

This period saw significant changes in civil rights policy, with passage of the Civil Rights Act of 1964, Voting Rights Act of 1965, Elementary and Secondary Education Act (which used federal funds to push schools toward desegregation), Fair Housing Act of 1968, and other measures. A constitutional amendment banned the poll tax and legislation banned literacy tests, which had often been used to prevent blacks from voting.

Education

Head Start put the federal government into the realm of preschool, and the ESEA represented the first broad foray of the federal government into K–12 education. Federal student financial aid gave a boost to college and university enrollment.

Environment

Going beyond conservation, federal policy began moving toward environmental protection, attempting to control a variety of pollutants.

Moral/cultural issues

Upsetting broad social consensus, the Supreme Court opened up this policy area with decisions banning school prayer, loosening restrictions on obscenity, and strengthening protections for the accused. Crime and drugs surged, putting new issues on the legislative agenda, and Barry Goldwater put the "moral issue" on the electoral agenda.

Federalism

Intergovernmental relations continued to change, with the federal government involving itself deeply in areas previously reserved to states and local government, such as education, mass transit, and urban planning. Increasingly, the federal government interacted directly with cities, bypassing state governments altogether. The "marble cake" federalism hinted at in the New Deal became fully evident in the Great Society through programs such as Model Cities, urban mass transit assistance, the Elementary and Secondary Education Act, and Medicaid.

The Great Society demonstrated how Theodore Lowi's categories of policy can be difficult to keep distinct. On one hand, redistributive policy was given new emphasis, as the War on Poverty created a network of redistributive programs. However, many of these can be seen as also constitutive, redefining American federalism. Civil rights and environmental changes were fundamentally regulatory in nature, but also had constitutive effects on federalism, and civil rights was widely viewed as part of a broader redistributive anti-poverty program.

The flood of new policy was the output of a **rare alignment of inputs**. The change frameworks make sense of the era. Intellectually, the Great Society had its foundation in a combination of FDR's New Deal thinking and the insistence of thinkers including John Kenneth Galbraith, Michael Harrington, and Rachel Carson that it was time for an emphasis on redirecting, rather than creating, affluence. A series of **events**—the recession of 1958, the Cuban missile crisis, and the Kennedy assassination—led to the creation of a **political environment** in which activist presidents eventually governed with large, liberal Democratic majorities. (However, in contrast with the New Deal, most of these events were not logically connected to the programs that resulted.) The mobilization of political movements interacted with events including the attacks in Selma, Alabama, and the assassination of Martin Luther King Jr. to contribute to the politics of the moment, as well. Not least, the **people** involved were crucial. In particular, Lyndon Johnson put to use his vast experience and skill in the legislative arena to make the most of his party's strength in Congress. At the same time, other events (such as riots and the Vietnam War) led to a deterioration of Johnson's political position, which ended his ability to pursue further policy change. After 1966, he was mostly stymied. Supreme Court justices also increasingly acted as policy makers: unlike the New Deal, the Great Society coincided with a burst of liberal judicial activism on civil rights issues and a variety of other cultural questions, such as school prayer and the treatment of criminal defendants.

Among the key events, **events abroad** had a big impact on the Great Society. The Cuban missile crisis and Vietnam War affected elections that changed the partisan and ideological composition of Congress, and hence its disposition toward domestic policy as well. As in the 1950s, the global competition with communism influenced Americans' views on civil rights policy. In the end, Vietnam consumed Johnson.

These inputs meant that the New Frontier and Great Society years saw a shifting **policy agenda** that embraced civil rights, a War on Poverty, environmental protection, and other quality-of-life issues as central, alongside more traditional concerns with maintaining prosperity and promoting economic security. Cultural/moral issues also made their appearance for the first time since Prohibition.

As in the New Deal, **problem definition** was a crucial force behind the development of new policy. Galbraith's definition of "the problem"—a shortage of public sector, an excess of private—made clear the solution, at least in broad terms, for those who subscribed to it. Similarly, Harrington's identification of hidden poverty as "the" major problem facing America, and his identification of its source in social factors beyond individual control, was seized on by liberal policy makers.

The **policy baseline and path dependency** were evident factors. Some policies of the era, such as the Job Corps and Food Stamps, had precedents in the New Deal. Others could be seen as incremental in character, insofar as they added to existing federal commitments. ESEA added to the National Defense Education Act. Medicare was promoted as a logical extension of Social Security, and both Medicare and Medicaid were enacted as amendments to the 1935 Social Security Act. The tax cut of 1964 reduced the top marginal income tax rate from 91 percent to 70 percent—in one sense incremental (a modest but significant shift in an existing policy) but in another sense not (since the shift fundamentally reversed the trend of the previous three decades toward higher rates). Looking broadly, the Great Society took the New Deal commitment to a bigger and more powerful central government, and made it even bigger and even more powerful.

When taken as a whole, however, the Great Society must be seen as more than just an incremental shift in policy. There were simply too many new programs, and most observers at the time understood the revolutionary character of the program. Johnson himself certainly did, as he described the Great Society in quintessentially revolutionary terms: "But most of all," Johnson intoned in his 1964 Michigan address, "the Great

Society is not a safe harbor, a resting place, a final objective, a finished work. It is a challenge constantly renewed, beckoning us toward a destiny where the meaning of our lives matches the marvelous products of our labor."

The Great Society made obvious the **difficulty of assessing the success or failure** of a program. The overall poverty rate fell by about one-third between 1960 and 1970. In particular, Medicare's provision of health care to Americans over the age of 65 helped prevent the destitution of the elderly, whose poverty rate fell faster than the national average. The initial civil rights actions, especially the Civil Rights Act of 1964, were morally imperative and are now supported by a near consensus of Americans on both the right and left. Defenders of the Great Society also argue that air and water quality were raised, that federal anti-poverty programs tried to take greater account of the views of the poor themselves, and that federalism was strengthened by promoting greater cooperation between levels of government.[28] Some liberals argue that the Great Society was, on the whole, a good thing, but that it fell short of its potential because it was underfunded. The War on Poverty fell short, in this view, because the war in Vietnam drained money and attention from domestic concerns.[29]

Critics contend that the decline in poverty from 1960 to 1970 was primarily the result of a growing economy, not the anti-poverty programs, which they see as mostly ineffective. Moreover, despite the expenditure of what is now $21 trillion of dollars on Great Society programs, poverty has remained largely stuck at 1970 levels. Some sympathetic critics, such as LBJ advisor Daniel Patrick Moynihan, conceded that too much confidence had been placed in social science "experts."[30] Less sympathetic analysts argued that the Great Society programs carried a high cost in three areas—**all of them unintended and unanticipated consequences**. First, critics point to high economic costs. The expansion of domestic government in the 1960s put the nation on the course toward an explosion of spending and deficits in the 1970s, 1980s, and beyond. Inflation and an end to the seemingly effortless prosperity of the 1960s followed. For example, Food Stamps, which served fewer than half a million people in 1965, had ballooned to 2.2 million clients by 1969. The "automatic spending" of Medicare and Medicaid alone accounted for more than $1.2 trillion in spending in 2016, more than twice the size of the federal deficit that year. Those health care entitlements had another problematic economic effect, distorting the health care market and contributing to the rapid rise of health care costs.[31] Socially, critics contend that the War on Poverty changed the incentive structure for the poor by subsidizing poverty and poverty-inducing behaviors while reducing the stigma against long-term unemployment. As a result, the rate of entrenched, chronic poverty went up, not down.[32] Moreover, important structures of civil society, such as family and private associations, were weakened by the government takeover of so many new functions. The illegitimacy rate, only 5 percent in 1960, has gone steadily upward, reaching around 40 percent today. Politically, opponents conclude that the Great Society seriously undermined federalism, and that centralized, unlimited, and arrogant government posed an increasing threat to liberty.[33] Altogether, in the view of critics, the Great Society—leaving aside progress on civil rights, which is today generally conceded to have been a good thing—traded very high (mostly unintentional) costs for very uncertain benefits.

However one assesses the Great Society in terms of policy, it cannot be considered a success in terms of politics. Instead, it represents what one might call a negative feedback loop. Lyndon Johnson's attention to civil rights (and Barry Goldwater's vote against the 1964 Civil Rights Act on constitutional grounds) helped cement the loyalty of black voters for the Democratic Party, even though congressional Republicans played a crucial role in the passage of the Act. As late as the 1960 election, Republicans received about one-third of the black vote; from 1964 forward, Democratic candidates have typically received 9 out of 10 black votes. However, Johnson lost the solid South, which became unmoored from the Democratic Party. Southern states did not always vote for Republicans after 1964, but they could never again be taken for granted by Democrats. The urban-rural coalition fashioned by FDR collapsed, as Johnson's strong commitment to urban concerns upset the balance. And Democrats lost their hold on the middle class, and retained only a tenuous hold on the working class (especially the non-unionized working class). Some of these voters were alienated by the core of the civil rights program, others by more controversial additions to the civil rights agenda (such as affirmative action and school busing) that seemed contrary to the spirit of race-blind equality that the Civil Rights Act had promised. Voters were also increasingly concerned with the disorder, countercultural decadence, and anti-American radicalism that they came to identify with the Democratic Party. Johnson had seemed to preside over a federal government that was out of control, striking in some important way at what millions of Americans took to be a defining characteristic of their country. Not least, the Great Society struck many in the great American middle as poorly conceived and ineffective, if not counterproductive. On top of the domestic discontents was Vietnam, a big foreign policy problem and the source of enormous division at home. If this complex of issues did not completely supersede the Great Depression as a source of partisan loyalty in the electorate, at least it went a long way toward balancing it. Republicans would win 7 of the next 10 presidential elections.

4

The Nixon-Ford-Carter Equilibrium

★   ★   ★

A gas station attendant directs traffic toward the pumps. The 1970s confronted policy makers with a toxic combination of inflation, rising unemployment, and an "energy crisis," complete with long gas lines.

FOLLOWING THE FRANTIC ACTIVITY of the Johnson presidency, the next 12 years saw another period of rough equilibrium, during which the political backlash against the Great Society gradually caught up with the Great Society's policy momentum. The Great Society era as a period of consistently liberal domestic policy was over. The Democratic electoral coalition was in trouble. National traumas, prominent in the

65

previous decade, continued piling up. And conservatism, declared dead after Lyndon Johnson's 1964 landslide, was on the upswing but far from dominant. This tension produced a series of administrations mixing conservative and liberal rhetoric and policies in unpredictable ways. It also meant that incrementalism reigned; there was no breakthrough for either side. The necessary political and intellectual inputs were not present, and events did not drive a broad and coherent direction in policy. To the contrary, these inputs contributed to something of a policy vacuum that would only be filled in the next period.

Richard Nixon's election to the presidency in 1968 was, to many, a surprising comeback. Dwight D. Eisenhower's vice president, Nixon had followed up his very narrow loss to John F. Kennedy in the 1960 presidential race with a losing campaign for governor of California in 1962. In the wake of that defeat, Nixon seemed to slink off into permanent retirement from politics. Instead, he campaigned hard for Republicans in 1966, won the GOP nomination for president in 1968, and beat Hubert Humphrey, the Democratic nominee, by a margin almost as narrow as the one he lost by in 1960.[1] The Republican Party Nixon led had changed since 1960. When he first ran, he secured his nomination by making a deal with liberal New York governor Nelson Rockefeller; the second time, his nomination was saved by a deal made with Strom Thurmond (now a Republican) and Barry Goldwater.[2] Nixon adopted part of Goldwater's "Sunbelt strategy" of appealing to the South and West, and added to it an appeal to blue-collar ethnic voters disturbed by the counterculture.[3] On Nixon's coattails, Republicans gained seats in the House and Senate, though they remained far from a majority in either chamber. On balance, the Senate remained controlled by liberals, while the House was more evenly divided between liberals and a bipartisan coalition of Republicans and conservative Democrats. If Eisenhower's 1956 reelection gave a taste of divided government, Nixon's 1968 election was the harbinger of an era dominated by it. Even Nixon's 1972 landslide against liberal Democrat George McGovern, in which he won 49 states (including McGovern's home state of South Dakota), did not disturb this picture, as Democrats remained in control of Congress. Consequently, Nixon was swimming in a sea of contention, which ultimately ended in his resignation from office due to the Watergate scandal. Biographers have long struggled with Nixon, who combined great political skill, perceptiveness, and flexibility with a sometimes brooding or even paranoid style.[4]

Foreign events proved a preoccupation for Nixon. On one hand, he was determined to achieve "peace with honor" in Vietnam, which meant continuing to fight (and sometimes even escalating) the war until South Vietnam could defend itself and the North Vietnamese politburo was willing to accept the independence of its neighbor. As a result, the antiwar movement grew angrier, and sometimes more violent; there were around 2,500 political bombings in the United States in an 18-month period in 1971–1972.[5] However, US casualties declined markedly after 1969, and by 1973, Nixon could claim to be a peacemaker, having reached an agreement with North Vietnam and having attended high-profile summit meetings with Soviet and communist Chinese leaders. The bulk of Nixon's memoirs are focused on foreign affairs.[6]

Moreover, there was no new intellectual force to cause a dramatic change in the trajectory of policy. To the contrary, some of the liberal assumptions that propelled the Great Society remained intact among policy makers, though largely exhausted. Nixon himself remarked, "In economics, I am now a Keynesian."[7]

None of this is to say that domestic policy was ignored by Nixon. In fact, the public policy agenda continued expanding.[8] Recessions in 1969–1970 and 1973–1974 put basic economic growth—not merely how to use affluence—back on the table as a major issue. For the first time since the early 1950s, inflation began to seriously rear its head, though signs had been detected in the late Johnson years. Quality-of-life issues, such as the environment, consumer protection, and women's rights, took an even more prominent place, as did law and order. Starting in 1973, when the Arab states enforced an oil boycott against the United States in response to US support for Israel during the Yom Kippur War, energy became a major issue. The resulting "energy crisis" further worsened the economic picture. Social and cultural issues with their origins in the 1960s, particularly crime and drugs, demanded a response. And in January 1973, abortion became a heated national issue when the Supreme Court rendered its *Roe v. Wade* decision.

In addition, a number of secondary civil rights issues arose and stirred enormous controversy. Affirmative action, which was started by Lyndon Johnson's executive order in 1968, was expanded by Nixon. At the same time, courts began ordering the forced busing of schoolchildren to produce the racial integration of schools; policy shifted from preventing forcible segregation to forcibly imposing integration. Additionally, a number of political reforms were advocated by Americans acting in the experimental spirit of the 1960s. Constitutional amendments were proposed guaranteeing 18-year-olds the right to vote and abolishing the Electoral College, both endorsed by Nixon (only the amendment on voter age was adopted). Finally, partly as a result of tensions between the Republican president and Democratic Congress, a number of constitutional issues arose regarding the federal budget and the separation of powers (including war powers).

Some of Nixon's domestic policies reflected a conservative turn away from the Great Society. He made liberal Supreme Court decisions an object of criticism and promised to reshape the federal judiciary to serve a more limited judicial role. He opposed school busing, which he made a key point of distinction between himself and McGovern in the 1972 election. Nixon also tried to abolish the Office of Economic Opportunity (OEO), which Lyndon Johnson had made the centerpiece of his "War on Poverty." Gerald Ford finally succeeded in 1974, though many of the programs under the OEO survived.

After his reelection in 1972, Nixon also became more confrontational with Congress, in an attempt to curtail federal domestic spending. In particular, he used a mechanism known as "impoundment" to refrain from spending money that had been appropriated by Congress. Impoundment had a long history but had generally been exercised with the quiet agreement of Congress. Nixon changed the character of impoundment, using it like a line-item veto to excise spending because of policy disagreements with Congress. Congress, seeing Nixon's use of impoundment as an affront to its power of the purse, passed the Budget and Impoundment Control Act of 1974, which curtailed impoundment, created a new budget process, and reasserted congressional authority over spending.[9]

Early in his presidency, Nixon also made an effort to craft a domestic policy agenda built around a revitalization of federalism, which Nixon judged to have been harmed by the Great Society's centralization. In 1971, he built his State of the Union address around what he called "New Federalism." Saying "I reject the patronizing idea that the government in Washington, DC, is inevitably more wise, more honest, and more efficient than government at the local or State level," he proposed and attained passage of the General Revenue Sharing program as a supplement to the highly structured "categorical grants" of the Great Society.[10] Revenue sharing provided states and local governments with a blank check to be used as they saw fit. He also proposed consolidating many categorical grants into broader, less-restrictive block grants.

At the same time, Nixon pursued policies that would universally be recognized as liberal today, although at the time, some liberals did not think Nixon went far enough. Indeed, economist Herbert Stein remarked that the Nixon era was characterized by "conservative men with liberal ideas."[11] He embraced and broadened the regulatory push of the Great Society, advocating the creation of the Environmental Protection Agency (EPA) and the Occupational Safety and Health Administration (OSHA). The EPA was granted broad powers to issue environmental regulations (such as clean air standards), and OSHA gained equally broad powers to regulate the workplace for employee safety. Both the EPA and OSHA were examples of broad congressional delegation of legislative authority to an administrative agency.

When it came to spending, taxing, and macroeconomic policy in general, Nixon had a record that tilted in the liberal direction, notwithstanding his brief assault on discretionary domestic spending. In 1969 and 1971, Nixon backed significant tax increases.

Perhaps his most important decision affecting fiscal policy was his agreement in 1972 to a 20 percent increase in Social Security retirement benefits, followed by annual cost of living adjustments (COLAs) that would take place automatically. Congress no longer had to act; benefits would rise automatically with inflation. The deal also transferred supplemental security income (SSI) for the needy aged, blind, and disabled from states to the federal budget. Nixon subsequently argued that he was defending fiscal probity by taking discretion out of the hands of Congress, but the bottom line was that a large and growing portion of federal spending was set to increase automatically.[12]

Nixon also took a regulatory rather than free-market approach toward fighting inflation. As public concerns about inflation mounted in 1971, Nixon announced a policy of wage and price controls. Specifically, utilizing emergency powers that had been employed by Franklin Roosevelt in World War II, Nixon declared a 90-day wage and price freeze. The idea was that inflation was driven by "inflationary expectations" that became self-perpetuating; a freeze would alter the inflationary psychology and break the cycle. The 90 days then turned into almost 1,000 days of wage and price controls that came in four phases. From a rate of 6 percent in 1970 and more than 4 percent in 1971, inflation had reached double digits by 1974, when the wage and price controls were mostly ended. By then, the notion that wage and price controls could cure inflation "was thoroughly discredited" (though some liberal politicians continued to advocate them), and focus turned to monetary policy.[13] Many reasons have been offered for the failure, including the Nixon administration's decision to remove the United States from the Bretton Woods financial agreement using a form of gold standard; rapidly rising federal spending; the lack of an anti-inflationary monetary policy; and, by 1973, the oil crisis. Free-market advocates argue simply that government control of prices will always be doomed to fail when tested against the realities of supply and demand.[14]

Dwarfing the more or less liberal domestic policies that Nixon enacted were the ones he tried but failed to enact. One was national health insurance, a goal that liberal Democrats had long deduced from FDR's Economic Bill of Rights and that Harry S. Truman had proposed. Another was a guaranteed income, under the rubric of the "Family Assistance Plan" (FAP). Liberals had also long hoped for a government-guaranteed income. Nixon offered both, which would have moved American domestic policy significantly to the left, and yet failed to achieve victory in a Congress controlled by Democrats. The more liberal Senate and less liberal House had difficulty finding common ground. Moreover, many Democratic liberals miscalculated. Nixon's plans were, in their view, not generous enough. They believed that Nixon was an aberration, a fluke who only won in 1968 because of Democratic disarray, and was likely to be defeated in 1972. They could not foresee that there would not be another liberal Democratic president until 2009.

When Nixon was forced to resign in the wake of Watergate, Gerald Ford took his place. Ford served only two-and-a-half years as president, and was immediately weakened by both the adverse public reaction to his preemptive pardon of Nixon and by the midterm elections of 1974, in which Democrats gained 47 seats in the House and 5 in the Senate. The new, much more liberal House did not shy away from conflicts with the president.

Consequently, gridlock ruled the day and nothing much of substance came of Ford's presidency in terms of domestic policy. Ford was a fiscally conservative midwesterner who had served as House Minority Leader before being appointed by Nixon to serve as vice president when Spiro Agnew resigned in 1973.[15] As president, he took up the battle against spending and vetoed 66 bills, mostly on fiscal grounds. Of these, 12 were overridden.

A highly visible sign of Ford's determination to restore fiscal restraint came in 1975, when New York City was on the verge of bankruptcy and came to the federal government for a bailout. Ford refused, leading a New York daily newspaper to shout in its headlines: "Ford to NY: Drop Dead." This stand was not very popular in New York, which then scrambled to cut its budget, but was not unpopular in much of the rest of the country.

Otherwise, Ford proved largely hapless. Widely considered "the accidental president,"[16] Ford's domestic presidency reflected his circumstances. Nothing better symbolized this reality than his anti-inflation program, "Whip Inflation Now," which was announced with great fanfare but amounted to little more than the red and white WIN pins that citizens were urged to wear. The appearance of presidential impotence was deepened by the response of Congress to events abroad. When North Vietnam attacked South Vietnam in March 1975, Ford asked Congress to increase aid to the South in order to enforce the peace agreement; Congress answered by cutting off all aid and letting the South fall. When Cuban troops flooded into the former Portuguese colony of Angola, Ford hoped to send aid to the pro-Western forces fighting there; Congress responded by cutting them off, too. And, politically, Ford found himself warding off a strong challenge for the 1976 Republican presidential nomination by Ronald Reagan, who came within 71 votes of defeating Ford at the

Republican convention. Reagan's challenge pulled Ford to the right and farther away from the Nixon approach to domestic policy.

Nevertheless, when Ford faced Democrat Jimmy Carter in November, he nearly prevailed. The final nationally aggregated popular vote tally was 50.1 percent to 48.0 percent, with Carter winning 297 electoral votes and only 24 states. Carter succeeded in cobbling together a large part of the old New Deal coalition, but just barely. And he did it with a very un-New Deal approach, running against Washington as an outsider who would restore honesty, common sense, and a more humble presidency to the capital.

As the Nixon-Ford years came to a close, three broad trends were observable. First, despite Ford's efforts, budget deficits continued to grow. After a small surplus in 1969, the deficit reached $74 billion by 1976. (Indeed, 1969 would show the last balanced federal budget until 1998.) Second, due to the explosion of domestic spending emanating from the Great Society and early Nixon years, domestic social spending exceeded defense outlays for the first time since before World War II. (That has remained true ever since.) Not least, this period proved to be the pinnacle of Keynesian intellectual dominance. The so-called Phillips Curve, developed by Keynesian economists, held that there was a mathematical trade-off between unemployment and inflation. As the demand curve moved up, employment would rise but so would prices; as demand fell, prices would fall but so would employment. Yet the experience in the 1970s was increasingly one of "stagflation," combining inflation and recession. For this dilemma, the Keynesians had no easy explanation and no plausible solution.

THE CARTER PRESIDENCY

If Richard Nixon's domestic presidency was the beginning of a transitional period, owing more to the liberal era that was ending than to the conservative era that was on the horizon, Jimmy Carter's was a mirror image. Just as Nixon disappointed many of his conservative supporters, Carter ended up disappointing many of the Democratic Party's liberal stalwarts.

Carter, the former one-term governor of Georgia, was trained as an engineer at the US Naval Academy and served seven years as a naval officer. He was an active Southern Baptist, and in the wake of Watergate, he ran by saying that he would never lie to the American people. Carter was the first candidate from the Deep South to be elected president.[17] Like Nixon, Carter was a bundle of contradictions: wanting to piece back together the New Deal coalition, he also vowed to rein in the bureaucracy and called the federal tax code (written mostly by congresses of his own party over the previous half century) "a disgrace to the human race."

In this, Carter was taking advantage of a populist unhappiness with Washington that George Wallace had recently exploited and that Ronald Reagan would soon tap into.[18] Carter added a technocratic 1960s "new politics" style endorsement of "limits to growth." In contrast to Nixon, who was perceived by many to lack an ethical core, Carter proved rigid and severe, more like Herbert Hoover than Franklin Roosevelt.

Carter also resembled Hoover in another respect—he presided over economic circumstances that continued to deteriorate until they were judged by many Americans to have been the worst since the Great Depression. By 1980, unemployment reached a postwar high of 8.5 percent nationally, far from the Depression-era peak (though certain industrial cities saw Depression-era levels of 15–25 percent unemployment). In addition, inflation reached double digits, hitting an annualized rate of 18 percent in February 1980, the worst inflation rate since the Civil War. Contributing to these ills was a new spike in energy prices, driven by the Iranian Revolution, which replaced the pro-American Shah of Iran with the anti-American Ayatollah Khomeini. This new phase of the energy crisis led, as in 1973, to gasoline lines and oil shortages. Interwoven with these economic problems was a severe decline in the automobile industry, exemplified by the near-bankruptcy of the Chrysler Corporation. For a time, almost everything seemed to be going wrong: Three Mile Island nuclear plant in Pennsylvania suffered a partial meltdown and leaked radioactive material; wildcat strikes by truckers protesting high gas prices led to riots, as did a racial incident in Miami; and Carter himself invited ridicule when he confessed to having to fight off a rabbit with his oar while fishing (the "killer rabbit" episode).

The sense that the administration, and perhaps the nation, was unraveling was strengthened by events abroad. As Carter unilaterally canceled or postponed weapons systems such as the MX missile, the B-1 bomber, and the neutron bomb, the Soviets continued an unrelenting military buildup. Nicaragua fell to the communist-led Sandinista Front, Cuban troops intervened in Ethiopia, and a communist coup put Afghanistan into the Soviet orbit. The two biggest blows came in late 1979. Ten months after the Iranian revolution, Iranian radicals supported by Khomeini invaded the US embassy in Tehran and took the staff hostage. Less than two months later, with its client tottering in Afghanistan, the Soviet Union invaded that country directly. The immediate response by Americans was to rally around the president, whose approval ratings shot up. Over time, however, the incidents only reinforced the image of Carter as weak and unable to defend the nation's interests.[19]

Carter's domestic policy, as one might expect, had many liberal elements.[20] His top two domestic priorities were a comprehensive energy bill that mostly relied on top-down centralized approaches and a welfare reform bill that had more liberal than conservative elements. After enormous wrangling, the energy bill passed; the welfare reform bill did not. Carter also proposed a form of national health insurance, which went nowhere, and endorsed and signed the 1978 Humphrey-Hawkins Full Employment Act, which emphasized federal responsibility for the economy. Humphrey-Hawkins established a set of economic goals, advocated a balanced budget and non-inflationary monetary policy, and required the federal government to provide jobs in times of high unemployment. Reality did not conform itself to legislation. Federal deficits rose further under Carter, and overall federal regulation exploded, especially in areas of environmental, consumer, and workplace safety regulations.[21]

Social Security, which had last made an appearance when COLAs were guaranteed in 1972, reappeared as a major issue in 1977, when calculations showed that the Social Security Trust Fund was nearly broke. The solution agreed to by Carter and Congress was to increase the FICA tax and correct an error in the 1972 calculation for COLAs. This "fix," Carter promised at the time, would see the program through 2030.[22]

Despite the overall growth of spending and regulation, Carter also endorsed some movements in the opposite direction. In his 1978 State of the Union Address, he argued that "government cannot solve our problems, it can't set our goals, it cannot define our vision."[23] His energy plans, while government-centered, nevertheless included a partial deregulation of oil prices. When Nixon rescinded most of his wage and price controls in 1974, controls on oil prices were left in place and contributed to oil shortages in the late 1970s. Carter proposed to relax those controls, though simultaneously insisting on a "windfall profits tax" to confiscate part of the profits that oil companies might make as a result (thus, critics complained, taking away with one hand what he was giving with the other). He also oversaw a process of deregulation in some key industries, such as airlines and trucking, that had been heavily regulated since the Depression. Deregulation came to be thought of as a conservative policy, but during the Carter years it briefly enjoyed support across the ideological spectrum from figures including Carter, conservatives like Ronald Reagan, and liberals like Edward Kennedy, who concluded that regulatory structures had impeded innovation and artificially raised costs to consumers.[24] Not least, under political pressure from his right, in 1980 Carter proposed spending cuts in domestic programs, including Food Stamps, in an attempt to balance the budget, though the attempt proved futile due to the deepening recession.

Carter's approach to fighting inflation eschewed wage and price controls, which had failed under Nixon, and embraced instead a combination of fiscal belt-tightening and tight monetary policy restricting the money supply. Carter appointed Paul Volcker as chairman of the Federal

Reserve Board in 1979. Volcker, a conservative Democrat, took a hard line against inflation, driving the prime interest rate up to a peak of 21.5 percent in order to wring excess demand out of the economy. It was these interest rates that helped drive the economy into deep recession in 1979–1980 (and then again in 1981–1982).

These changes also (along with the rest of Carter's deviancies from liberal orthodoxy) helped drive Edward M. Kennedy into a primary challenge against Carter in the 1980 Democratic primaries. Carter's deviance was perhaps best shown not by anything he did but by what he did not do. He was the first Democratic president since Grover Cleveland in the 1890s to not tout some new comprehensive program of activist government, and to not achieve passage of any significant new program of government benefits. Woodrow Wilson had the New Freedom, FDR the New Deal, Harry Truman the Fair Deal, JFK the New Frontier, LBJ the Great Society. Carter had a sprawling but ineffective energy program, higher and lower spending, more and less regulation, and a monetary policy that helped produce the highest unemployment rate since 1939.

Carter's incrementalism and limited and conflicted agenda was in no small part a product of the mixed political environment, which featured large but divided Democratic congressional majorities, continued bureaucratic momentum for Great Society regulation, a growing public conviction that government had grown too big and unaccountable, and a growing intellectual and organizational capacity of the conservative movement. As political scientist Stephen Skowronek argues, Carter had the misfortune of serving at a time of political "disjunction" as the once-solid New Deal coalition was splintering.[25] (Skowronek notes that Herbert Hoover, too, governed in a moment of coalitional "disjunction.") Think tanks on the right like the Heritage Foundation and the American Enterprise Institute were fully engaged in the "war of ideas." Led by conservatives, Republicans made modest but important gains in the midterm elections of 1978 and used Congress as a platform to propose deregulation and big tax cuts, such as the 30 percent across-the-board Kemp-Roth income tax cut. Kemp-Roth was just one sign of a growing "tax revolt": sensing the heat, Congress had passed the Steiger amendment cutting capital gains taxes, and state voters in California and Massachusetts passed ballot initiatives cutting taxes. Not least, religious conservatives upset by abortion, the banning of school prayer, threats to the traditional family, and proposed IRS regulations that endangered the tax exempt status of Christian schools began organizing en masse through groups such as the Religious Roundtable and Moral Majority. Energetic conservatives succeeded in blocking the ratification of the Equal Rights Amendment, despite Carter's vocal support for it, in addition to blocking promulgation of the IRS regulations on schools.

By the summer of 1979, the president's approval rating had fallen below 30 percent in some polls, reaching a nadir lower than Richard Nixon's rating in the Watergate scandal. Though Carter recovered in the early stages of the Iranian and Afghan crises, by mid-1980 he was languishing again with low popularity. This meant that Carter's leverage with Congress, especially on domestic policy issues, was very limited.

Though he ultimately fought off the Kennedy challenge, Carter would face an even tougher foe in November. Ironically, he considered Ronald Reagan the easiest Republican to defeat and welcomed Reagan's nomination by the Republicans. The Nixon, Ford, and Carter era of equilibrium and transition ended on November 4, 1980, exactly one year after the start of the Iranian hostage crisis, when Carter was decisively beaten by his preferred opponent.

EQUILIBRIUM, 1969–1981: SUMMARY AND ASSESSMENT

In this period, some consequential policies were enacted, but at a much slower rate than in the heyday of the Great Society. Incrementalism returned to the forefront; government spending and regulating continued growing, though largely as a result of momentum rather than new programs.

Economic policy

Policy makers veered from one approach to another as Keynesianism lost its explanatory power. Overall federal spending increased again, from 19.8 percent of GDP in 1968 to 21.1 percent in 1980—another 46 percent increase in real terms. After a brief surplus in 1969, deficits reigned for the rest of this period (and consistently until 1998). Non-defense spending exploded from 10.7 percent of GDP to 16.3 percent; spending on "human resources" became more than half of all federal spending for the first time since World War II, going from 33 percent of all federal spending to 53 percent. Regulatory activity also exploded. From 20,466 pages in 1969, the *Federal Register* passed 30,000 pages in 1973, 40,000 in 1974, 60,000 in 1975, and 70,000 in 1979, landing at 87,012 pages in 1980. At the same time, though, certain specific industries such as airlines and trucking were deregulated.

Social welfare

Payments to individuals exploded from 5.6 percent of GDP in 1968 to 10 percent of GDP in 1980, but most was the result of the forward momentum or expansion of existing programs (including the Social Security amendments in 1972). Attempts to fashion extensive new programs in health or welfare failed, and policy makers began to confront the fiscal realities of uncontrolled social spending.

Civil rights
Both courts and elected officials pushed civil rights policy into new territory, but starting from a familiar base—from desegregation and non-discrimination into forced integration and affirmative action.

Education
After the Great Society established a broad federal interest in K–12 education, more incremental change in education followed. The most important new policy was the Individuals with Disabilities Education Act (IDEA) of 1973, mandating a certain level of special education services across the country. In 1980, the cabinet-level US Department of Education was created.

Environment
Pushed by the growing environmental movement, creation of the Environmental Protection Agency and passage of the Clean Air Act were features of the Nixon administration. During the Carter administration, the Superfund was created to facilitate cleanup of toxic waste sites.

Moral/cultural issues
"Law and order" was a major Nixon theme, and the Supreme Court nationalized the debate over abortion with *Roe v. Wade*. By the end of the 1970s, a full-fledged political backlash had developed in defense of traditional moral values and family structures.

Federalism
Nixon proposed the "New Federalism" in an attempt to reverse the centralization of government since the 1930s. His goal was to revive the capacity for action at lower levels by sending more federal resources to state and local governments, with fewer federal strings attached. From 1968 to 1980, federal grants to state and local governments surpassed 1 percent of GDP for the first time.

The combination of **inputs** in this era led to incrementalism and a lack of policy coherence. Conservative ideas were slowly gaining strength, New Deal visions had lost potency, and Keynesianism was increasingly discredited, but no set of **ideas** had firmly established itself. Political scientist Samuel Beer asked in 1980 whether America had any longer a "public philosophy" capable of serving as a coherent guide for policy makers. Beer's conclusion was "no."[26] **Events** including stagflation and the energy crisis contributed to the sense of confusion—a disassembling of the old order. Watergate and Nixon's resignation cut short his attempt to form a new, eclectic approach, and stagflation and Iran did the same to Carter. **Politics** reflected this reality. In a sense, the entire 12-year period was characterized by one version of divided government or another: first Republican presidents and Democratic congresses, followed by an outsider president trying and failing to work with an establishment congress. The heated political atmosphere of the 1960s and early 1970s gave way to increased public cynicism and apathy; many of the social movements of the previous era lost steam, though the environmental movement gained momentum and leverage within the policy process. The growing political vacuum was also a product of the personalities of the **people** involved— the secretive and self-destructive Nixon, decent but nondescript Ford, inexperienced and rigid Carter. Political scientists Michael A. Genovese, Todd L. Belt, and William W. Lammers classify both Nixon and Carter as "low-opportunity presidents."[27] To put it another way, the streams of politics, ideas, and events did not give them much to work with.

With a few exceptions, the **baseline** dominated. On the rare occasions presidents tried to break out in a more fundamental way, such as health care and welfare under both Nixon and Carter, they failed. The elimination of the Office of Economic Opportunity was a rare case of a government office being eliminated; otherwise, the programs and structures of the Great Society endured and its regulatory activity accelerated, despite its much weaker political foundation.

The agenda of this period was likewise heavily influenced by the Great Society, either positively or negatively. Sometimes policy makers sought to complete its unfinished business. Sometimes they grappled with the problems the Great Society left behind, including inflation and ineffective programs and strategies. Additionally, stagflation, the energy crisis, and environmental issues either joined the agenda or gained importance. Moral issues, which had appeared in the 1960s, expanded to include abortion, family, and religious freedom, catapulted to prominence by the Supreme Court and a fracturing social consensus.

The importance and difficulty of **problem definition** could be seen in the varying approaches to inflation from Nixon to Carter. Was inflation the result of inflationary expectations, too much money circulating, or too much federal spending? Depending on the answer, the result was wage and price controls, tightening monetary policy, and federal spending cuts.

Unanticipated consequences abounded. Wage and price controls did not solve inflation, but may have contributed to oil shortages and gas lines a few years later by curtailing supply. Economists estimated that the explosion of regulation in the 1970s may have reduced GDP by a full percentage point. Perhaps equally important, liberal Democrats clearly miscalculated regarding Nixon's proposals for national health insurance and guaranteed income. In that case, their policy decision—to not enact Nixon's proposals—carried consequences far removed from their intentions.

Finally, **assessments of policy** in this era are not uniform. The predominant view has been that the 1970s represent a failure of economics and a disaster of national morale, accompanied by a number of foreign policy catastrophes. An alternative minority view, seen in John E. Schwartz's *America's Hidden Success: A Reassessment of Public Policy from Kennedy to Reagan*, is that the economy in the 1970s was better than generally portrayed. In particular, despite recessions in 1974–1975 and 1979–1980, average economic growth was solid and workers' wages increased during most of this period.[28]

This optimistic picture, however, was clearly not adopted by voters. It also was not adopted by most analysts at the time. At a minimum, stagflation (which afflicted not just the United States but other industrialized democracies) was sufficiently serious to call into serious question the dominant economic paradigm of Keynesianism. To some, the seemingly intractable character of stagflation called into question the viability of the market as a way of organizing societies economically. Numerous observers raised the question in the late 1970s and early 1980s whether, in the midst of the economic crisis, capitalism itself could survive.[29]

Intertwined with this era of incoherent and largely unsuccessful policy was a growing crisis of American institutions. Richard Nixon fully embraced what some came to call the "imperial presidency," or the modern presidency as it had grown up since Franklin Roosevelt. After the trauma of Vietnam and in the midst of Watergate, Congress finally pushed back, passing legislation to curtail the president in both foreign and domestic realms. After Nixon's forced resignation due to impeachment proceedings, Ford and Carter sought to take a reduced symbolic if not actual role. However, many concluded that they had overcompensated. The result was a concern by 1980 that presidential contraction had gone too far. Some asked the question: Is the presidency still an effective institution?[30] Alongside lost confidence in the presidency was a widespread loss of public confidence in American institutions more generally.

Tied up with all of these concerns, which were mostly domestic in nature, was the biggest question of all, raised by analysts such as Ben Wattenberg, a moderate Democrat, who contended that the free West was on the verge of staring into an abyss: Soviet victory in the Cold War (or perhaps even a hot one) was a real possibility.[31] The next era of policy making would have to address these questions.

5

The Reagan Revolution

★ ★ ★

President Reagan went on national television to promote his major tax-cutting plan, which Congress approved in August 1981. The tax cut was an important prong of Reagan's economic plan, which also included domestic spending restraint, deregulation, an anti-inflationary monetary policy, and free trade.

THE QUESTIONS LEFT OPEN at the end of the 1970s (Could the presidency work? Could capitalism survive as a viable economic system? Could free society survive in a hostile world?) were addressed by a new era of policy making. Sometimes called the "Reagan Revolution," this burst of conservative policy making aimed to reduce the role of government in the economic affairs of the nation, reversing the general direction of policy since the 1930s. It was made possible by a confluence of ideas,

79

events, politics, and people. At the same time, the gravity of "path dependency" pulled the "revolution" back to earth.

Both the politics and intellectual tenor of the time favored a major conservative reappraisal of policy. The ideas that served as a basis for Reagan's policy shift had developed over several decades since the onset of the New Deal, starting with the foundation laid by Friedrich Hayek. Hayek, an economist who considered himself a classical liberal, wrote *The Road to Serfdom* in 1944, arguing that central economic planning was both economically inefficient and a threat to liberty.[1] Although Hayek's argument ran against the dominant grain at the time, it became a rallying point for supporters of limited government and free markets.

As the economic problems of the 1970s called into question the assumptions of Keynesian economics, there was an intellectual rebirth of classical economics, building on Hayek's broad insights. This took two distinct and sometimes competing directions, though all were agreed that free markets should be preferred over government intervention for both economic and political reasons. One important form of what became known as neoclassical economics took the form of "monetarism," advocated most stoutly by Milton Friedman. Friedman first gained notoriety by contending in his 1965 book *The Great Contraction* that the Great Depression was the result of destructive monetary policy by the Federal Reserve Board rather than the excesses of unregulated capitalism, as New Dealers had argued.[2] His overall economic view was that government's role should be limited and that the true cure for inflation would not be found in short-term manipulations of fiscal policy but in maintaining a stable money supply.[3]

The second version of neoclassical economics to emerge in response to stagflation came to be known as "supply-side economics." Promoted by thinkers such as Jude Wanniski, Arthur Laffer, Paul Craig Roberts, and Robert Bartley, supply-side economics urged that policy makers focus on microeconomic incentives rather than macroeconomic aggregate demand. To supply siders, the fatal flaw of Keynesianism flowed from its neglect of the role of supply in the economy. The tradeoff between unemployment and inflation was not inevitable; if you could push up the supply curve, you could produce higher employment *and* lower prices. Conversely, stagflation, which baffled Keynesians, could be explained by a downward slide of supply that resulted in both lower employment and higher prices. The solution lay in policies that encouraged production by reducing government obstacles and disincentives to economic activity. This understanding pointed to deregulation and to cuts in marginal income tax rates, or the rate charged on the last dollar of income.[4] It also led to a very different view of tax cuts for Keynesians and supply siders.

Keynesians preferred temporary tax rebates aimed to benefit lower income people who would spend them; supply siders preferred permanent cuts in marginal tax rates for all taxpayers to increase incentives for additional work and income.

In concert with these theories was an intellectual move remoralizing capitalism. Works such as *Wealth and Poverty* published by George Gilder in 1981 and *The Spirit of Democratic Capitalism* published by Michael Novak in 1982 contended that a free market economy was not only more economically efficient but was more moral than its critics credited.[5] Gilder argued that to be engaged in business is to attempt to understand and meet the needs of your fellow human beings. Economic freedom also promotes character traits of responsibility, creativity, forward thinking, and deferral of gratification. In this view, from thriving on greed, capitalism makes greed unprofitable in the long run.

A conservative policy thrust was reinforced by social science research suggesting that the War on Poverty had not only failed but had been counterproductive. Charles Murray's *Losing Ground*, published in 1984, served as a warning against the unintended consequences of government activism and a call for a drastically reduced government role in fighting poverty.[6]

On a parallel track with the intellectual revival of free market economics was another strand of conservative thinking, exemplified by Russell Kirk, sometimes called "traditionalism." Kirk's contention, found in *The Conservative Mind* and other writings, was that modern liberalism threatened free society by undermining the cultural basis for freedom, which was found in property rights, family, and the moral virtues advanced by religion.[7] Kirk drew heavily on Edmund Burke's view that utopian, top-down social change was unworkable and bound to produce tyranny.

These ideas had been brought together under the rubric of the conservative movement, which had been active for a quarter-century. Economic conservatives formed one element of the movement, Kirk's traditionalists formed another, and anti-communists, whose chief concern was in confronting the Marxist-Leninist threat emanating from the Soviet Union, were a third element. By 1980, the increasingly mobilized and organized forces of religiously oriented social conservatives, including evangelical Protestants, conservative Catholics, and Mormons, were instrumental in putting social issues higher on the national policy agenda.[8] Finally were the neoconservatives, often former liberals (or even former Marxists) who had been, as they put it, "mugged by reality." Neoconservative intellectuals had come to embrace a strong American posture in the world and conservative views on issues such as crime and welfare.[9] The conservative movement had its divisions, but they were generally exaggerated, and most conservatives saw no conflict. (Evangelicals, for example, proved to be strong advocates for "Reaganomics."[10])

As a result of national problems widely perceived to be the consequence of liberal policy, conservative ideas increasingly resonated in the electorate. By 1980, a solid majority of Americans had come to say that the government had "gone too far in regulating business and interfering with the free enterprise system," that "the best government is the government that governs least," and that the states had a better understanding than Washington, DC, of "real people's needs"—a complete reversal of public opinion since the 1960s and early 1970s.[11] Indeed, since the mid-1960s, Americans had identified themselves as "conservative" over "liberal" by a ratio of about three to two.

The events of the 1970s, at home and abroad—from stagflation, energy crises, and social deterioration to the fall of South Vietnam, the Soviet run, and the Iranian Hostage Crisis—gave the strengthened conservatives an opportunity to make their case.[12] Reagan's win in 1980 opened up a conservative window of opportunity that arguably had not existed since Calvin Coolidge was president. Reagan's presidential landslide—44 states, 489 electoral votes, and 51 percent of the vote in a three-way race (topping Carter, his nearest competitor, by ten percentage points)—was accompanied by significant coattails in Congress. In the Senate, Republicans picked up 12 seats, enough to give them a majority for the first time since 1954. Liberal stalwarts such as George McGovern, Birch Bayh, Frank Church, John Culver, and Warren Magnuson lost their seats to mostly conservative challengers. On the other side of the Capitol, Republicans gained 33 House seats, not enough for a partisan majority but enough to revive the conservative coalition between Republicans and conservative Democrats that controlled the House from 1938 to 1958 and intermittently since then.[13]

At the center of this moment stood Reagan himself. Two weeks from turning 70, Reagan on the day of his inauguration was the oldest man sworn in as president of the United States. He had become famous as a movie actor in films such as *Knute Rockne, Hellcats of the Navy*, and *King's Row* and then had served as a traveling spokesman for General Electric. Politically, he had begun adult life as a New Deal Democrat, but had changed his party affiliation as he came to conclude that Democrats no longer represented Jeffersonian ideals. In 1964, he launched his national political career by delivering a well-received televised speech for Barry Goldwater (called "A Time for Choosing"). Two years later—in that 1966 midterm election year that marked the effective end of Lyndon Johnson's Great Society aspirations—Reagan ran for governor of California against incumbent Pat Brown and won by a million votes, his first of two gubernatorial wins. After failing in a half-hearted run for the GOP presidential nomination in 1968 and a hard-fought battle against Gerald Ford in 1976, Reagan finally got the Republican nod in 1980 on his way to the White House.[14]

Reagan was drawn to conservatism by both reflection and experience. Though he was often derided by his foes as unintelligent, he was well-read in such thinkers as Hayek, Friedman, Kirk, and Alexis de Tocqueville, the nineteenth-century French observer who discovered the virtues of decentralized government and civil society while writing his classic *Democracy in America*. Reagan's life experience was also important. As a college student he majored in economics at a time when the curriculum was still dominated by classical free-market ideas. As an actor he saw firsthand the disincentive effects of high marginal tax rates, writing later about colleagues who decided not to shoot another movie because the 91 percent top income tax rate made it not worth the effort. Not least, he later described his GE speaking tour as "a postgraduate course in political science."[15] Often compared to Franklin Roosevelt, Reagan was widely admired for his confidence, dignity under pressure, and communication skills that allowed him to connect with Americans and make a persuasive case for change. He also usually had a keen sense of when compromise was necessary, and he was not averse to it as long as it could advance his objectives.

Like major policy innovators before him, Reagan was working within a window of opportunity that closed over time due to shifting politics and events. His biggest moment of opportunity came in the first year of his presidency, when he had a Republican majority of the Senate and working control of the House. The window shut a bit as deep recession took a new hold in late 1981 after a brief respite, the second half of the "double-dip" recession that started in 1979–1980; shut quite a bit more when Democrats gained 26 House seats in the midterm elections of 1982, putting the liberal Democratic leadership back in full control of the chamber; and shut most of the rest of the way in the 1986 midterms, when a Democratic wave put the opposition party back in the majority in the Senate. The day after the 1986 elections, the Iran-Contra scandal broke, a foreign policy misstep that further crippled Reagan for most of 1987.

Like Franklin Roosevelt and Dwight Eisenhower, Reagan found that a big reelection victory gave him another four years in the White House but did not translate into a new burst of domestic policy making. Running in 1984 against Democrat Walter Mondale, who had served as Jimmy Carter's vice president, Reagan won nearly 60 percent of the vote, 49 states, and 520 electoral votes. However, Reagan ran a mostly retrospective campaign, taking credit for defeating stagflation, restoring America's position in the world, and reviving national morale, and he had limited congressional coattails.

THE REAGAN ECONOMIC BREAKTHROUGH

To Reagan, "no problem the country faced was more pressing than the economic crisis—not even the need to modernize our armed forces— because without a recovery, we couldn't afford to do the things necessary to make the country strong again or make a serious effort to lessen the dangers of nuclear war."[16] In September 1980, the Reagan campaign released an economic plan which consisted of four pillars: (1) reduce the rate of growth of federal spending, (2) cut tax rates significantly, (3) proceed with deregulation, and (4) attain a stable growth in the money supply.[17] As he took office, Reagan declared that "in our current crisis, government isn't the solution to our problems. Government is the problem."[18] Reagan then proposed to Congress a tax and spending plan that formed the centerpiece of his economic policy.

The spending blueprint called for a $42 billion reduction in federal domestic spending for the next year (compared with the "current services baseline"). After considerable haggling, Congress approved budget cuts of $38 billion for the next year and a total of $140 billion over three years. Overall, from 1980 to 1989, discretionary domestic spending fell by one-third as a percent of GDP, its lowest level since before the Great Society. Reagan found it much more difficult to restrain entitlement spending than discretionary domestic spending. Nevertheless, despite a bulge in the middle of the decade, by 1989, entitlement spending too had fallen relative to 1980. Reagan's 1981 budget victory was made possible by the cooperation of the "Boll Weevils," a bloc of conservative Democrats in the House who broke with their party's leadership to support deeper spending cuts. Key was Rep. Phil Gramm of Texas, a conservative Democrat (until he switched parties in 1983), a former economics professor at Texas A&M, and chair of the House Budget Committee. Reagan was also able to mobilize public opinion on behalf of his proposals; when he made speeches calling on Americans to tell Congress that they supported his plan, they responded in unprecedented numbers.[19] Demonstrating the power of unforeseen events to influence policy outcomes, the unsuccessful attempted assassination of Reagan by John Hinckley Jr. on March 31, 1981, in which Reagan was shot near the heart and exhibited determination and humor in adversity, clearly strengthened his political position as well.

The tax legislation, initially modeled on the Kemp-Roth tax cut bill calling for a 30 percent reduction in income tax rates, passed shortly after the budget. The Economic Recovery Tax Act (ERTA) included these elements: a 25 percent across-the-board reduction in individual income tax rates over three years (5–10-10), reduction of the top rate from 70 percent to 50 percent, a tax cut allowing businesses to deduct more from their taxes for capital investments, and indexing of income tax rates to inflation. The last piece was added to solve the problem of "bracket creep": due to inflation, millions of households were being driven into higher tax brackets even though their real income (that is, their income after inflation was taken into account) had not risen.

Liberals attacked the tax and spending cuts as unfair, cutting spending on programs for the poor while cutting taxes for the rich (although the *New York Times* praised tax indexing as "one of the fairest pieces of tax law in many a year"[20]). Conservatives answered that redistribution of income was not a proper role of government and that all taxpayers benefitted from the tax cuts. They also argued that the Reagan tax cuts bore a striking resemblance to the Kennedy tax cuts—both lowered the top rate as part of a permanent across-the-board reduction in marginal tax rates for all income taxpayers.[21] Reagan's tax and budget changes marked a dramatic move toward a limited government approach to economics.

Reagan's views on taxation were advanced further in 1986, when Congress passed the Tax Reform Act, which represented a hard-won deal between liberals, conservatives, and moderates. Though Reagan's working House majority had been lost in 1982, Republicans still held a Senate majority. Democrats, including House Ways and Means chair Dan Rostenkowski and Sen. Bill Bradley, worked with the administration and Republicans, including Senate Finance chair Bob Packwood, to forge an agreement. The income tax base was broadened by eliminating dozens of special deductions and exemptions. At the same time, the tax structure was flattened and simplified, going from 14 brackets with a top rate of 50 percent to a total of 2 brackets, 15 percent and 28 percent. Larger standard exemptions meant that about four million working poor taxpayers were removed from federal income tax. The Tax Reform Act was the biggest structural change in federal income tax since the Sixteenth Amendment was enacted and was Reagan's most important second-term domestic policy achievement.[22]

Similarly, the Reagan administration made considerable strides toward reducing the burden of regulation on the economy. Reagan supported continuation of Carter's efforts to deregulate industries such as airlines and trucking. He also did something Carter did not do, which was to try to reduce the overall level of regulation on business. Unlike tax and spending changes, which required agreement by Congress, the attack on regulation could be carried out by the executive branch. In the first 10 days of his presidency, Reagan froze more than 170 pending regulations. In his first term, Reagan's administration, using more rigorous cost-benefit standards, imposed 6,000 fewer rules than had Carter. Antitrust regulators interfered less often with mergers deemed economically efficient. Overall, by 1986, pages in the *Federal Register* shrank by 46 percent since the record high in 1980 before bumping up a bit in 1988, still ending 39 percent below the 1980 level.[23] Reagan utilized the Office of Management and Budget to impose "central clearance" of proposed new regulations, a mechanism that led to the modification of about one quarter of all new regulations. For the first time since environmental regulation became a major agenda item in the 1960s, policy shifted toward attempting to limit the economic costs of regulation and the restraints on individual freedom and property rights imposed by regulation. In the West, where most land is owned by the federal government, Reagan was sympathetic to the "Sagebrush Rebellion" of farmers and ranchers who demanded fewer government restrictions on land use. He also applied free-market principles to the energy crisis, completing the decontrol of oil prices and decontrolling natural gas. In contrast to Carter, Reagan's energy plan was to have no plan, in the expectation that the market would bring supply and demand into line with each other better than any centralized bureaucratic approach could accomplish.

Finally, although the president has limited control over the monetary policy adopted by the Federal Reserve Board, he can affect policy through his appointments and by publicly exerting or resisting pressure on the Fed to alter its course. As the Federal Reserve Board continued its policy of fighting inflation, Reagan took the politically risky posture of publicly backing Fed Chairman Paul Volcker, and then reappointing him in 1983. In the words of Reagan biographer Lou Cannon, "Reagan stuck by the Fed chairman when it counted."[24] In the end, the Federal Reserve policy was not exactly what Milton Friedman had ordered—having discovered that money supply was too difficult to manipulate directly, the Fed used the lever of interest rates—but it served the same objective.

Aside from these four key pillars, Reagan's economic policy included some other important elements. For example, he promoted a policy of free trade, negotiating the Caribbean Basin Initiative and a US-Canada trade agreement that later served as the foundation of the North American Free Trade Agreement (NAFTA). Stifling a protectionist backlash, Reagan also succeeded in blocking demands for "industrial policy" and higher trade barriers. Faced with an illegal strike by air traffic controllers in 1981, Reagan fired them, reducing the power of public sector unions for the next quarter century. The minimum wage was frozen for a decade, and the system of comparable worth proposed by feminists, who wanted equal pay not only for equal work (which was already required by federal law) but for different work deemed equivalent by a government board, was buried. Significantly, tax policy also shifted to encourage greater saving for retirement. ERTA established tax-deferred Individual Retirement Accounts to encourage private savings for retirement, and the IRS made a ruling that employees' income could be considered tax-free if matched by employers and put into private retirement accounts (so-called 401(k) plans). Thus Reagan-era policies were largely responsible for the subsequent "democratization of the stock market," featuring a large new class of small investors.[25]

THE LIMITS OF LIMITED GOVERNMENT

Despite Reagan's general direction, his policies were not always consistent with a tax-cutting, limited-government approach. One big failure came in late 1981, when Reagan proposed cuts in Social Security benefits that would have saved $50 billion by 1986 alone and would have forestalled gathering financial problems in the system. After having supported one big round of spending cuts earlier in the year, Congress rebelled, with the Senate rejecting the plan 95–0. In the aftermath of his rebuke, Reagan convened a bipartisan commission headed by economist Alan Greenspan to find a solution that could be sold to Congress. By early 1983, only six years after Jimmy Carter's fix promised to put the system on a sound footing, Social Security was again facing insolvency. The Greenspan Commission suggested, and Congress approved, an acceleration of the payroll tax increase approved in 1977 combined with a gradual increase in the retirement age to 67. The Greenspan compromise was sufficient to build a large surplus in the Social Security Trust Fund for several decades.[26]

Reagan also agreed to increases in excise taxes in 1982, 1984, and 1987 as part of deficit reduction agreements with Congress. The largest of these was the 1982 Tax Equity and Fiscal Responsibility Act (TEFRA), which was pushed both by Democrats and Senate Republican Finance Committee chair Robert Dole, who feared long-term deficits. TEFRA raised $98 billion of revenue over three years, recapturing around one-third of the projected revenue loss due to ERTA and causing a split between Reagan and congressional supply siders such as Jack Kemp. He was, however, able to maintain his income tax cuts, the core of his tax policy, against numerous proposals to undo or limit them. As part of the TEFRA deal, Congress also agreed to cut $3 of spending for each $1 of tax increase; Reagan would later complain bitterly that Congress did not keep up its end of the deal, though others disputed that interpretation.

What Reagan called "one of my biggest disappointments" was the growth of the federal deficit after 1981.[27] He had long complained about Washington's deficit spending, and had taken office promising to balance the budget by 1983 (he soon revised the date to 1984). Instead of the deficit being eliminated, however, it expanded to a high of $220 billion in 1985. The rise of the deficit inaugurated nearly two decades of policy making largely dominated by the question of how to control it.

The tax increases that Reagan signed onto were part of the policy response. Critics argued that he should have agreed to larger tax increases (usually an argument made by liberals), vetoed more congressional appropriations bills for overspending (usually argued by conservatives), or both. When Senate Republicans came close to reaching an agreement to curtail Social Security COLAs in 1985, Reagan backed away, remembering the political punishment inflicted by Democrats in the wake of his aborted 1981 Social Security proposals. However, he ultimately embraced the Gramm-Rudman-Hollings Act (or GRH), which was attached to a 1985 bill increasing the federal debt limit. The first version of GRH passed in 1985, setting deficit targets for each year declining over five years to zero in 1990. If the targets were not reached, a "sequestration" of spending would take place—an automatic across-the-board spending cut by whatever percentage was necessary to meet the deficit target. Half of the cuts were to come from defense spending, the other half from discretionary domestic spending. The mechanism used by GRH I to impose the sequestration was deemed unconstitutional by the Supreme Court on separation of powers grounds in 1987, so Congress passed a revised version (GRH II) with a new mechanism and revised targets calling for a balanced budget by 1993. Throughout this period, Reagan and state governments pressured Congress by supporting an amendment to the US Constitution that would have required the federal government to balance its budget except in times of national emergency. By the late 1980s, 32 of the 34 states that were required had called for a convention to consider such an amendment. Not least, from 1983 on, the economic rebound itself produced waves of new revenue.

Finally, developments abroad helped in the search for deficit reduction in the late 1980s (and would help much more in the 1990s). The international threat posed by the Soviet Union began to ebb, first slowly and then with increasing speed. Reagan's supporters contended that his tough anti-communist policies were working. Skeptics argued that the process leading to the disintegration of Soviet power was mostly internal.[28] Either way, defense spending, which had risen dramatically under Reagan at the beginning of the decade, stabilized and then began to fall.

Altogether, by the end of the decade, the federal deficit had fallen back to roughly where it had been in 1980 as a proportion of the national economy, and federal spending was rising at the slowest rate since the 1950s. However, in the meantime, the national debt had risen from about $1 trillion to about $3 trillion.

SOCIAL POLICY

The change in the public policy agenda since the time of the Great Society was evident in the way the economic issue had changed—from "what do we do with prosperity?" to "can we cope with stagflation?"—but it was also evident in the way a whole new realm of social and moral issues had come to the fore. Reagan emphasized a conservative approach to fighting crime with longer sentences and tougher policing. He and First Lady Nancy Reagan also reinvigorated the War on Drugs, a term initially used by Richard Nixon, to fight the rise in illegal drug usage since the 1960s. (In this, he was urged on by black pastors and inner-city mayors who feared that the crack cocaine epidemic was destroying their communities.[29])

Reagan also promoted a socially conservative response to what he and other conservatives saw as the breakdown of the family. In Reagan's view, the combination of Great Society government programs and the 1960s cultural assault on traditional notions of morality had inflicted considerable damage on the family as an institution. This was, to him, a matter of profound social impact. Statistically, children growing up in one-parent households are significantly more likely to commit crimes, drop out of school, have out-of-wedlock children themselves, use drugs, and commit suicide. They are also much more likely to be abused. Reagan also saw the family as a social institution that served as a buffer between individuals and the power of the state. Where Jimmy Carter had sponsored a White House Conference on the Family that had endorsed the liberal and permissive family trends of the 1960s and 1970s, Reagan formed a White House Working Group on the Family that recommended restrictions on divorce, abortion, and government-subsidized day care.[30]

The Reagan Administration and Democratic Congress also reached agreement in 1988 on a welfare reform bill (the Family Support Act), the first major welfare reform bill enacted since the Great Society. The main focus of the bill was to impose greater parental responsibility for children and to reduce government barriers to the exercise of that responsibility. The Family Support Act strengthened child-support collection mechanisms, provided assistance for welfare recipients making the transition to work, required that welfare cover two-parent (and not just one-parent) families, and allowed states to require minors with a child to live with relatives until they turned 18 years old. In many respects, the results of the Act proved disappointing to its advocates, but it was the starting point of the move toward more significant welfare reform that culminated in 1996.[31]

Reagan was also allied with the recently organized movement of social conservatives and promoted their causes. He embraced the pro-life cause on abortion and endorsed a constitutional amendment to overturn

Roe v. Wade (it came to a vote in the Senate but failed to receive the necessary two-thirds vote). He consistently mentioned this cause in speeches, allowed the Justice Department to argue in favor of overturning *Roe* in two different court cases, and even wrote a notable essay that was later republished as a book calling on the nation to turn away from abortion on demand (*Abortion and the Conscience of the Nation*). Another issue that occupied Reagan's attention was that of school prayer. Until 1963, it was not uncommon for school prayer and Bible readings to take place in public schools. At that time, Supreme Court decisions declared the practice unconstitutional. Reagan and other conservatives believed the decisions were based on an incorrect reading of the First Amendment's Establishment Clause and contributed to a moral decline in society. As late as the mid-1980s, about three-fourths of Americans supported a constitutional amendment to overrule the Supreme Court on that issue.[32] Reagan spoke about it often and supported a constitutional amendment that would have allowed voluntary school prayer. Like the anti-abortion amendment, the pro-school prayer amendment fell short in the Senate, and some social conservatives felt Reagan had not done all he could to pressure Congress. Nevertheless, he pushed the issue onto the legislative agenda in a way that was not done before or since.

Aside from the "moral issues" that concerned social conservatives, Reagan also signed a major immigration law in 1986. The Immigration Reform and Control Act was a compromise that required employers to verify that they were not hiring illegal immigrants while offering amnesty to illegal immigrants who had been in the country continuously since 1982 if they met certain requirements.

Broadly speaking, Reagan's social policy agenda was wrapped around a core of support for civil society as a necessary complement to limited government. In his 1980 nomination acceptance speech, Reagan said, "Let us pledge to restore, in our time, the American spirit of voluntary service, of cooperation, of private and community initiative."[33] To promote this outcome, Reagan established a White House Office of Private Sector Initiatives to provide organizational support and coordination for private-sector charities and nonprofit activities. As sympathetic commentator Dinesh D'Souza remarked, Reagan thought "that as citizens of a free country we should demand less of the state and more of ourselves."[34]

REAGAN AND THE CONSTITUTION

Closely intertwined with Reagan's domestic policy initiatives was a substantial institutional and constitutional shift.[35] In Reagan's view, the policy problems of the 1970s were a result of out-of-control government that spent too much, taxed too much, and regulated too much, as well as of a federal judiciary that had taken on an inappropriate policy-making role. The problem was not merely one of bad policy, but of a wrong constitutional understanding. At the same time, the presidency as an institution had, in the view of Reagan and many analysts, suffered a dangerous decline in prestige in the 1970s.

Consequently, Reagan's solution was heavily directed at constitutional and institutional factors. One of Reagan's first accomplishments was to restore the strength of the presidency. Altogether, noted presidential scholar Richard Neustadt concluded that Reagan had "restored the public image of the office to a fair (if rickety) approximation of its Rooseveltian mold: a place of popularity, influence, and initiative, a source of programmatic and symbolic leadership, both pacesetter and trendsetter, the nation's voice to both the world and us."[36] Where FDR, Truman, Kennedy, and Johnson had used a strong presidency to advance more powerful centralized government, Reagan used a revived presidency to try to re-limit the federal government.

Reagan's view was that the nation had taken a wrong constitutional turn with the Progressive and New Deal notions of a "living Constitution." To Reagan's thinking, the Constitution should be interpreted, as far as possible, according to the intentions of the founders, who had established a limited government of specified powers.[37]

Accordingly, Reagan sought to reestablish at least the metaphor of the doctrine of enumerated powers, or the idea that the federal government can only do the things that are specified in the Constitution. In practical terms, he proposed policies that put a higher priority on clearly constitutional functions of the federal government (such as defense) than on functions that he viewed as constitutionally dubious (such as federal education spending).

His traditional view of rights, emphasizing individual rights clearly found in the Constitution, meant that Reagan promoted policies that defended gun rights, rights of religious expression, and property rights, the latter of which Reagan (in contrast to Progressives) saw as a subset of human rights rather than in competition with them. He opposed forced busing and other policies designed to treat people differently on the basis of racial classification.

Third, Reagan believed strongly in decentralization of government, and thus in constitutional doctrines of federalism (or states' rights). In Reagan's interpretation, the hyperactive federal government of the Great Society had pushed aside the legitimate authority of the states in the federal system. In response, he proposed a sweeping "New Federalism" initiative in his 1982 State of the Union address. Though it used the same label as Richard Nixon's federalism proposal, Reagan's idea was based on a significantly different conception of a healthy federal system.

Rather than direct more federal money to state coffers, as Nixon had done, Reagan wanted to create greater definition between federal and state roles. In other words, he hoped to move federalism back in the direction of the "layer-cake federalism" model and away from the New Deal/Great Society's "marble cake federalism." His 1982 New Federalism proposal suggested a trade that would be appropriate to the dual federalism model: the federal government would take over the whole responsibility for Medicaid, and the states would take over full responsibility for Aid to Families with Dependent Children, Food Stamps, and 44 other programs mainly in the areas of education, community development, transportation, and social services. Revenue from a number of federal excise taxes would go into a trust fund to be distributed to the states for these purposes, but the taxes would be phased out over a period of eight years, leaving the states with responsibility for both funding and delivering the programs.[38]

This effort at a grand refashioning of American federalism was not enacted. State governors were afraid that they would end up with more responsibility but less money, and never signed on. Despite the failure of the New Federalism plan, Reagan did a great deal to advance federalism incrementally. He gradually cut grants to states, making them more dependent on their own exertions. In 1986, he and Congress also agreed to terminate the General Revenue Sharing program started under Nixon. Reagan's administration worked to modify the remaining federal grants to state and local governments in two ways. First, in keeping with his state-centered philosophy of federalism, he shifted the balance of grants in the direction of state governments and away from local governments; in a major change from Great Society tendencies, he did not believe it was constitutionally appropriate for Washington to turn local governments into federal clients, bypassing the states. Second, he sought to convert so-called categorical grants, in which grants from the federal government come with a large number of very specific conditions attached, into block grants, with fewer strings and more flexibility. For example, the 1981 Education Consolidation and Improvement Act (ECIA) consolidated 29 categorical grants for K–12 education into one educational block grant. In health care, the 1981 budget act fashioned four block grants out of around 20 categorical grants. Overall, in 1981, a total of 9 new block grants were formed by consolidating 27 categorical programs and terminating another 62. Over time, additional flexibility was granted to states to design their Medicaid and welfare programs.[39]

Perhaps the most important thing that Reagan did to strengthen the role of the states was to pursue retrenchment of the federal role in American life. Reagan himself saw his economic plan—with the federal government cutting taxes and limiting its domestic spending—as a "quiet federalist revolution" because of the way it left an opening for a bigger state role. In 1992, Alice Rivlin of the Brookings Institution, who would later serve in Bill Clinton's administration, would say that "in the last decade, the tide of centralization has turned and the balance of power has generally shifted from the federal government toward the states."[40]

Pursuing this constitutional shift required a number of strategies from Reagan, including consistent rhetorical attention to federalism, legislative proposals, and administrative action (such as Executive Orders 12372 and 12612, which required executive branch agencies to consider the impact on federalism of proposed policies). It also required a judicial strategy, which took the form of an unprecedented effort, directed by presidential counselor and then attorney general Edwin Meese, to try to ensure that judicial appointees were on board with the president's conservative judicial philosophy. By the end of his presidency, Reagan had appointed three Supreme Court justices (O'Connor, Scalia, and Kennedy) and 49 percent of the entire federal judiciary. One constitutional law scholar noted that "Reagan's administration had a more coherent and ambitious agenda for legal reform and judicial selection than any previous administration."[41] Not all of these appointments turned out as Reagan had hoped, but he clearly moved the judiciary in a conservative direction.

Altogether, no president since the New Deal gave as much consideration as Reagan to the constitutional and institutional aspects of policy. From the New Deal through George W. Bush, Reagan talked more than any other president about the Constitution in his major addresses to the nation.[42] He did not just have incidental effects on federalism, separation of powers, or a constitutionalism of limited government; he deliberately aimed to achieve those changes as an important and integrated part of his domestic policy program.

THE REAGAN REVOLUTION: SUMMARY AND ASSESSMENT

Ronald Reagan's presidency represented the third great burst of policy making since the onset of the Great Depression, and the first coherent and substantial change of direction since the consolidation of the New Deal. If Franklin Roosevelt had sought to save capitalism by taming it, Reagan sought to save it by freeing it.

Economic policy
Reagan's free-market policies included elements of monetarism, supply-side economics, and traditional conservative spending reduction policies, and economic policy was made less redistributionist. From 1980 to 1988, overall federal spending fell from 21.1 percent of GDP to 20.6 percent

and revenue fell from 18.5 to 17.6 percent of GDP. A major tax cut in 1981 coupled with tax reform in 1986 reduced the top income tax rate from 70 percent to 28 percent and took several million of the working poor off the tax rolls. Adjusted to inflation, total federal spending rose only 22 percent in that time, the slowest rate of increase since the 1950s. Non-defense spending fell from 16.3 percent of GDP to 15.0 percent; discretionary non-defense spending fell by one-third, from 5.1 percent to 3.4 percent of GDP, a reversal of the trend since the early 1960s. Moreover, pages in the *Federal Register* fell from 87,012 in 1980 to 53,376 in 1988, the first substantial decline since the *Federal Register* was introduced in 1936. Fully regulated industries accounted for 17 percent of GDP in 1977, but only 9 percent by 1988.[43] Reagan also promoted free trade and pushed back attempts by Democrats in Congress to impose protectionist policies.

Social welfare

Payments to individuals held steady, falling from 10.0 percent to 9.9 percent of GDP, while human resources spending fell from 11.2 to 10.3 percent of GDP, a stabilization or reversal of spending trends that had been increasing rapidly since 1950. No new social welfare programs were established, with the exceptions of the catastrophic health plan, which was repealed the next year, and the Jobs Training Partnership Act, which replaced the Comprehensive Employment and Training Act. Welfare was reformed in the Family Support Act, laying the groundwork for further conservative welfare reforms in the 1990s. Discretionary social spending was cut, as was spending on welfare and Food Stamps entitlements. Social Security retirement was put on a sounder financial basis for the next several decades though a combination of an accelerated tax increase and a significant cost control measure.

Civil rights

Race-based policies such as forced busing were challenged, though Reagan stopped short of abolishing federal affirmative action programs. Opponents of the new policies saw them as back-tracking on civil rights progress; defenders saw them as restoring civil rights policy to its original color-blind thrust.[44]

Education

Reagan was unable to fulfill his campaign pledge of abolishing the federal Department of Education, which he saw as beyond the federal government's constitutional purview. However, federal education funding was cut and a 1981 law turned many federal categorical grants for education into block grants to the states. The 1983 report *A Nation at Risk* launched a national, state, and local debate over how to improve the rigor of American education.[45]

Environment
The focus of environmental policy shifted to reducing the economic burdens of environmental regulation, which had grown tremendously in the 1970s, and making natural resources under federal control more accessible to the private sector. Resistance by Congress and environmental groups limited the administration's freedom of action, but the direction of policy represented a major change.

Moral/cultural issues
Reagan embraced a conservative counter-revolution against the 1960s counterculture and the permissive decisions of federal courts. In some cases, such as drugs and federal criminal sentencing, policy changed accordingly. In others, such as school prayer or abortion, Reagan was unable to dislodge liberal policy imposed by courts, though he provided symbolic leadership.

Federalism
Reagan made a concerted effort across many fronts to decentralize power from Washington to state governments. For their parts, states were prepared to accept greater policy responsibility due to measures they had taken to strengthen their administrative and fiscal capacities. Reagan's grand "New Federalism" plan was not adopted, but the restoration of the states to an autonomous place of policy prominence remained a high priority throughout the Reagan administration. In Theodore Lowi's terms, Reagan arguably paid more attention to constitutive policy than any other modern president.

In each area, the Reagan policy sought to reverse the dominant trends of the Great Society (and even, in philosophical terms, the New Deal). Many of the changes that actually occurred were less dramatic than Reagan had proposed, but were nevertheless significant. That policy shift was possible because of a window of opportunity that opened up with the confluence of ideas, events, people, and politics. **Events** were crucial: the merging of economic crisis, foreign policy crisis, social crisis, and crisis of morale called into question the reigning doctrines of liberalism and made the public receptive to an alternative. An alternative was available in the form of conservative **ideas** expounded by economists like Friedrich Hayek, Milton Friedman, and Jude Wanniski, social scientists like Charles Murray, and thinkers such as George Gilder, Russell Kirk, and Michael Novak. That conservative intellectual framework was accompanied by the growing political organization of the conservative movement, which by 1980 was a quarter-century old. As in 1932, ideas met the moment. A failed assassination attempt helped move Reagan's program forward, the double-dip recession helped stall it, and the economic recovery that started in 1983 was an event that seemed to validate Reagan's policy departure and helped secure his reelection and continuation of his policy drive.

As in 1933, ideas and events would not have carried the day without the **right individuals** and the **right political circumstances**. Reagan was, in most respects, the right individual. His political skills were crucial, though his inattention to detail and "lack of programmatic ambition" (as two political scientists put it) was sometimes costly.[46] It is difficult to imagine any of Reagan's 1980 primary opponents—men including Howard Baker, George H. W. Bush, John Connolly, and Robert Dole—conceiving, articulating, and pressing a comprehensive challenge to the Great Society ethos as Reagan did. And, of course, Reagan was not the only individual to make a difference. Jack Kemp's commitment to supply-side doctrine, Bob Dole's commitment to deficit reduction, Phil Gramm's willingness to cross party lines and support Reagan's 1981 budget cuts, and House Speaker Tip O'Neill's pugnacious defense of the New Deal ethos all contributed to the mixed outcome of the decade.

Not least, the 1980s showed once more how reliant policy is on **politics**. Reagan accomplished as much as he did because he won two landslide presidential victories, won control of the Senate for six years, had a working majority in the House for his crucial first two years, and was supported by a rising movement and, most of the time, public sentiment. He fell well short of many of his policy goals in no small part because of the political limitations imposed by a hostile House of Representatives from 1983 to 1989, only a modest Senate majority while it lasted, and public reluctance to scale back entitlement programs. The **multiple streams** of ideas, politics, events, and people explain both the Reagan breakthrough and its limits.

As in other eras, **foreign policy** had a direct impact on domestic policy (and vice versa). Most notably, the trajectory of defense spending—first up to counter the Soviet threat, then down as that threat diminished—had a noticeable impact on the nation's overall fiscal picture. And, as usual, consequences flowed in the other direction, as well. As Reagan had hoped, the economic recovery supplied the economic means to support the defense buildup. It also reportedly had the effect of demoralizing the Soviet leadership, which had until then believed the capitalist economy was close to collapse. At the outset, the end of the Iranian hostage crisis gave Reagan early momentum, while the Iran-Contra scandal paralyzed him through much of 1987. The successful invasion of Grenada in October

1983 pushed Reagan's approval back over 50 percent just in time for the election year, and might be considered partially responsible for Reagan's second term domestic policy departures, including deficit reduction and tax reform. Throughout his presidency, Reagan was influenced by his conservative soul-mate Margaret Thatcher, who became British Prime Minister nearly two years before Reagan became president and blazed the trail in the Anglo-American world with much the same approach.

The limited reach of the Reagan Revolution is also a testament to the power of **path dependency**. Unlike Franklin Roosevelt, who was largely starting from scratch, or Lyndon Johnson, who was in many ways accelerating and broadening the course Roosevelt had already set, Reagan sought to reverse a course that was by 1980 well-entrenched. The welfare and regulatory state that Reagan hoped to trim had built up its own expectations, had a "current services baseline" pointing ever upward, and was well defended by its many organized clients. Though domestic spending was limited, no departments and hardly any programs were eliminated; the compromise saving Social Security involved marginal changes in taxes and the retirement age; Reagan's moves toward decentralization were incremental, not radical.

The **policy agenda** shifted as problems were solved and new problems arose. Stagflation was the number one domestic agenda item at the beginning of the 1980s, but by mid-decade it had been supplanted by bipartisan concern with the deficit. Energy was high on the agenda until deregulation (and behind-the-scenes deals with Saudi Arabia) made oil relatively cheap again. Driven by new movements, social and moral issues arising from the 1960s and 1970s occupied greater attention, and largely because the president was ideologically committed to them, so did constitutional and para-constitutional reforms (such as New Federalism).

Though they did not achieve all they had hoped, conservatives largely succeeded in imposing their **definition of the problem** (too much government, too arrogantly applied), which in turn led inexorably to a policy conclusion (less, and more humble, domestic government). Having lost the battle of problem definition in the late 1970s and early 1980s, liberals were on the defensive throughout this era, navigating "a new politics in which Democrats talk like Republicans to survive."[47]

As with other eras of policy making, Reagan's demonstrates how complicated it can be to **assess the success or failure** of public policy departures. Reagan succeeded politically in strengthening the Republican electoral coalition, making it more competitive at all levels, yet he failed to bring about a full-fledged realignment as Franklin Roosevelt had done. He succeeded in attaining the most sweeping shift in domestic policy since the Great Society, but failed to bring about the degree of change he and many of his supporters had hoped. And the results of the policies themselves were open to a variety of interpretations, as had been the results of the New Deal and the Great Society.

Most obviously, Reagan's supporters noted that the economic crisis of the 1970s and early 1980s was overcome. Inflation was defeated, unemployment fell to 5.3 percent in 1989, and the economy created 20 million jobs in what became the longest period of economic expansion in US history to that point. After a period of decline from 1973 to 1982, family incomes in all quintiles rose through 1989. Conversely, poverty rates, which peaked in 1982, fell for the rest of the decade. Despite a momentary drop in October 1987, the stock market ended the decade at a value triple that at the beginning. Moreover, the energy crisis subsided, as oil prices fell and gasoline shortages ended. By virtually every measure of economic well-being, the nation was much better off at the end of Reagan's presidency than at the beginning. In this respect, economic policies in the 1980s were arguably more successful than those in the 1930s at producing the desired result.[48]

Nevertheless, some critics argued that the economic expansion was unrelated to Reagan's policies. Alternately, others contended that, even if the recovery was driven by policy changes made under Reagan, the side-effects were costly. In particular, they pointed to rising income inequality, the undeniable existence of homelessness among some of the poor (although the number of homeless was often exaggerated greatly), and what they considered the costs of deregulation, including the collapse of the savings and loan industry, an event that cost taxpayers $132 billion to correct (perhaps the best example in the 1980s of the **law of unanticipated consequences**).[49] Reagan's defenders can note that some of the claims of critics are simply inaccurate. For example, it is not true that the "rich got richer and the poor got poorer" in the Reagan recovery; the rich and poor both got richer, though top incomes grew faster than incomes at the bottom.[50] Most critiques, however, depend not on faulty facts but on a judgment about whether to place a higher value on economic equality or on liberty and economic growth. Others trod a middle path, noting sound policy adjustments, improvements in key economic indicators, and both theoretical and practical imperfections of "Reaganomics" as implemented.[51]

Likewise, many analysts see the deficits of the 1980s as a direct result of Reagan's tax cuts and defense spending increases. Others blame the continued momentum of domestic spending, especially entitlements such as Social Security, Medicare, and Medicaid. One can find evidence for either proposition, depending on the measures one uses. In either nominal or constant (inflation-adjusted) dollars, from 1980 to 1990 tax revenues rose substantially and domestic spending increased more than defense spending. Measured in terms of GDP, revenue as a proportion of the economy fell because the economy grew faster than revenue; likewise total domestic spending fell as a proportion of GDP while defense spending grew. However, if one compares spending and revenue in the 1980s with that in 1960, at the end of the Eisenhower presidency—the last era when the budget was consistently at or close to balance—defense spending was only half as high in the 1980s as it had been in 1960, while revenue was higher and domestic spending much higher. Taking this long view, domestic spending rather than tax cuts or defense spending emerges as the prime driver of the deficit in the 1980s. Politicians, analysts, and ordinary citizens trying to make sense of these alternative measurements undoubtedly applied their own political values to the exercise.[52]

Such disputes about political values similarly color assessment of Reagan policies in other areas. At the end of the 1980s, many aspects of the quiet social crisis had stabilized or improved for the first time since its onset in the 1960s. From 1980 to 1990, crime rates and violent crime rates stabilized, murder rates fell, divorce rates fell, the abortion rate stabilized, drug usage fell, SAT scores rose, and the nation experienced a surge of voluntarism and charitable giving. Illegitimacy rates continued climbing, and the AIDS epidemic began, showing that all was not well; even measures that improved by 1990 remained significantly worse than they had been in 1960.[53] Yet arguably Reagan's social policies were a locus of contention primarily because they represented the fault line between the permissive culture of the 1960s and the culturally conservative reaction of Middle America. Likewise, his constitutional views brought a sharp rebuke from liberals who saw them as unacceptable for philosophical reasons: Reagan's emphasis on limited government, enumeration of powers, individual (rather than group) rights, property rights, and federalism posed a serious challenge to the liberal project, enunciated in Roosevelt's "Economic Bill of Rights," of constructing an all-encompassing centralized welfare state built on a fluid conception of constitutional limits and substantial delegation of power to bureaucratic experts.

The election of 1988 would be an explicit test of Reagan's enduring popularity and the apparent revival of national morale. When his vice president, George H. W. Bush, won a solid victory, political scientist Gerald Pomper called it "Ronald Reagan's third term."[54] The next two decades would see ups and downs for Reagan's domestic policy legacy, but throughout a rough equilibrium dominated in which his influence continued to loom large.

6

The Bush-Clinton Equilibrium

★　★　★

House Speaker Newt Gingrich and President Bill Clinton fought but eventually reached agreements reforming welfare and balancing the federal budget for the first time since 1969.

WHEN GEORGE H. W. BUSH WON the 1988 presidential election, political scientist Gerald Pomper declared it to be Ronald Reagan's third term. When Bush was swept out of office by Bill Clinton in 1992, many observers saw the event as the end of the Reagan era and the beginning of a new era of Democratic governance. In reality, the period 1988–2000 represented a modification and, to some extent, consolidation of the Reagan Revolution in sometimes surprising ways. If Bush did less to cement

Reagan's legacy than many originally expected, Clinton did much less to undo it. Bush claimed fealty to Reagan's ideas, while Clinton drew from an intellectual movement advocating a rightward shift in the Democratic Party. Most of the time, politics pointed to stalemate, and both Democratic and Republican attempts at a policy breakout were blocked, though Republicans shifted the policy agenda to the right again after 1994. The biggest events were abroad, as the Soviet Union collapsed and the Cold War ended. By the end of the 1990s, a Democratic president pushed by a Republican Congress would balance the federal budget.

THE BUSH PRESIDENCY

George H. W. Bush was the son of Prescott Bush, a US Senator from Connecticut in the 1950s. Before becoming Ronald Reagan's vice president, Bush had served two terms in the US House and then in a number of executive positions, including director of the Central Intelligence Agency, US Ambassador to the United Nations, and US envoy to communist China. In World War II, he had served with distinction as the youngest aviator in the navy; he would end up being the last World War II veteran to become president. Bush was widely known as a non-ideological "pragmatist" who aimed to manage government more than transform it. He was also noticeably more interested in foreign affairs than in domestic matters.[1] As president, Bush sought to distance himself from the more conservative Reagan and filled his cabinet disproportionately with like-minded moderates from the old Republican establishment (Secretary of Housing and Urban Development Jack Kemp, of Kemp-Roth tax-cutting note, was an exception). Bush nevertheless ran on Reagan's record and popularity, famously calling on congressional Democrats to "read my lips—no new taxes."

Just as Bush's personality and limited domestic interest had an impact on domestic policy, so did the political environment. Bush's presidential victory was solid but not overwhelming, and he was accused by the supporters of Democratic nominee Michael Dukakis of running an unfair negative campaign. Moreover, these same Democrats retained strong majorities in both houses of Congress; unlike Reagan in 1980, Bush enjoyed no congressional coattails in 1988. Congressional Democrats were well aware of Bush's relatively weak political position, and made the argument that he *and* they enjoyed equally valid popular mandates.[2]

In this context, budget issues dominated Bush's term. The federal deficit, which had fallen after 1986 and then stabilized for the remainder of the 1980s, started swinging upward again. By 1990, it was clear that the Gramm-Rudman-Hollings (GRH) deficit reduction scheme, which had helped hold the deficit in check, was about to run headlong into major challenges. Three important events worked together to push Bush into a new deficit-reduction agreement with Democrats. First, a financial crisis in the savings and loan industry forced the federal government to bail out failing thrifts at a cost that ultimately reached $132 billion. Second, after more than seven years of economic growth the economy began to slip into a recession. Although the recession proved to be relatively short and mild, unemployment rose and federal revenues fell, exacerbating the deficit problem. Finally, on August 1, 1990, Saddam Hussein's Iraq invaded the neighboring country of Kuwait. After a brief hesitation, Bush declared "This will not stand," sent US troops to Saudi Arabia, and began preparing for war. Bush was reluctant to risk the cuts in defense spending that would have happened if the GRH sequestration actually took place.

Driven partly by Budget Director Richard Darman's desire to reach a comprehensive "grand bargain" with Democrats that would solve the deficit problem once and for all, the Budget Enforcement Act of 1990 was passed. Bush agreed to a large increase in taxes, including creation of a new 31 percent rate for high earners, while Democrats agreed that GRH's deficit targets would be replaced with caps on discretionary spending that would be enforced by sequestration. Any increase in entitlement programs would have to be paid for with tax increases or spending cuts elsewhere.[3] Although many analysts credit the BEA with contributing to lower deficits later in the decade, the short-term outcome was a near doubling of the deficit, as the economy continued to weaken. Bush's credibility with the public was severely damaged, and Republicans were split. In both the House and the Senate, a majority of Democrats supported the deal, while a majority of Republicans opposed it.[4]

There were some other notable domestic policy departures in the Bush years, many of which tilted toward bigger or more centralized government.[5] For example, the Americans with Disabilities Act was passed in 1990 with Bush's support requiring government and private businesses to make accommodations for people with disabilities (such as handicapped parking, restrooms, ramps, and elevators). Likewise, the Clean Air Act Amendments were enacted in 1990, imposing strict new air pollution standards, though the administration was able to include a new, market-oriented concept to pollution control alongside the older regulatory approach. Bush declared himself to be the "education president" and proposed "America 2000," an educational strategy that included school choice, "break the mold" schools given more bureaucratic flexibility, national testing, and alternative teacher certification. However, America 2000 was brushed aside by Congress.

Overall, federal spending and regulation grew considerably under Bush, as pages in the *Federal Register* expanded from about 53,000 in

Reagan's last year to about 68,000 in 1991. In response to the alarm of economic conservatives, the last year of Bush's presidency the *Federal Register* fell back to about 61,000 pages, still about 15 percent more than in 1988. After the flat spending of the late 1980s, non-defense spending under Bush also grew from 15 percent of GDP in 1988 to 16.8 percent in 1992. This expansion of government was more the result of a drift than that of a deliberate preference by Bush.

In other ways, Bush represented significant continuity with Reagan's domestic policy. He was strongly supportive of free trade, and negotiated the North American Free Trade Agreement with Mexico (though it was not approved by Congress until after he left office). He emphasized, as Reagan had, the importance of charity and voluntarism in civil society (what Bush called the "thousand points of light"). He maintained a generally conservative social policy, particularly upholding Reagan's position against abortion. In 1992, Vice President Dan Quayle criticized the sitcom *Murphy Brown* because the main character was portrayed having a child as an unwed mother, arguing that such a portrayal was irresponsible when children in intact two-parent families fare much better than children in single parent families.[6] However, Bush disappointed conservatives when he failed to act decisively against the National Endowment for the Arts, which had funded photography by Robert Mapplethorpe that was widely deemed obscene.

Perhaps because Bush did not aggressively pursue a well-developed domestic agenda, the vacuum was filled by the political reaction to a number of Supreme Court decisions. One, *Texas v. Johnson* in 1989, ruled that burning the American flag was a constitutionally protected form of political expression. Bush endorsed a constitutional amendment to overturn it, but, lacking the two-thirds majority needed, Congress passed an ordinary statute, which the court promptly struck down. Another 1989 case, *Ward's Cove*, stirred anger among liberals. There the court ruled that businesses could not be sued under anti-discrimination laws just because the number of racial minorities who were employed did not match their proportions in the surrounding population (called "disparate impact"). Democrats in Congress passed the "Civil Rights Restoration Act" in 1990 aiming to reverse the court's decision, but Bush vetoed it on grounds that the disparate impact rule led to racial quotas. The next year, Congress passed a slightly modified version, which Bush signed. In 1990, in response to a court case, Congress overwhelmingly passed the Religious Freedom Restoration Act, stating that government was required to find methods of achieving its objectives that placed the smallest possible burden on individuals' religious practices. Finally, two cases reached the Supreme Court that gave the court an opportunity to overturn *Roe v. Wade*. However, in *Webster* (1989) and *Casey* (1992), a majority of justices voted to retain *Roe* while narrowing it, deeply disappointing social conservatives.

During his presidency, the chief success for Bush came in foreign policy, with the fall of the Berlin Wall, a crushing victory against Iraq in the first Gulf War, and the collapse of the Soviet Union itself. Bush hoped that he could translate the 90 percent public approval ratings he enjoyed at the end of the first Gulf War into a new push on domestic policy. Yet he could never gain traction, and Congress took action on almost nothing he proposed. A year later, with Bush's approval ratings around 40 percent, the pattern repeated: at his 1992 State of the Union address, Bush again demanded that Congress take action on the economy, including tax cuts in investments and capital gains.[7] However, after his two-month deadline had passed and Congress had not acted, the president did not press the matter.

Of course, Democrats in Congress had their own domestic policy agenda. Congress passed a number of pieces of liberal legislation that pushed Bush into unpopular vetoes and set the stage for the next administration. These included the Family and Medical Leave Act of 1993 and the National Voter Registration Act (the so-called Motor-Voter Act). By the end of the Bush presidency, the sense of stalemate in Washington was complete.

As a result of Bush's reversal on taxes and quotas, his relative passivity in the NEA controversy, and the overall growth of government under his watch, many conservative Republicans were ready to revolt. The slide into recession in 1990 and weak recovery from mid-1991 on meant that many other Americans were ready to revolt, too. This broad revolt of "outsiderism" took a number of forms. Conservative commentator Patrick Buchanan unsuccessfully challenged Bush in the Republican primaries. Texas businessman H. Ross Perot, an apostle of the "radical center," launched the most successful non–major party bid for the presidency since Theodore Roosevelt's in 1912, aimed at the federal deficit, trade and economic competitiveness, and political reform. Not least, Arkansas Governor Bill Clinton received the Democratic nomination as a moderate Democrat and an outsider to Washington. In the end, Bush simply could not persuade enough Americans that he merited a second term.[8]

THE CLINTON PRESIDENCY

Bill Clinton was the first Democrat to win a presidential election since Jimmy Carter in 1976, 16 years before. He had cracked the supposed Republican lock on the Electoral College, winning several states in the West and South that had long disdained Democratic presidential candidates. Yet he prevailed with only 43 percent of the nationally aggregated popular vote, the third-lowest of any winning candidate since 1828. Nearly one in five American voters chose Ross Perot, who remained a pivotal figure for some time. Meanwhile, like Bush in 1988, Clinton had no coattails; Democrats gained no seats in the Senate and lost 10 seats in the House. The Democratic Party retained large majorities in Congress, but most had no reason to believe that they owed anything to Clinton politically.

In contrast to Bush's patrician upbringing, Clinton had grown up lower middle class in Arkansas in a household headed by an alcoholic stepfather. He went through a hippie phase and took steps to evade the Vietnam-era draft, but also attended Yale law school and was elected attorney general of Arkansas and then governor at the young age of 32. He lost a gubernatorial reelection bid in 1980, but mounted a successful comeback in 1982 (earning the appellation "the comeback kid"). Intensely interested in the details of policy and often a highly disciplined campaigner, he was also noted for lack of personal discipline and had gained a reputation as a womanizer.[9]

Clinton was influenced significantly by a set of ideas promoted by moderate Democrats in and out of Washington. In the mid-1980s, after Walter Mondale's drubbing at the hands of Ronald Reagan, a group of moderate and conservative Democrats (mostly from the South) formed the Democratic Leadership Council (DLC). Other entities such as the Progressive Policy Institute joined the movement. The DLC gradually became a force within the Democratic Party arguing for a "Third Way" between Reaganism and McGovernism.[10] Bill Clinton was an early member, and served as DLC Chair. When he ran for president, his campaign bore the DLC stamp. Clinton explicitly ran as a "New Democrat" focusing on the middle class and issues of economic security. He supported the death penalty, pledged to cut the deficit in half, and promised to "end welfare as we know it." At the same time, he ran on a platform of universal health care and measures supported by unions. He said abortion should be "safe, legal, and rare."

In domestic policy, where Bush ran as a continuation of Reagan, Clinton repeatedly criticized the "failures of the past twelve years," but ended up consolidating Reaganism more than overthrowing it. To understand this outcome, it is important to make a distinction between Clinton's first term and his second term. Although he was reelected—making him the first Democratic president since Franklin Roosevelt to serve two full terms—his two policy terms did not coincide with his two constitutional terms. It was the midterm election of 1994 that marked the dividing line between his policy terms.

Clinton's first "term." Bill Clinton's first two years in office were dominated by big policy proposals with high political stakes.[11] First,

Clinton decided, upon the advice of Treasury Secretary Robert Rubin (and against the recommendation of Labor Secretary Robert Reich), to focus on deficit reduction ahead of most other spending priorities. He did propose a $16 billion fiscal stimulus plan with the aim of cutting unemployment, but a Republican-led filibuster in the Senate killed it. On grounds of fiscal probity, Clinton announced that he was unable to pursue the middle class tax cut he had promised in the campaign, and he proposed a deficit reduction package totaling about $500 billion over five years, called the Omnibus Budget Reconciliation Act of 1993.

The package was split roughly half and half between tax increases and spending cuts, mostly in defense. Hopes by liberals that the end of the Cold War would produce a giant "peace dividend"—a shift of resources from defense to a cornucopia of domestic programs—were not fulfilled. On the tax side, critical provisions included two new tax rates for upper-income earners (36 percent and 39.6 percent), a 4.3 cent per gallon gas tax increase, an increase in corporate taxes and taxes on Social Security benefits, and elimination of the cap on income subjected to the Medicare tax. According to projections by the Office of Management and Budget, the package would reduce the deficit from $290 billion in 1992 to $212 billion in 1996, though it would begin to rise again after that. By the time Congress voted on the bill in August 1993, public opinion had largely turned against the tax increase. In the end, the budget measure passed 218–216 in the House and 51–50 in the Senate, with Vice President Gore casting the tie breaking vote.

At the same time, First Lady Hillary Rodham Clinton was put in charge of a task force to design the administration's health care proposal. This issue had been at the top of the liberal wish list since FDR's Economic Bill of Rights in 1944, and the president calculated that the time was right, with big Democratic majorities in both houses, to act. The Health Security Act, proposed in early 1994, mandated that individuals purchase health insurance and that businesses with more than 5,000 employees be required to provide coverage. It established subsidies for those too poor to buy insurance, created regional health alliances in each state to offer insurance, created a Medicare prescription drug program, and funded a variety of rural health programs, physician training, and related services. It would also have created a National Health Board to monitor health care quality. The White House was unable to entice any congressional Republicans to add their names to the legislation, which they saw as too expensive and centralized. As with the budget a year before, public opinion, originally receptive to the Clinton plan, soured. Facing a tough election two months away, congressional Democrats announced they were putting off a vote until the next year. It would actually be another 16 years before a similar bill would be considered for passage.

Although the budget and health care reform debates consumed the greater part of the domestic agenda for the first two years of the Clinton presidency, some other important domestic policy changes were enacted. One of the first things done by Congress in early 1993 was to send to Clinton a variety of bills that had earlier been passed but vetoed by Bush, including the Family Medical Leave Act and Brady Handgun Control Act.

Three other legislative measures merit note. Part of Bill Clinton's "New Democrat" appeal was based on his willingness to support free trade agreements, and in late 1993, Clinton brought a revised NAFTA to Congress for its consideration. In contrast with the budget bill earlier that year, Clinton worked closely with Republicans to secure passage, a rare instance in his first two years in which Clinton forged a bipartisan coalition on behalf of a centrist program.

Another measure of note was the Omnibus Crime Act of 1994. The crime bill was also meant to underscore Clinton's credentials as a "New Democrat." It included significant expansion of the death penalty for federal crimes, funding to help local communities hire 100,000 police officers, major social spending for community projects such as midnight basketball leagues aimed at occupying otherwise crime-prone youngsters, and a ban on so-called assault weapons (loosely defined as semi-automatic rifles with a military appearance). However, liberals disliked the death penalty provisions, fiscal conservatives decried pork barrel spending, and the National Rifle Association mobilized its millions of members against the assault weapon ban. Clinton and Democratic leaders pushed it through, but at a high political cost. The predominant picture in the public eye became one of gun control and pork-barrel spending.

Third, George Bush's America 2000 educational proposal morphed into Clinton's Goals 2000 contained in the Educate America Act passed by Congress in 1994. The goals included demonstrated student competency in a variety of key subject areas, a framework that influenced state standards and future federal legislation.

As chief executive, Clinton also ordered a reappraisal of federal operations under the rubric of the "Reinventing Government" project headed by Vice President Al Gore. The project was partially inspired by the 1993 book *Reinventing Government: How the Entrepreneurial Spirit Is Transforming Government* by David Osborne and Ted Gaebler, and Osborne served as an advisor.[12] The project led to a federal personnel reduction of over 350,000 and saved an estimated $168 billion over five years.[13] The Reinventing Government project was a logical follow-up to the Grace Commission appointed by Ronald Reagan in the 1980s, which made nearly 2,500 recommendations for administrative efficiency and cost saving.[14]

All of this took place in the context of an international environment that was relatively quiet. There were a number of brushfires in the Balkans, Haiti, North Korea, and Somalia, but nothing resembling the intense confrontation of the Cold War or even the war against Saddam in 1991. The world influenced domestic policy by allowing near-complete focus on domestic issues for the first time since the 1930s, a reversal of preceding years in which foreign policy crises pushed domestic policy to the back burner.

THE 1994 ELECTIONS AND BILL CLINTON'S SECOND TERM

Republicans had last won control of the House in 1952, and had been out of power in the Senate for eight years. Organized by House Minority Whip Newt Gingrich, Republicans announced a ten-point "Contract with America" as part of a nationalized campaign to swing the House to the GOP in 1994. The Contract listed legislative items that Republicans pledged to bring to a vote in the House within 100 days of taking office. Contract items, determined through a process of consultation with party members and pro-Republican constituency groups, included a balanced budget and line item veto, a tough anti-crime bill, welfare reform with a two-year time limit for welfare recipients, middle class tax cuts, a capital gains tax cut and regulatory reform, tort reform aiming to limit lawsuits, and term limits for members of Congress. Overall, the Contract with America represented a strike in the direction of conservative governance focused almost entirely on domestic issues. On election day, Republicans gained 52 seats in the House and 9 in the Senate, enough to gain control of both houses of Congress. Although surveys showed that specific Contract items had limited effect on voters, the goal of nationalizing the elections was achieved. As importantly, the Contract gave the incoming GOP majorities a ready-made agenda.[15]

The election results and the new Congress dramatically changed the direction of domestic policy. For a time, Newt Gingrich was the center of attention, becoming the most powerful House Speaker since 1910. The Republican Congress drove policy, while Clinton became a bystander reduced to pleading that he was still relevant. Any large scale expansion of government, such as the Clinton health care plan, was out of the question, and the administration began backtracking on a number of other liberal policies.[16]

House Republicans kept their promise and brought to a vote all the items on the Contract within the first 100 days of the 104th Congress. Most passed, though the term limits constitutional amendment failed to garner the necessary two-thirds vote. However, as Gingrich would discover, this was the easy part. Two major obstacles remained to achieving this conservative revolution in policy.

One was the Senate, where the rules allowed greater influence by the Democratic minority. Moreover, many Republican Senators did not share Gingrich's fervor. These included Majority Leader Robert Dole, a cautious Kansan who had spent a career in the Senate forging legislative compromises. As a consequence, many bills languished in the Senate after a quick passage in the House.

The other obstacle was Clinton, whom Republicans mistakenly believed could be "rolled" by determined action. In reality, Clinton was biding his time and would employ a skillful combination of accommodation and confrontation, "triangulating" his position between Republicans and congressional Democrats. Accommodation took several forms. Clinton signed some of the early products of the 104th Congress, including the "Freedom to Farm Act," which phased out New Deal–era farm subsidies in favor of a free-market agricultural approach, and a measure that made it more difficult for Congress to impose "unfunded mandates" on state and local governments. Rhetorically, Clinton embraced a new limited government ethos, proclaiming in his 1996 State of the Union address that "[t]he era of big government is over."[17]

At the same time, Clinton fought Republican plans to shrink the federal budget and the scope of federal regulatory authority.[18] The flashpoint came when Congress passed and presented to the president an omnibus reconciliation bill making a multitude of big changes in federal policy. The bill would have cut federal spending by about $500 billion, cut taxes by $245 billion, and balanced the budget in seven years. It would also have eliminated the federal departments of Energy, Education, Commerce, and Housing and Urban Development. It envisioned savings in Medicare totaling $250 billion over seven years, the elimination of hundreds of smaller federal programs, significant reductions in the budgets of regulatory agencies, and changes requiring regulators to meet a higher burden of proof before adding new regulations. Because these changes were attached to an increase in the federal debt limit necessary to keep the federal government operating, Republicans believed that Clinton would have no choice but to sign the bill. Had Republicans succeeded, they would have fundamentally altered the trajectory of federal policy in the direction of a more limited scope and cost of government.

However, Clinton vetoed the bill, leading to two federal government shutdowns in short order. Although both sides bore responsibility, Clinton was largely successful in the public relations war at the center of the struggle. For their part, Republicans were divided, and finally agreed to end the shutdown without having reached a comprehensive balanced budget agreement. Instead, both sides agreed to continue negotiations and fund the government with a continuing appropriation based on the last year's spending minus 10 percent. Clinton appeared the victor and avoided the deep structural changes Republicans hoped to make. However, in a major concession to Republicans, Clinton also agreed to submit a seven-year balanced budget proposal of his own. Republicans also got $53 billion of spending cuts and elimination of some three hundred federal programs.[19] Both sides hoped the issue would be settled by the upcoming presidential election between Clinton, Dole, and (once again) Ross Perot.

While the upcoming 1996 elections served as an excuse to put off further action on the budget, they served as a prod to policy in other areas. This was especially true in welfare reform. Clinton had set the issue aside in order to focus on health care reform. After gaining congressional majorities, Republicans twice passed conservative welfare reform bills, only to have them vetoed by Clinton. In the summer of 1996, a breakthrough occurred. As both Clinton and congressional Republicans looked for a major pre-election accomplishment, they reached a deal, enacting the biggest change in welfare policy since the New Deal.

The Personal Responsibility and Work Opportunity Reconciliation Act of 1996 (PRWORA) revised the Social Security Act of 1935, ending Aid to Families with Dependent Children (AFDC) as an entitlement program and replacing it with Temporary Assistance to Needy Families (TANF). TANF would operate as a fixed block grant to states, which would design their own welfare programs. Most recipients would have a two-year continuous limit on welfare and a five-year lifetime limit, and would face work requirements. States could (but did not have to) bar additional welfare money to women having additional illegitimate children. The welfare reform act was the culmination of a long process in the world of ideas and a period of considerable experimentation at the state level prodded by the 1988 federal welfare reform.

The summer of 1996 also saw Clinton sign the Defense of Marriage Act (DOMA), which established a federal definition of marriage as between one man and one woman and exempted states from being required to recognize same-sex marriages from other states. DOMA was the first major federal response to the rise of the issue of same-sex marriage. Some of Clinton's liberal allies were outraged by his conservative moves on welfare and gay marriage, but those moves may also have ensured his reelection.

Clinton gained a solid but unexceptional reelection win against Dole and Perot, garnering 49 percent of the vote after running a campaign based on mini-issues such as school uniforms and labeling of violent television programming, alongside a promise to defend Medicare, Medicaid, education, and environment programs. Republicans held on to their congressional majorities, losing only a handful of seats in the House and actually making a small gain in the Senate.[20]

Having failed to win undivided power in the elections, both sides resumed budget negotiations. Helped along by economic growth, Clinton and congressional Republicans finally reached a balanced budget deal in the summer of 1997. The deal included domestic spending cuts, a set of spending caps, a $500 per child tax credit, and a cut in the capital gains tax—all Republican priorities. However, the tax and spending cuts were smaller than Republicans had proposed two years before, and Clinton was satisfied that his spending priorities in Medicare, Medicaid, education, and environment were protected. No federal departments were abolished. The plan envisioned a balanced budget within seven years. In actuality, due to the strong economy, the goal was achieved by the end of 1998. It was the first time since 1969 that the federal budget had been in balance.

Clinton hoped that the balanced budget and the strong economy would provide a springboard for major new policy departures in a number of areas, but most of these efforts were stymied. He signed the Kyoto Protocol committing the United States to take measures to reduce carbon emissions, but never introduced it to the Senate after Senators voted 99–0 to oppose any agreement (such as Kyoto) that excluded the participation of China and India. He was able to win reluctant congressional approval for providing funds to help school districts hire 100,000 new teachers, but little else of note after 1997. A push for gun control, inspired by the Columbine High School massacre in April 1999, failed, though Congress did repeal the Glass-Steagall Act of 1932, which had required banks to separate commercial and investment banking. In a dramatic turnaround, the biggest domestic policy issue became what to do about the burgeoning federal budget surpluses. Clinton's plan—to pour it into shoring up Social Security—never advanced very far, nor did Clinton's suggestion that a broader bipartisan deal might be made safeguarding Social Security's future. The Republican plan—tax cuts passed in 1999 and again in 2000—were vetoed by Clinton. All that was left was a series of minor skirmishes over the margins of federal spending. The elections of 1998 only confirmed the stalemate, as Republican attempts to exploit the Monica Lewinsky scandal backfired and Democrats escaped with small House gains—the first by a president's party in a midterm election since 1934.[21]

Clinton's policy ambitions, already diminished considerably by the 1994 elections, were dealt a deathblow after 1997 for a number of reasons. Clinton's relatively weak reelection mandate did not help matters, and he was distracted enormously in 1998 and early 1999 by the Lewinsky scandal, which ultimately led to his impeachment by the US House, though the Senate did not muster the two-thirds vote needed to remove him from office. Other lesser scandals, including one involving his 1996 reelection fundraising, also weakened him.

BUSH-CLINTON EQUILIBRIUM: SUMMARY AND ASSESSMENT

Although it was a rocky period of increasing partisanship and political drama, the George H. W. Bush–Bill Clinton era of policy making was predominantly a period of adjustment, consolidation, and stalemate. Incrementalism once again proved its worth as a way of describing policy. Taking a long view, it is best seen as a rough continuation of the Reagan era, with adjustments at the margins. Altogether, political scientist Bert Rockman noted that "[l]ike Eisenhower, Clinton may be known for having put a tepid but confirmatory seal of approval on popular policies of the other party."[22]

Economic policy

Both Bush and Clinton sponsored large tax increases, but so did Reagan (in 1982). Under Clinton, the top marginal tax rate reached 39.6 percent, well below the 70 percent it had been in 1980. Despite Clinton's best efforts, no major new entitlement programs were created, and after 1994 non-defense spending was cut considerably, reaching a 27-year low of 14.7 percent of GDP in 2000. Under the post-1994 Congress, both income taxes for families and capital gains taxes were eventually cut. Both Bush and Clinton adhered to Reagan's pro–free trade stance. And the administrations of the 1990s embraced the monetary policies of Reagan's Federal Reserve Board chairman, Alan Greenspan, who was reappointed once by Bush and twice by Clinton. Clinton declared that "the era of big government is over," reduced the federal workforce by over 350,000, and reached an agreement with Republicans that balanced the budget starting in 1998. However, pages in the *Federal Register* resumed their upward climb, at first slowly and then with greater speed as Clinton's presidency came to a close.

Social welfare

Though human resources spending rose from 10.3 to 11 percent of GDP from 1988 to 2000, it still ended the period lower than it had been in 1980. The Clinton attempt to enact universal health care failed, though more modest steps (such as creation of SCHIP, a children's health insurance plan) were adopted. In the wake of the 1994 congressional elections, welfare was dramatically reformed, cut and turned from an entitlement into a block grant with time limits and work requirements.

Civil rights

The Civil Rights Act of 1991 returned to the status quo before the *Ward's Cove* case, and not much else changed at the federal level. Opposition to affirmative action had some successes in states such as Michigan and California, but Clinton blocked change in Washington.

Education and environment

The biggest change was in a movement throughout the period toward federal encouragement of state education standards. The 104th Congress sought to abolish the Department of Education, and did cut spending on environmental regulatory enforcement, but Clinton made defense of federal education and environment programs a large part of his re-election campaign. For the most part, stalemate ensued. When Clinton signed the anti-global warming Kyoto Pact, he did not have enough Senate support to bring it to a vote.

Moral/cultural issues

Battles over gay rights surged to the forefront, but Clinton signed DOMA, and promised that he would make abortion "rare" as well as "legal" and "safe." The religious right became more organized and active. The "culture war" raged on, but policy was stalemated.

Federalism

The most important constitutional shift in this period was the continued diffusion of power to the states, especially in the area of welfare. Federalism was a major theme of the 104th Congress and Republicans at all levels, and Clinton signed a bill restricting unfunded mandates. Some Supreme Court decisions contributed to this shift by emphasizing the Tenth Amendment or placing limits on the use of the Commerce Clause to justify expansive federal authority (*United States v. Lopez* and *United States v. Morrison*).

At the same time, the 1990s showed the ongoing limits to Reaganism. Clinton did not succeed in overturning it, but Bush was a lukewarm advocate and Clinton successfully prevented Newt Gingrich from pushing Reaganism much further. Had Gingrich prevailed in 1995, the era would have been one of major change rather than incrementalism. As it was, only welfare reform (and perhaps the Freedom to Farm Act) stepped outside of the incrementalist framework, and welfare reform was an example of policy change bubbling up from state experiments in a federal system. It also corresponded with more dramatic results than anyone expected; a decade after passage of PRWORA, welfare caseloads had declined by 60 percent nationally and work participation rates had surged.[23]

These policy outputs made sense: Policy **inputs** almost all worked in the direction of a period of consolidation rather than radical change. Bush showed little interest in **ideas** except to perfunctorily endorse Reagan's, while Clinton was most influenced by the Democratic Leadership Council's ideas promoting a new, less liberal Democratic policy approach and Osborne's promoting more efficient administration. **Events** played an idiosyncratic role: the Oklahoma City bombing in April 1995 by a pair of anti-government radicals allowed Clinton to regain his place on the front page and to tar by association those promoting limited government, while the funeral of Yitzhak Rabin in November led to Gingrich's self-destructive petulance when Clinton would not discuss the budget impasse with him on Air Force One. Later, the Lewinsky scandal shut down any hopes of a grand deal on Social Security. In general, though, no domestic event was dramatic enough to significantly alter the political or policy landscape. The most important events had taken place **abroad**, with the end of the Cold War and the threat of Soviet communism. For most of this period, foreign policy was the dog that did not bark. The nation did benefit from a "peace dividend" but not as liberals had hoped, with a shift of spending from defense to domestic programs. Instead, Republicans, now willing to accept deep cuts in defense, were able to press for deep cuts in domestic spending, as well.

The **politics** of the Bush-Clinton era were also well suited for incremental policy change. There was divided government in Washington, with a president of one party and a Congress controlled by the other party, in 10 out of 12 years. Moreover, the parties were increasingly polarized, and party-line voting grew throughout the era. Bush's 1988 presidential victory was solid but tainted in the eyes of Democrats by the sharp-elbowed campaign he ran; Clinton won twice, but without ever receiving a majority of the popular vote (43 percent in 1992, 49 percent in 1996). The impeachment and Senate trial of Clinton put the exclamation point on the new political atmosphere. The election of the first Republican Congress since 1952 ended Clinton's foray into anti-Reaganism, contributing to an extension of Reaganism instead. In what Stephen Skowronek calls "political time," Bush and Clinton were a reasonable facsimile of Harry S. Truman and Dwight D. Eisenhower—with not dissimilar results.

Not least, the **people** who were making policy at the top inclined the era toward an incrementalist result, though they were not all incrementalists themselves. Bush was notably non-ideological and uninterested in domestic policy. Clinton wanted to make big changes, but was undermined by lack of personal discipline and by the (relatively conservative and non-crisis) nature of the times. Gingrich, too, wanted to make big changes (in a different direction), but was also immature and was prone to gamble when a more cautious approach might have been in order. Dole, like Bush, was a natural compromiser. No one consistently possessed the combination of conviction and compromise shown by a Roosevelt or a Reagan and arguably necessary to navigate major policy change.

Maintenance of economic growth remained high on the **policy agenda**: Bush took office near the end of a nearly eight-year stretch of economic growth, while Clinton left office near the end of a ten-year stretch of growth that began in 1991 and did not draw to a close until 2001—a new record for the longest expansion in US history. Some things, though, changed dramatically. Above all, the nation's deep concern with its decades-old budget deficit turned into an unexpected struggle to determine how to allocate budget surpluses that were projected to reach a cumulative $2.3 trillion over the next decade. By 2000, energy had returned to some prominence as a policy issue, and global warming had made its entrance. Education was embraced as a key federal issue by both Bush and Clinton. Health care surged forward as an issue, then collapsed just as abruptly. Cultural issues such as affirmative action, immigration, and gay marriage came to the fore but were largely fought out at the state level. Family and the social problem of the illegitimacy rate received increased attention. Some issues also dropped down the list of policy concerns. Crime rates improved, for example, so crime as a policy issue declined in saliency. However, post-Columbine, gun control briefly occupied center stage. The Contract with America dominated the congressional agenda for more than a year.

Whatever the dramatic hopes of Clinton or Gingrich, **path dependency** dominated. Under Bush, the ADA was seen by disabled-rights activists as an extension of previous civil rights efforts and the Clear Air amendments simply built upon the previous Clean Air Act. Even the balanced budget agreement of 1997 was a more moderate version of the changes Republicans had proposed in 1995.

The battle over **problem definition** was particularly notable in budget and crime policy. Was the deficit mainly a spending problem or a revenue problem? Neither Bush nor Clinton succeeded in persuading most Americans that the problem was insufficient revenue, and they paid a heavy political price for their support of large tax increases. With the help of Ross Perot, Republicans won the battle to define the deficit as a problem requiring a solid plan to balance the budget. And was crime mainly the result of social deprivation or recidivism and weak law enforcement? This was one of the key questions framing the debate over the 1994 crime bill.

Perhaps the best example of the problem of unanticipated consequences was the 1990 "luxury tax," which was meant to raise revenue by establishing a special tax on expensive automobiles and yachts. As a result, the demand for American-made yachts fell by 70 to 80 percent and at least 30,000 boat workers (possibly many more) lost their jobs. Since fewer yachts were sold, the government made little revenue on the luxury tax; moreover, the laid-off workers were not paying income or payroll tax anymore, but instead were receiving unemployment benefits. Within a short time, the luxury tax was costing the federal government more than it was raising.[24] (It was repealed in 1993.) Additionally, some analysts would later point to the 1999 revision of the Glass-Steagall Act as a ticking time bomb that contributed to the financial meltdown of 2008.[25]

And, as always, debate raged over the actual **effects of policy**. Analysts debated how much of the sharp decline in welfare caseloads was due to PRWORA and how much was due to other factors, such as a growing economy.[26] Similarly, though the balanced budget of the late 1990s was welcomed by most observers, there was little agreement on why it happened. Bush boosters argued that it was their president's 1990 budget deal that did the trick over the long run, though the deficit doubled within three years of the BEA's enactment. Clinton claimed credit for his 1993 budget, though that budget was only projected to reduce the deficit to $212 billion. Critics also noted that the bill only produced 49 percent of the predicted revenue in 1993–1996 and claimed it reduced employment and economic growth compared to what it would have been.[27] Newt Gingrich and congressional Republicans took credit, pointing out that they had forced a reluctant Clinton to accept the principle of a balanced budget and had imposed significant discipline on domestic spending. Economists generally agreed that the most important factor was the return of economic growth after the recession of 1990–1991.[28]

The key question, then, was why the economy did so well in the late 1990s. Here the debate was largely between those who credited Clinton's innovations and those who credited the continuation of Reagan's basic framework, including relatively low marginal tax rates, free trade, Alan Greenspan's monetary policy, and a political atmosphere that welcomed entrepreneurialism.[29]

7

George W. Bush and the Republican Non-Breakout

★ ★ ★

The terrorist attack on September 11, 2001, abruptly changed the public policy agenda. Issues such as the federal budget surplus were immediately supplanted by a renewed focus on national security.

AS THE CLINTON YEARS DREW to a close, both parties struggled to find their footing. The nation seemed to have settled into an era of modest change. The economy, though showing signs of trouble, had not yet slipped back into open recession, large budget surpluses were projected far into the future, and both parties had recently been rebuffed in attempts to force dramatic changes. Most Americans approved of Bill Clinton's job as president, but disapproved of his character. Some Democrats chafed

119

under what they saw as post-1994 Clintonism's unprincipled centrism, while Republicans searched for a new political formula, especially after the disappointing midterm election results in 1998.

In 2000, Democrats nominated Vice President Al Gore as their presidential candidate. Gore won the nomination against former New Jersey senator Bill Bradley, who ran against Gore from the left. Republicans nominated Texas governor George W. Bush, son of former president George H. W. Bush. Governor Bush was propelled to the lead in the Republican nomination race in the wake of the 1998 elections, which convinced many Republicans that the congressional GOP was too hard-edged and that the party needed to look outside of Washington for leadership. Having won his first term as Texas governor in the Republican wave of 1994, Bush provided a rare bright spot for Republicans in the much tougher year of 1998 by winning a landslide reelection victory, including a majority of the women's vote and the Hispanic vote.[1]

Bush was in many ways the Republican version of Clinton, who sought to change the direction of his party, making it more acceptable to moderate voters. Just as Clinton was heavily influenced by the ideas of the Democratic Leadership Council, Bush was influenced by the concept of "compassionate conservatism" promoted by professor Marvin Olasky and others.[2] Olasky became an adviser to Bush as governor, who adapted Olasky's ideas to his presidential campaign. As Bush constructed it, compassionate conservatism (or, as some later called it, "big government conservatism") was represented by a combination of proposals meant to hold the allegiance of the Republican base while appealing to women and racial minorities. The "conservatism" took the form of support for a large tax cut; Bush had taken the lesson from his father's presidency that tax increases could be fatal to a Republican president. The "compassion" was emphasized by support for liberal immigration reform, acceptance of a growing federal role in K–12 education, endorsement of a new Medicare prescription drug program, and criticism of congressional Republicans for cutting anti-poverty spending. Bush also embraced conservative stands on social issues and supported federal funding of faith-based social service providers, which appealed to both the Republican base and blacks and Hispanics, who are often deeply religious even when they are economically liberal.

Bush's domestic policy record was conditioned by his "compassionate conservative" campaign commitments and by politics more generally. Above all, most of his presidency was conducted in an atmosphere of partisan rancor owing partly to the circumstances of Bush's election. The final results were very nearly a tie: Gore finished with 48.4 percent of the popular vote, Bush with 47.9 percent. The 25 electoral votes from

Florida, where Bush led Gore by only a few hundred votes, decided the winner. After a bitter month-long legal battle over recounts, the US Supreme Court ruled for Bush, who won Florida and with it the election.

At the same time, Republicans suffered small losses in both the House and the Senate, maintaining a narrow majority in the House and holding only a 50–50 tie, which could be broken by Vice President Dick Cheney's vote, in the Senate. In May 2001, Republican Senator James Jeffords of Vermont switched parties, giving Democrats a slim majority. Republicans regained their own slim Senate majority in 2002, and expanded their majorities in both houses in 2004. Bush also won reelection in 2004 against Democratic Senator John Kerry of Massachusetts, and he expanded his votes among blacks, Hispanics, and women. However, the 50.7 percent of the popular vote that he won was the smallest share won by a reelected president in a two-way race since Woodrow Wilson in 1916. What had become known in 2000 as the "red-blue" divide (red for Republicans, blue for Democrats), changed hardly at all from 2000 to 2004. Only two states shifted from blue to red, one from red to blue.[3] In 2006, a backlash against widely perceived Republican misrule in Congress and mistakes by the Bush administration in Iraq and elsewhere brought Democrats into power in both houses. Republicans hoped at two different points in Bush's presidency—from January to May 2001 and from the 2002 midterm elections through the 2006 midterm elections—that they had made a political and policy breakthrough that signaled a new GOP era, but those hopes proved illusory.

If policy making in the George W. Bush years took place in the shadow of the politics made by the contentious 2000 election, most of it also took place under the influence of one of the most dramatic events in American history, the terrorist attacks of September 11, 2001. Bush ran his campaign and began his presidency with a domestic policy focus, but 9/11 radically altered the public policy agenda.

OPENING MOVES

When Bush took office in January 2001, he had two major domestic priorities.[4] One was a significant tax cut that he touted during the 2000 campaign, the "conservative" centerpiece of compassionate conservatism. The other was a package of education reforms, the "compassionate" centerpiece of his formula. Bush argued that without the tax cut government would end up draining away the projected surplus with higher spending. Additionally, by early 2001, it was clear that the economy had slowed.

The stock market had peaked in January 2000 at the height of the "dot-com bubble" and had lost about 20 percent of its value one year later; manufacturing employment began falling in the summer of 2000. Bush argued that his proposed tax cut could avert or mitigate a recession.

With modest Democratic support and nearly unanimous Republican support, Congress passed a $1.35 trillion/ten year tax cut (the Economic Growth and Tax Relief Reconciliation Act). Provisions included a reduction in the top rate from 39.6 percent to 35 percent; moving a large number of taxpayers from the 15 percent rate into a new, lower 10 percent rate; increasing the child tax credit from $500 to $1000 per child; creating a $10,000 tax credit for adoptions; and gradually phasing out the estate tax. Senate Democrats insisted on adding a Keynesian pump-priming provision—an immediate $300 per taxpayer rebate considered an "advance" on next year's tax cut—in the expectation that consumers would spend this money and stimulate the economy. Senate rules required the tax cuts to expire after 10 years, guaranteeing that there would be a fight over renewal sometime in the next decade. To supporters, the tax cut was a fair policy of "tax relief" that allowed taxpayers to keep more of what was rightfully theirs; to opponents, it was an unfair "giveaway" of public resources to people who already had enough.

Bush also succeeded in obtaining passage of his other big initial domestic priority, the package of education reforms that was labeled the "No Child Left Behind Act" (or NCLB).[5] Central to Bush's attempt to cast himself as a different kind of Republican, Bush discarded the traditional Republican hostility to federal involvement in K–12 education. Instead, Bush proposed increased federal education funding, linked with a requirement that states measure educational outcomes in schools with standardized tests and publicize the results to their communities. Schools that consistently failed to educate students could lose funding and be turned into charter schools. NCLB was the culmination of several years of experimentation with standards at the state level, and of federal programs such as America 2000 and Goals 2000.

Many conservatives disliked the intervention of the federal government in education, which they saw as a state and local responsibility. Many liberals opposed the use of standardized tests or the threat of a funding cutoff. Bush, however, was able to fashion a bipartisan congressional majority, working with Senator Edward Kennedy of Massachusetts (who successfully insisted that a proposal for school vouchers be dropped from the bill). In the end, as with the tax cut, Bush won, though more Democrats than Republicans voted for NCLB in the House. Just as Clinton had done with his 1993 budget bill and NAFTA, Bush won the tax cut and NCLB with two very different legislative coalitions.

THE AFTERMATH OF TERROR

The primary effect of the September 11 terrorist attacks was to focus attention on war and foreign affairs. Within a month, US troops were fighting al Qaeda and the Taliban in Afghanistan. In March 2003, the United States launched an invasion of Saddam Hussein's Iraq. The two wars, as well as the general campaign against al Qaeda, would continue for the remainder of the Bush presidency, and would consume the greater part of the president's energy.

However, some new domestic issues also surged to the fore with 9/11. First, the attacks deepened the recession, causing a big sell-off on Wall Street, costing a million jobs over the next four months, and seriously threatening the solvency of the airline industry. The president and Congress responded with a $15 billion bailout plan for struggling airlines, $20 billion to aid New York, and additional tax cuts in 2002 and 2003. The tax cut in 2003, which cut capital gains and dividends taxes by an estimated $350 billion in hopes of spurring investment, was especially contentious, receiving almost no Democratic support. It was politically possible only because Republicans had regained control of the Senate in 2002. As a proportion of the economy, the 2003 Bush tax cut in combination with the 2001 tax cut was the third largest since 1960, behind only the Kennedy-Johnson tax cut in 1964 and the Reagan tax cut of 1981.[6] Under the guidance of Alan Greenspan, who remained chair of the Federal Reserve Board, the Fed fought the sharp downturn by dramatically lowering interest rates.

Second, intertwined with the new War on Terror was a renewed emphasis on internal security, an issue that had been largely dormant since the 1950s. This new policy focus included passage of the USA PATRIOT Act weeks after 9/11, federalization of airport baggage screening, creation of the Department of Homeland Security, and a secret domestic surveillance program run by the National Security Agency. The PATRIOT Act added a number of law enforcement and intelligence tools to the fight against terrorism within the United States, and facilitated communication between competing agencies, such as the Federal Bureau of Investigation and Central Intelligence Agency. Although the measure passed 98–1 in the Senate and 357–66 in the House, it soon came under attack from civil libertarians who feared that it gave too much power to law enforcement. Some measures, including the federal takeover of baggage security and the creation of the Homeland Security Department, were originally proposed by Democrats and only reluctantly taken up by Bush.[7]

While recession and internal security had a much higher profile because of 9/11, other domestic issues, prominent on September 10, fell by the wayside. Immigration reform was one, but perhaps the biggest issue in Washington had been how best to preserve the $1 trillion of projected budget surpluses that remained after the tax cut. On the eve of the terrorist attack, members of Congress debated whether to place the portion of the surplus attributable to Social Security tax in a "lock box" that could not be spent. Within 24 hours, the country was at war and fiscal restraint was no longer a concern. Between tax cuts, recession, war, and the costs of rebuilding lower Manhattan, the surplus had turned into a deficit. The nation's brief moment of fiscal sobriety was over.

BIG GOVERNMENT CONSERVATISM IN ACTION

The decline of fiscal restraint as an issue, though driven by 9/11, dove-tailed with Bush's domestic policy agenda.[8] Looking for crucial votes in the agricultural Midwest and Rust Belt in 2002, Bush signed an expensive farm bill that essentially undid the 1996 Freedom to Farm Act, reinstating a much heavier government role in agriculture, and imposed higher tariffs on foreign steel. He also secured passage of the first major new entitlement program since the 1960s in the Medicare prescription drug program, an idea originally proposed by Bill Clinton. Medicare Part D, as it was called, offered subsidized insurance coverage for prescription drugs to people on Medicare, at a cost estimated in December 2003 at more than $400 billion over the next two decades. The legislation used competition among private providers to hold down costs, and included an option allowing taxpayers to save money for medical expenses in tax-free accounts (Health Savings Accounts, or HSAs). These innovations were an attempt to construct the program in a manner that would take advantage of free-market principles. Bush and the Republican congressional leadership pushed reluctant Republicans to vote in favor of the plan, while most Democrats voted against it, preferring a more expensive alternative shorn of free-market competition and HSAs.

Bush had less success with the faith-based initiatives program. The idea of allowing religious social services organizations to apply for federal money was not new and it had broad support in the abstract—so-called Charitable Choice provisions in the 1996 welfare reform allowed this in some cases, and the idea had been broadly supported by Clinton and Gore. However, it foundered over congressional disagreements about whether religious organizations receiving federal funds should be allowed to proselytize or discriminate in employment on the basis of religious beliefs. As a result, the president turned to executive orders to effect part of his program, placing it on a weaker footing.[9]

Even less successful were attempts to promote Social Security reform and comprehensive immigration reform.[10] Bush had highlighted

Social Security reform as a major goal during the 2000 election campaign and again in 2004, when he touted it as part of his "Ownership Society" program. The idea was to allow workers to put some portion of their Social Security tax in a personal account which would grow like an investment and be available for withdrawal during retirement—something like a 401(k) plan channeled through Social Security. Supporters of the idea hoped that it would reduce the fiscal pressures on Social Security, which were going to become severe in the foreseeable future, while improving Americans' rates of savings and investment and making them somewhat more self-reliant. As conceived by Bush, the accounts would belong to the taxpayer and could be passed on to his or her heirs. In general outlines, the idea of personal accounts had at one point received support from Democrats such as Senators Joseph Lieberman, Bob Kerrey, and Daniel Patrick Moynihan. After the 2004 election, which saw Bush reelected with larger congressional majorities, he was convinced that the moment was right to tackle the long-term problem of Social Security financing, and he made Social Security reform the number-one domestic priority of his second term. As he said shortly after the election, "I earned capital in the campaign, political capital, and now I intend to spend it."[11] The decision to lead with Social Security reform in 2005 meant that other Bush priorities, such as immigration reform and tax reform, would have to wait, although each had its advocates. Bush would have to focus the nation's attention on a real but distant problem while the present war in Iraq deteriorated and often dominated the news.

Rather than offer a detailed legislative proposal, Bush launched his drive for Social Security reform by laying out his view of the long-term threat to the program and a set of principles which he hoped would guide Congress in its deliberations. By 2018, Bush argued, the Trust Fund would be paying out more money than it was bringing in, and by 2042 it would be emptied altogether. According to polls, a major speaking tour by Bush convinced Americans that the crisis was (or would be) real, but they were unconvinced by his remedy.[12] Democrats closed ranks against Bush and promised to filibuster any bill that contained personal accounts. Their flirtation with personal accounts had ended, and they saw Bush's plan not as the means of saving Social Security but as a threat to the cornerstone of Franklin Roosevelt's welfare state. For their part, Republicans were divided. Fiscal conservatives did not like the up-to-$2 trillion "transition costs" of continuing to pay full benefits while reducing FICA revenue, and many in the GOP were nervous about touching the famed "electric third rail" of American politics with no Democratic support. Attempts by Bush to negotiate came to naught, and his attempts to pressure moderate

Democratic senators by holding rallies in their states may have backfired. Bush had tried to do too much with too little capital: his Senate majority was not large enough, his 50.7 percent reelection was too narrow, and his reelection campaign, though he mentioned Social Security, was predominantly focused on national security.

Then yet another major event put the final nail in the coffin of Social Security reform, as well as inflicting serious damage on Bush for the remainder of his presidency. When Hurricane Katrina made landfall on the Gulf Coast on August 29, 2005, it set in motion a series of events that led to the flooding of New Orleans, the deaths of nearly 1,900 people, and at least $80 billion worth of damage. Responses by federal, state, and municipal authorities were all initially slow and ineffective, but blame was quickly focused on the White House.

Katrina gave Republican leaders in Congress, already nervous, a reason to set Social Security aside, and it was never revived for the remainder of the Bush presidency. The effects of Katrina went beyond the death of Social Security reform, though.[13] The crisis in the Gulf, and the public perception that the president had failed to respond well, had numerous other consequences for Bush's domestic agenda. For one thing, it eclipsed Bush's bipartisan commission on tax reform, which had submitted a report that Bush hoped would serve as the basis for action on his second domestic priority. For another, it severely undermined the political coalition Bush hoped to forge for compassionate conservatism. Outrage over the plight of poor blacks in New Orleans made any alliance with Bush by black pastors and other community leaders impossible. Bush's promise that the federal government would spend whatever it took—some thought it would be up to $200 billion—to rebuild the Gulf Coast might have been the last straw for conservatives increasingly concerned about Bush's lack of fiscal discipline. Federal deficits had reached $413 billion in 2004. Republicans in Congress finally pushed back, responding with the Deficit Reduction Act of 2005 (signed by Bush in early 2006), which cut spending on Medicare, Medicaid, federal student loans, and other domestic programs by $40 billion over five years.

A final piece of the compassionate conservatism agenda was put to the test in 2006 and 2007, and failed both times. Bush had long hoped to improve the standing of Republicans among Hispanic voters and also wanted to cultivate the US relationship with Mexico. To this end, he had begun discussions about some sort of comprehensive immigration reform in 2001, but this thrust had been shut down by the concern with border security that was stimulated by 9/11. In 2006, Bush brought the issue back with a plan that combined enhanced border security, a guest worker program, and a "path to citizenship" for illegal immigrants. Opposition among congressional Republicans was too strong, however, as the Republican voter base preferred to focus on border security and was strongly averse to anything that appeared to be amnesty for illegals. Instead, shortly before the 2006 midterm elections, Congress passed and the president signed (with reservations) a bill authorizing a 700-mile-long security fence along the border with Mexico. When Democrats took control of Congress in those elections, Bush hoped he might have better luck on immigration reform. On this issue, as with No Child Left Behind, Democrats rather than Republicans were his natural partners. However, Republican opposition in the Senate and public skepticism doomed the effort again.

ENERGY AND ENVIRONMENT

Increasing oil prices combined with fears of global warming brought new attention to the issue of energy at the very end of the Clinton administration, and energy remained an important but secondary issue throughout this Bush administration.[14] Environmental groups were critical of Bush for removing the United States from the Kyoto Protocol early in 2001 and for approaching global warming cautiously. However, Kyoto was already stalled and ratification by the Senate was extremely improbable regardless of what Bush did.

Shortly after taking office, Bush also appointed an energy task force to propose a broad energy program. Headed by Vice President Dick Cheney, the task force became controversial for its secrecy. Its recommendations combining enhanced energy production, updated energy transmission, and conservation, were fashioned into a bill early in the Bush presidency but was stalled. Also stalled were Republican attempts, which dated back to the Reagan administration and were renewed under Bush, to allow oil exploration in the Arctic National Wildlife Refuge, an area that some experts believed contained large reserves of oil.

However, Bush did secure a large new stream of funding for research in hydrogen-powered cars, and two major bipartisan energy bills were passed during his watch. The first, in 2005, included tax incentives and subsidies for energy production, consumer conservation, and alternative fuels, as well as more stringent energy efficiency rules for appliances. Second, the "Energy Independence and Security Act of 2007" (EISA), passed by the new Democratic Congress, lacked any new incentives for producers, taking a purely regulatory approach. EISA called for a 500 percent increase in the use of alternative fuels by 2022, an increase in fuel efficiency standards for cars, increased efficiency standards for appliances, a carbon-neutral rule for federal buildings by 2030, and the banning of incandescent light bulbs after 2014. Altogether, the policy approach to energy during the Bush years was far removed from the laissez-faire policy of the Reagan administration, which had ended price controls, reduced government funding of alternative fuels, and relied on the free market to set prices and levels of production.

SOCIAL ISSUES

In the mix of social issues that define what is sometimes called the "culture war," there were a number of important but divergent developments.[15] After regaining control of the Senate in 2002, Republicans succeeded in passing a federal law prohibiting "partial-birth" abortions, a particularly gruesome method typically used late term. (Bill Clinton had vetoed such a law when it passed in the late 1990s.) Congress also passed legislation protecting the lives of babies born despite a botched abortion and making it illegal to transport a minor across state lines to get an abortion without the consent of the parents.

At the same time, though, same-sex marriage advanced. Most notably, in November 2003 the Massachusetts Supreme Judicial Court ruled that limiting marriage to a man and a woman violated the state's constitution. In response, Bush proposed that Congress take up a federal constitutional amendment stipulating that marriage was solely for one man and one woman, in order to negate the Massachusetts decision and, more importantly, cut off any attempt by federal or state judges to impose same-sex marriage elsewhere. This Federal Marriage Amendment failed to receive the requisite two-thirds vote in Congress in 2004 and again in 2005. Citizens in 31 states succeeded in changing their state constitutions to incorporate similar language, but the battle continued. Bush promoted conservative family views in other ways, as well. When the 1996 welfare reform act was reauthorized in 2006, it included tougher work requirements and $150 million for a "Healthy Marriages Initiative" aimed at promoting marriage.[16]

Finally, Bush also attempted to address new ethical issues arising out of modern biotechnology. In 2001, he announced that federal money would be available for the first time to fund embryonic stem cell research. However, he limited the research to a contained group of lines from embryos that had been frozen and were already slated for destruction. Bush's aim was to preserve respect for the sanctity of human life. Critics believed that such considerations were outweighed by the potential for medical discoveries, though that potential was highly speculative. As public opinion moved against Bush's position, he was forced to veto bills that would have funded wider research. Embryonic stem cell research offered an illustration of policy making at its most difficult, with policy makers forced to weigh important but competing ethical claims amid uncertainty about the practical consequences of their decisions.

RESPONSE TO ECONOMIC CRISIS

As the Bush presidency was winding down, policy makers faced a major challenge in the form of a slowing economy and, ultimately, a near meltdown of the financial system. Economists would later conclude that the economy had slipped into recession in December 2007 after six years of growth. Unemployment began to increase, but the biggest threat came in the financial sector, which experienced serious problems due largely to the bursting of the housing bubble that had been created over the previous several years. Many homeowners with "subprime" mortgages (given to borrowers who could not qualify for regular mortgages) found themselves unable to pay, foreclosures grew, and housing prices began to recede. This threatened banks and other mortgage lenders, as well as other financial institutions that had invested in complicated financial instruments that included portions of mortgages bought from the lenders.

Early in 2008, Bush and the Democratic Congress agreed on an economic stimulus package that sent $600 checks to most taxpayers. At first, the Bush Treasury Department and the Federal Reserve Board tried to prevent a financial panic by bailing out individual financial firms such as Bear Stearns and Goldman Sachs. By mid-September 2008, this ad hoc approach could no longer keep up with events. As Lehman Brothers and American International Group (AIG) lurched toward insolvency, Treasury Secretary Henry Paulson proposed a comprehensive program costing roughly $700 billion to prevent the collapse of the financial system. Paulson's initial plan, a spare three-page document putting tremendous discretion in the Secretary of the Treasury to disburse funds as necessary, was not agreeable to Congress. After a failed vote and long negotiations, Congress passed the Troubled Assets Relief Program (TARP), authorizing $800 billion in funds to help salvage troubled financial firms and restore liquidity to the financial system—reminiscent of the Reconstruction Finance Corporation and Emergency Banking Act of the Depression era. Eventually, most TARP funds were repaid.[17] At the same time, new Federal Reserve Board chair Ben Bernanke, whose academic study focused on the Great Depression, adjusted monetary policy to provide liquidity in the economy. While TARP and Bernanke may have blunted the crisis, economic indices continued to deteriorate.

POLICY IN THE GEORGE W. BUSH YEARS: SUMMARY AND ASSESSMENT

For the first time since the Eisenhower administration, the GOP controlled the presidency and both houses of Congress at the same time. George W. Bush hoped that he was launching a new policy era, in concert with a new political era featuring dominance by a Republican Party that retained its traditional base but added more women and racial minorities. In the end, though, Bush's Republican breakout was not to be, and policy bore some resemblance to the incoherence of the 1970s.

Economic policy

Economic policy combined Keynesian and neoclassical elements. Tax cuts combining supply-side and Keynesian principles reduced the proportion of the national economy taken by federal revenue from 20 percent of GDP to an average of 17 percent from 2001 to 2008. (Tax reform and permanent extension of the Bush tax cuts failed.) Spending was the mirror image, moving from 17.6 percent of GDP to 20.2 percent. While much of this overall increase was in defense, non-defense spending also rose from 14.7 percent of GDP to 16 percent; non-defense discretionary and programmatic mandatory spending both rose. After 9/11, the deficit returned, receded a bit, then exploded in 2008. Responses to the recession by president and Congress were strongly interventionist, including stimulus spending and TARP. There was a slight reduction in annual pages in the *Federal Register*, which numbered 83,294 in 2000 and 80,700 in 2008, with most years in between in the high 70,000 page range. Bush, like his immediate predecessors, embraced free trade, but often accommodated himself to liberal calls for increased regulation. (An example was his embrace of the Sarbanes-Oxley Bill of 2002, which responded to accounting scandals at major companies by instituting a new and complicated system of financial regulation.)

Social welfare

The 1996 welfare reform was reauthorized and strengthened. In health care, a prescription drug benefit was added to Medicare along with some free-market reforms. Faith-based service providers were given greater federal assistance through executive order, but legislation failed. Social Security reform, Bush's number one second-term domestic priority, failed.

Civil rights

There was little change, as the Supreme Court upheld affirmative action and no major civil rights statutes were passed.

Education

The No Child Left Behind Act represented a significant centralizing step in the evolution of federal education policy.

Environment

Bush withdrew the United States from the Kyoto Protocol on global warming. Two energy bills included restrictions on certain sources of carbon emissions and promoted energy production, conservation, and "green" energy technologies. Oil drilling in ANWR was prevented by Congress.

Moral/cultural issues

This area, too, saw an eclectic mixture of policies, including new restrictions on abortion, a rear-guard action against gay marriage that failed at the federal level but largely succeeded at the state level, and allowance of some embryonic stem cell research but with serious limits.

Federalism

Bush's domestic policy largely neglected constitutional issues of federalism or limited government. In fact, Bush talked about constitutional issues in State of the Union addresses less often than any other president since Franklin Roosevelt, and rarely seemed to take them into account in policy development.[18] In particular, NCLB—although building on previous departures such as Goals 2000 and America 2000—was a major step in interjecting the federal government more deeply into K–12 education. Trends toward greater centralization seem to have resumed after a two decade recess. Like Reagan, Bush paid close attention to judicial appointments and presidential powers, but his constitutionalism seemed to end there.

In addition, Bush constructed a new institutional and legal framework for dealing with terrorism, perhaps the most non-incremental domestic policy departure during his presidency, but immigration reform was denied twice. Altogether, Bush's domestic policy was not without significant accomplishments, but he failed to achieve a large number of his highest priorities.

The importance of **path dependency** was reaffirmed, as changes to taxes, education, and Medicare, among many others, essentially built on (while modifying) existing policy. Social Security was so entrenched that even modest change proved impossible. In most areas, **incrementalism** was the order of the day.

The important policy **inputs** were all visible. Bush was also influenced by the **idea** of compassionate conservatism, which he made his own. However, compassionate conservatism, like many "third way" attempts, fell victim to the difficulties inherent in trying to satisfy varying constituencies with different, if not irreconcilable, policy preferences and priorities. For liberal commentators, George W. Bush as compassionate conservative was a "largely fictional" figure.[19] For many conservatives, it was "big government" that defined Bush, who in their view had betrayed the Reagan legacy.[20] Compassionate conservatism was not a powerful enough new paradigm to bring another moment of major change.

People were also important. Bush himself applied lessons from his father's experience and had his own style, convictions, and strengths and weaknesses. While some of his domestic policies (as in education and immigration) were not terribly different from Al Gore's proposals, policy on taxes, global warming, and social issues would doubtless have been quite different from 2001 to 2009 had Gore found an extra thousand votes in Florida; even Bush's main competitor in the 2000 Republican primaries, Arizona Senator John McCain, would likely have pursued distinct policies, including smaller tax cuts, less domestic spending, opposition to the Medicare prescription drug entitlement, and support for more embryonic stem cell research. It may have been fortunate that Ben Bernanke, who was a student of the Great Depression, directed the Federal Reserve Board when the financial crisis of 2008 exploded.

The **politics** of the era opened a window for policy change, especially during the periods of unified Republican control of Congress and the presidency, but also placed limits on the size and duration of that window. Many Democrats rejected Bush's legitimacy because of the circumstances of his initial election. His re-election was narrow, and even at its best, the Republican congressional edge was too narrow and partisan animosity too great for the sort of major changes Bush hoped to make.

Far from least, **events** played a major role. September 11 not only immediately rearranged the domestic agenda but pushed most domestic issues to the back burner. Subsequently, the unfolding Iraq War, Hurricane Katrina, and the financial crisis of 2008 all impacted domestic policy in crucial ways. Domestic policy was heavily influenced by **foreign and national security issues**. The fight against terrorism drove major portions of the domestic policy agenda. National security was the ground on which Republican political victories were built in 2002 and 2004, and hence could be considered indirectly responsible for domestic policies enacted by Bush and Congress between 2002 and 2006. Conversely, failures in Iraq cost Bush important leverage on Social Security and immigration starting in 2005 and were largely responsible for the reversal of congressional power in the 2006 elections, and hence for greater policy confrontation between president and Congress, and for a more interventionist domestic policy, in 2007–2008. Though Bush was classified by Michael A. Genovese, Todd L. Belt, and William W. Lammers as one of only four "high opportunity" presidents since 1933 (Roosevelt, Johnson, and Reagan being the other three), the "multiple streams" leading to domestic policy outputs in the Bush years were not nearly as propitious.[21]

Driven by key events, the Bush years saw several dramatic shifts in the nation's domestic **policy agenda**. From September 10, 2001, to September 12, the agenda abruptly changed from dispensing the surplus to focusing on internal security against terrorism. In a matter of days in September 2008, the focus shifted to the threat of financial meltdown. Immigration, health care, Social Security, and energy came, went, and sometimes came back, depending on political factors and events (such as Hurricane Katrina). Midway through the Bush presidency, deficits again briefly drew attention and response.

The **difficulty of assessing policy success** was manifest in competing evaluations of homeland security policies. From September 11 through the remainder of the Bush presidency, there was no major terrorist attack in the United States. One school of thought held that this period of safety was the result of Bush's policies, which had diagnosed the threat and met it appropriately. Another school of thought contended that Bush had exaggerated the threat and his policies represented overkill.

The financial crisis of 2008 showed the importance of **unanticipated consequences**, and the difficulty of tracing cause and effect when attempting to define policy problems. The predominant liberal explanation for the crisis was Wall Street greed combined with deregulation of the financial industry. Many pointed to the 1999 Act that deregulated commercial banking, allowing banks to dabble in derivatives and other risky financial instruments.[22] Former president Clinton, who signed the bill, disagreed with this interpretation of the reform, which he argued had mitigated the crisis by allowing banks to spread risk.[23] Many conservative and libertarian analysts blamed government policies, especially reckless behavior by federally underwritten agencies Fannie Mae and Freddie Mac, which (they argued) created a demand for subprime mortgages, and federal banking laws from the 1990s that encouraged banks to lend to unqualified borrowers for the sake of racial diversity.[24] Others contended that the Federal Reserve stimulated the housing bubble by keeping interest rates too low after 2001, and pointed out that both Clinton and Bush had made it a policy aim to increase home ownership beyond what market conditions would normally allow. Rather than Wall Street greed, Wall Street ignorance may have played a part, as firms dabbled in complicated financial instruments without understanding the risks involved. Some brave observers even held that ordinary Americans were to blame for irresponsible borrowing.[25] Needless to say, these explanations are not mutually exclusive.

To the extent that government policy contributed to the financial breakdown, whether through too little government (deregulation gone awry), too much government (subsidies and mandates to lenders), or not the right kind of government (low interest rates), no one in government pursued those policies in hopes of creating a financial crisis. To the contrary, those policies were driven by noble motives of enhancing prosperity and expanding home ownership to the poor or lower middle class.

Finally, as demonstrated during the Great Depression, there is enormous policy leverage in successfully **defining the problem**. If one can impose a definition of the problem as private greed and too little government, it provides a powerful foundation for an expanded regulatory state and higher taxes on the wealthy. If one defines the problem another way, it could lead to very different policies. The 2008 election and the policy efforts that followed would show again the importance of controlling problem definition.

8

New Directions in the Wake of the Great Recession? The Obama and Trump "Transformations"

★ ★ ★

Courtesy of Richard Drew/Associated Press

Stock traders react in horror and exhaustion during the financial crisis of fall 2008. The crisis and its aftermath brought forth a new policy-making environment with new challenges. Both President Obama and President Trump sought to capitalize.

THE "GREAT RECESSION" that threatened the country as George W. Bush left office altered the policy-making environment tremendously, shaking up political coalitions and presenting new opportunities for policy-making entrepreneurs. First Barack Obama, then Donald Trump, sought to capitalize. However, both engendered bitter opposition which hindered their projects. At times, both Obama and Trump seemed to have the potential to move policy in a fundamentally different direction—to drive an era that might punctuate the policy equilibrium in a fundamental way for the first time since Reagan.

As Barack Obama took office on January 20, 2009, the policy inputs were aligned to open a window for a major domestic policy transformation. Moreover, the new president clearly saw himself as a figure who could someday take his place in the nation's pantheon of political leaders, including Reagan, Franklin Roosevelt, and perhaps even Abraham Lincoln.[1]

An event of considerable significance—the financial meltdown of 2008 and corresponding deep recession—demanded a major policy response and provided an opportunity for policy makers to change the direction of the country. Obama's interpretation, that the economic crisis was the result of Wall Street greed and insufficient regulatory zeal, could serve as justification for more liberal policies. Obama's White House chief of staff Rahm Emanuel even declared, "You never want a serious crisis to go to waste," though Emanuel allowed that the crisis was big enough that there might be room for ideas from both parties.[2]

The politics of the moment were also propitious for a big policy shift. Obama's victory, though not quite a landslide, was the most solid victory by a Democratic presidential candidate since Lyndon Johnson's in 1964. Obama won 53 percent of the nationally aggregated popular vote and 365 electoral votes against Republican John McCain. In the process, Obama won several states, such as North Carolina, Virginia, and Indiana, that had been solidly Republican in presidential elections for four decades or more, as well as key swing states like Ohio and Florida. His coalition depended heavily on minority voters and young and first-time voters. After their gains of 2006, congressional Democrats added to their majorities in 2008, adding another 24 seats in the House and 8 seats in the Senate.[3] After Republican Senator Arlen Specter of Pennsylvania switched parties and their Minnesota win was confirmed by a contentious recount, Democrats had 60 Senators, a filibuster-proof majority if all Democrats stuck together. Neither party had held 60 Senate seats since Democrats had done so prior to the 1978 midterm elections 30 years before. Although these Democrats had won the crucial House seats to put them over the top by fielding moderate or conservative candidates in swing districts, the Democratic caucus in both houses was arguably more ideologically unified than it was the last time it held a majority in the early 1990s. Moreover, exit polls in 2008 showed a small majority of voters favoring a government that did more, for the first time in decades.[4]

And then there was Obama himself. The president was famed for his ability to inspire a variety of Americans. He had first gained national attention when he delivered a prime-time address to the 2004 Democratic national convention declaring that "there's not a liberal America and a conservative America; there's the United States of America."[5] Yet his 2008 nomination was won largely by mobilizing the Democratic left and distancing himself from Clintonian centrism. He favored a policy of liberal government activism and redistribution of income. The son of a Kenyan immigrant and a white mother, he would also come into office as the first African American president in American history. Obama himself spoke of his desire to be a "transformative" president. Critics noted Obama's thin governing experience—no executive experience and only four years in the US Senate—and associations with left-wing extremists such as Reverend Jeremiah Wright and William Ayers, a former anti-Vietnam War terrorist.[6]

Ironically, given his connection with young voters, Obama was not influenced by recent ideas like the program of the Democratic Leadership Council or Marvin Olasky's compassionate conservatism. Rather, he looked back to progressivism and the New Deal. His campaign autobiography, *The Audacity of Hope*, was filled with praise of Woodrow Wilson and Franklin Roosevelt. Obama was also heavily influenced by the writings of Saul Alinsky, a 1960s activist who offered tactical advice for those seeking radical change. In economic terms, there was no question that Obama was most strongly influenced by the ideas of Keynesianism. Economist Thomas Piketty's influential critique of income inequality, published in 2015, imbibed and amplified the intellectual thrust of the Obama administration.[7]

The issue most responsible for propelling him to the Democratic nomination was his opposition to the war in Iraq, but the issue most responsible for electing him president in November was a domestic issue, the economic crisis. On the general election campaign trail in 2008, Obama emphasized the need to raise taxes on couples making more than $250,000 a year (while refraining from tax increases below that level), health care reform, a stronger fight against global warming, a focus on alternative energy, and aggressive government intervention to right the economy. By the time he took office, it was clear the economy would have to be his first priority.

ECONOMIC CRISIS

Obama and the Democratic Congress moved quickly to pass a large economic stimulus package, the American Recovery and Reinvestment Act.[8] At a two-year cost of $787 billion, the ARRA included $288 billion (37 percent) for "tax cuts," though much of this was devoted to refundable tax credits that pay people who do not owe taxes; $144 billion (18 percent) to relieve budgetary pressures on state and local governments, primarily in the areas of education and Medicaid; and $357 billion (45 percent) allocated to federal social programs and other federal spending. That spending included the following items:

- extension of unemployment benefits;
- additional funds for Food Stamps (now called Supplemental Nutrition Assistance Program, or SNAP), welfare payments, and child nutrition programs;
- increased teacher salaries;
- increased Pell Grant payments;
- housing programs;
- scientific research;
- infrastructure construction and maintenance;
- government facilities and vehicles; and
- energy programs in conservation and alternative energy.

The administration claimed that the bill would "create or save" 3.5 million jobs, holding the unemployment rate short of 7 percent before it would start falling again. In the end, the ARRA passed with no Republican votes in the House and only three in the Senate. Republicans argued that the bill was too expensive, that it contained too much pork barrel spending, and that it would do too little for the private economy. Economists were divided about the value of the stimulus package: some supported it as necessary for economic stabilization, some considered it too small or not directed enough toward infrastructure and job creation, and some, pointing to the failure of such programs in the Great Depression and in Japan in the 1990s, considered the Keynesian approach as the wrong direction altogether. Cynics noted that Democratic-leaning interests such as green energy companies and public employee unions were major beneficiaries. Within a year, the administration was on the defensive, as unemployment climbed over 10 percent (and reached 17 percent if one added discouraged workers who had stopped looking for employment); Obama said that he had underestimated the depth of the recession but that unemployment would have been even worse without ARRA.

The fiscal stimulus promised by the ARRA was supplemented by a monetary stimulus in the form of the so-called quantitative easing policy of the Federal Reserve Board, which entailed the central bank purchasing government securities or other assets to inflate the money supply. The policy actually began in November 2008 and was expanded in 2009, 2010, and 2012; when the purchases were halted in October 2014, the Fed had accumulated at least $3.8 trillion in additional assets since the beginning of the program.[9]

A second area where Obama proposed federal intervention to address the economic crisis was mortgage relief for homeowners who were now facing the threat of foreclosure. Unlike ARRA, this effort was directly related to the proximate cause of the financial crisis.

Third, Obama authorized a series of emergency steps, not unlike the ad hoc steps taken by Bush in early 2008, to shore up specific institutions that he considered "too big to fail," such as Bank of America and General Motors. Alongside these steps, the Treasury Department continued disbursing TARP money to troubled financial institutions and conducted a "stress test" of banks to assess how solid they were.

REFORM

As steps were taken to stabilize the economy, Obama also took advantage of his overwhelming congressional majorities to pursue longer-term reforms. The thrust of these reforms was to centralize economic and political power in Washington.

The centerpiece of these efforts was health care reform, a long-standing objective of liberals and one of the unfinished items on Franklin Roosevelt's Economic Bill of Rights. Democrats took steps in this direction in early 2009 by passing a bill, vetoed twice by George W. Bush, that expanded the SCHIP program subsidizing insurance for families with children by including families with an income up to 300 percent of the poverty level. By the summer of 2009, comprehensive health care reform was the central domestic policy thrust of Obama and the Democratic congressional leadership.[10] The aims were much the same as those enunciated by Bill Clinton during his failed drive for health care reform in 1993–1994: to guarantee close to universal health insurance coverage while holding down rapidly rising health care costs. The Democratic approach also drew heavily on Clinton's proposed mechanisms. However, seeking to avoid the same fate as "Clintoncare," Obama took a different legislative strategy. Instead of proposing detailed legislative language, as Bill Clinton had done, Obama established broad principles but left the drafting of legislation up to Congress. Republicans favored a more incremental approach focused on reform of medical lawsuits, lowering costs by permitting insurance competition across state lines, and providing tax credits for private insurance. However, they were largely shut out of the process.

Critics feared that Obama's plan would lead to a total government takeover and rationing of health care over time, and some pointed to the enormous costs of the program, estimated at over $1 trillion over the next decade. Despite an ongoing public relations offensive that included an estimated 54 speeches by the president, Obamacare struggled in public opinion polls after September 2009, while a Senate vacancy election in Massachusetts in January 2010, occasioned by the death of Edward Kennedy, saw an upset victory for the Republican candidate, Scott Brown, who had pledged to stop Obamacare.

Nevertheless, Obama and congressional Democrats moved ahead. The House narrowly passed its version in November 2009. On Christmas Eve, the Senate followed, passing a different version with exactly the 60 votes (all Democrats) needed to end debate. In March 2010, the House passed the Senate bill 219–212, hours after a small but pivotal group of pro-life Democrats accepted a deal brokered by Obama: he would sign an executive order stipulating that federal money would not fund abortions, and they would vote yes. Liberal Democrats were not fully satisfied with the final bill, which did not include a public option of government insurance, but generally congratulated themselves on achieving much of FDR's health care agenda. However, the bill remained unpopular, and not a single Republican voted for it in either house. Passage arguably represented the biggest expansion of the influence of the federal government since the Great Society.

The Patient Protection and Affordable Care Act (usually called Affordable Care Act, or ACA) mandated that individuals purchase health insurance. Government would also prohibit insurance companies from denying insurance coverage to people with preexisting conditions or capping lifetime insurance payments to individuals. Obama's embrace of an individual insurance mandate represented a reversal of his position in the 2008 Democratic primaries, when Hillary Clinton supported a mandate and Obama attacked it as coercive. But it was essential to gaining the support of key interest groups such as the insurance companies, pharmaceutical companies, and the hospital association. The law also included an employer mandate requiring businesses with more than 50 full-time employees (defined as employees working 30 hours a week or more) to provide health insurance to them, a major expansion of Medicaid, establishment of a defined set of minimum coverages required in every health insurance policy, and creation of the Independent Payments Advisory Board, the task of which was to determine which procedures would be approved for use. If not covered by the Medicaid expansion, the uninsured could obtain coverage through insurance exchanges established by states or by a federal exchange. Federal subsidies would be available to those who could not afford insurance on the exchanges. The plan was to be paid for over the next decade with a half trillion dollars in Medicare cuts and another half trillion in tax increases, ranging from an income tax surcharge to taxes on high-cost insurance plans to taxes on the manufacturers of medical devices.

The development of the Affordable Care Act demonstrated, among other things, the importance of path dependency. Obama's approach attempted to significantly modify the existing health care system that was built on a combination of private and government funding and centered on employer-provided insurance. Rather than either a totally government-run system, or a free-market alternative that would have replaced the employer-based system with an individual-based system by providing the tax benefit for health insurance directly to individuals, the ACA retained and tried to harness the employer-based system and supplement it by expanding an existing Great Society program, Medicaid.

Although the debate over health care dominated the policy making landscape for months, Obama pushed other major reforms, as well. In education, Congress approved an Obama plan to end all private federally guaranteed student loans. Instead, all federally guaranteed student loans would be folded into a government lending agency.

Later in 2010, Obama had success when it came to financial regulation, an issue that directly addressed the financial breakdown of 2008. This time, Obama sent detailed legislative language to Congress. His aim was to regulate complicated financial instruments like derivatives, give the government the authority to restructure or terminate financial institutions that appear to pose risks to the economy, and to establish a new independent (critics said unaccountable) consumer protection agency to monitor and regulate financial arrangements such as mortgages and credit cards. In summer 2010 the Dodd-Frank financial regulation bill was enacted.[11]

Obama also pushed for Congress to adopt a "cap-and-trade" system that would limit overall carbon emissions and allow companies to trade their carbon permits. Obama and many environmentalists argued that the bill was necessary to fight global warming and to help convince other industrial nations to do the same. Opponents claimed the measure would cost the average American family thousands of dollars and could lead to much greater government regimentation of the economy. In 2009, the House narrowly passed a cap-and-trade bill, but it died in the Senate a year later when it became clear the votes were not there.[12]

Overall, Obama and the 2009–2011 Democratic Congress significantly changed the fiscal and regulatory policies of the United States. Annual domestic spending rose by 20 percent in inflation-adjusted dollars from 2008 to 2011. Overall federal spending rose from $2.983 trillion to

$3.603 trillion, an increase of $620 billion in just three years, while the federal deficit reached $1.4 trillion in fiscal year 2010, the highest since World War II as a proportion of GDP. And the regulatory environment became more restrictive. Keynesianism had regained a dominant position in economic policy making, and the progressive affinity for empowering independent bureaucratic experts was given new life.

TRANSFORMATION STALLED

However, Obama's transformation encountered unexpected obstacles. The first was the rise of the Tea Party movement, a political movement that exploded on the scene in February 2009. In many ways, the movement had its roots in the final days of the Bush administration, in the form of an inchoate outrage over the TARP program to aid (or, as critics described it, "bail out") failing financial institutions. Obama's proposed mortgage relief program turned into the trigger when CNBC business correspondent Rick Santelli's on-air "rant" against irresponsible government bailouts led to spontaneous demonstrations. Within months, hundreds of state and local Tea Party groups had been formed by activists fearful of Washington's power grabs and rapidly accumulating debt. By 2010, the Tea Party was in full swing, mobilizing to affect the 2010 midterm elections.[13]

Ultimately, those elections significantly altered the trajectory of policy in Washington. Republicans gained 63 House seats, the most seats switched in a midterm election since 1938, returning Republicans to the majority they had held from 1994 to 2006. The bulk of Democratic losses were in the conservative and moderate districts that had given Democrats their majorities in 2006–2008; the liberal Obama agenda had imperiled, and ultimately lost, these seats. In the Senate, Republicans gained 6 seats, raising their total from 41 to 47 and putting them in striking distance of a majority.

In certain ways the 2010 elections were quite similar to the 1994 midterms. However, the gap between Obama and the House Republicans was bigger and more difficult to bridge than the gap between Bill Clinton and the 104th Congress. Obama was farther to the left and more fixed in his views than Clinton, and the parties as a whole had become more polarized in the intervening years. Democrats and Republicans were more different ideologically, culturally, and demographically than they had been. Voters from both parties identified themselves as farther from the center (Republicans farther right, Democrats farther left).[14] Polarization also took the form of competing movements, the Tea Party on the right and, starting in 2011, the redistributionist and anti-capitalist Occupy Wall Street movement on the left.[15]

Almost immediately upon taking office in January 2011, the new House began aggressively challenging Obama's fiscal priorities, and they clashed frequently over the next six years. In the most important clash, in summer 2011, the two sides were engaged in a standoff over spending and an increase in the debt limit. Republicans insisted on spending cuts equal in size to the increase in the debt limit, about $2 trillion over 10 years, enforced by automatic sequestration if spending limits were exceeded. Eventually abandoned by Senate Democrats, Obama reluctantly relented. Spending stabilized in constant dollars and gradually shrank as a proportion of GDP, as Keynesian economists such as Paul Krugman complained that "austerity" had taken hold.[16] In constant dollars, overall spending did not regain 2011 levels until 2016.

For the remainder of the Obama presidency, a fiscal stalemate took hold. Obama won reelection in 2012, but by a margin nearly identical to George W. Bush's modest margin in 2004, and was the first president to be reelected with fewer raw votes than he won in his first election. Indeed, Obama trailed challenger Mitt Romney in the polls a week before the election, until Hurricane Sandy intervened and gave him an opportunity to appear "presidential." He retained the loyalty of his core coalition, but his approval rating was "underwater" (below his disapproval rating) for almost all of his second term. Republicans held their House majority in 2012 and 2014, adding to it a majority in the Senate in 2014.[17] By the end of Obama's presidency, Democrats were also at their weakest levels in state government since before the Great Depression. The heady picture of Obama as the next FDR, entertained in 2009, had fully dissipated. Obama's policy window substantially closed in 2010, and the political environment never allowed it to reopen very far.[18]

With some tinkering at the edges, the budget sequestration of 2011 continued to restrain federal spending, but most of the big increase up to 2011 was locked into place. In the aftermath of the 2012 elections, when both sides saw that the other would not be dislodged, a compromise was reached on extension of the 2001 Bush tax cuts, which were made permanent for taxpayers up to $450,000. Attempts to address the looming entitlement crisis, including the $10.6 trillion unfunded liability on Social Security's books, were notably unfruitful, and Obama was never very interested in that issue. Early in his presidency, he appointed the bipartisan Simpson-Bowles Commission to examine deficit issues, but he never expended any political capital in defense of its recommendations, which died on the vine. In 2011, the budget sequestration deal was accompanied by creation of a congressional "supercommittee" tasked with finding entitlement savings, but again, Democrats and Republicans had incompatible views on how to address the problem and Obama let the committee quietly end its work without a resolution.

Other areas of conflict flared. Republicans introduced a measure repealing the Affordable Care Act (or "Obamacare") the day after it passed. After the 2010 elections, House Republicans passed a repeal measure, which the Democratic Senate ignored. In late 2013, House Republicans sought to force the issue by passing a budget bill that would have defunded Obamacare, but the Senate refused and, after a short government shutdown, Republicans retreated. After the 2014 elections, the House and Senate combined to pass a repeal measure, which Obama vetoed. The debate over the ACA reached the Supreme Court several times, as well. In 2012, the Court ruled that the individual mandate did not violate the Constitution but that the ACA could not punish states that refused to accept the Medicaid expansion with a complete loss of Medicaid funds. In 2014, the Supreme Court ruled that the Department of Health and Human Services could not issue ACA regulations that forced closely-held companies to provide abortifacients to their employees if it violated their religious principles. Not least, the battle involved the states. Roughly half of the states declined to form their own exchanges, and about as many refused to sign on to the Medicaid expansion. Republican state attorneys general also joined the lawsuits against the ACA.

In other areas of policy, Obama used unilateral executive actions to bypass Congress when it did not approve his proposals. Having failed to secure congressional approval of the cap-and-trade proposal, Obama's Environmental Protection Agency developed a regulatory scheme (the Clean Power Plan) that aimed to achieve major reductions in carbon emissions. The president also substantially reduced the number of permits available for oil and gas exploration on federal land and offshore, as well as nixing the Keystone XL pipeline and Dakota Access pipeline. In 2015, Obama committed the United States to the Paris Climate Accord and ordered the EPA to take steps to bring the United States into compliance while declining to submit the agreement to the Senate, saying it was a "framework" rather than a binding treaty.

On immigration, Obama threw his energy behind another attempt at comprehensive immigration reform. The Senate passed a bill, but the House did not come to agreement. Subsequently, Obama issued executive memoranda essentially legalizing the status of an estimated 3.7 million adults (under the Deferred Action for Parents of Americans program, or DAPA) and 800,000 youths (under the Deferred Action for Childhood Arrivals program, or DACA), an estimated 40 percent of the people in the country illegally.

As with health care, both environmental policy and immigration policy found their way to the federal courts. The administration won some of those battles, as when the Supreme Court ruled that the EPA was not exceeding its legal authority under the Clean Air Act when it sought to regulate carbon emissions; it also lost some, as when a federal court sided with the US House lawsuit arguing that DACA exceeded the president's authority.

Racial issues surged to the fore under Obama, as well, starting early in his presidency, when the president said a Boston police officer had "acted stupidly" by arresting black academic (and friend of the president) Louis Gates after an altercation. The administration advocated controversial policies in favor of racial preferences in housing and school discipline, and Obama embraced the radical Black Lives Matter movement that formed after a white Ferguson, Missouri, police officer shot and killed unarmed black teenager Michael Brown in 2015. (Both a local grand jury and the US Department of Justice later declined to indict the officer when evidence indicated that the shooting was justified.[19])

Overall, Obama's policies on crime deviated from criminal justice policy for the past several decades. The administration emphasized what it considered to be an "incarceration crisis" and relatively de-emphasized fighting crime, which had reached a 50-year low. Attorney General Eric Holder instructed US Attorneys to not prosecute minor drug offenses, and the administration ordered release of around 100,000 felons.[20]

Education policy was no less controversial. Building on the base of the state standards promoted by America 2000 and Goals 2000 and required by the No Child Left Behind Act, the Obama administration endorsed the Common Core Standards. Common Core was an attempt to create a set of common standards across states. Ostensibly, the standards were developed voluntarily by state governors, but Obama's Department of Education played a central role in coordinating the governors and using federal funds and NCLB waivers to push adoption. Initially 46 states signed on to the Common Core Standards, but by 2015 four had rescinded their support and others seemed poised to do so. A coalition of libertarians, social conservatives, and teacher's unions opposed the standards, seeing them as substantively flawed or a heavy-handed imposition of centralized control.

Then, in a rare (and barely noticed) moment of bipartisanship, the Republican Congress and Obama agreed on the Every Student Succeeds Act. The No Child Left Behind Act was allowed to expire and was replaced by the ESSA in 2015. The Act rescinded most of the NCLB mandates regarding state standards and testing, as well as the waivers granted by the Obama administration in exchange for states pursuing the administration's preferred education policies. With the exception of a provision creating a $250 million federal grant program for public preschool, the overall effect of the ESSA was to decentralize education power back to states and local school districts.[21]

Finally, social policies under Obama shifted significantly to the left. In contrast to the last avowedly pro-choice president, Bill Clinton, Obama made no effort to build rhetorical bridges to the other side; the "rare" was dropped from Clinton's "safe, legal, and rare" formulation. After running in 2008 as opposed to same-sex marriage, Obama declared himself in favor in early 2012. He also instructed the Justice Department not to defend the 1996 Defense of Marriage Act in federal court. In the end, Obama applauded when the Supreme Court ruled in 2015 that same-sex marriage was a constitutional right. The administration also consistently sought to redefine freedom of religion in a more constrained way.[22]

AN OBAMA TRANSFORMATION?
SUMMARY AND ASSESSMENT

Barack Obama came to the White House as the repository for high hopes by political liberals, by voters hoping for economic restoration, and by many Americans who saw in him the potential for a leader who could bridge the partisan and racial divides in the country. Like his predecessor but more so, Obama perceived an opening for major change. Like his predecessor, though, he saw the window close with an unexpected speed and forcefulness.

Obama won significant policy changes, but his goal of leading a political transformation to the left was unfulfilled, at least in the short term. Author Stanley Renshon titled the final chapter of his 2012 book on Obama "Transformation's Collapse."[23] Though he was narrowly reelected, his coalition shrank over time. In January 2017, when he handed the presidency over to Donald Trump, Republicans controlled the House, Senate, and two-thirds of state governments. Likewise, according to opinion surveys, both partisan and racial polarization clearly grew more severe during the Obama presidency, though academics debated who was more to blame.[24] However, other analysts cautioned that the long term policy and political impact of Obama was undetermined, that "it's premature to conclude that Obama won't eventually earn the same credit as FDR, and Democrats won't reap the same rewards, as the New Dealers did."[25]

Economic policy
Keynesianism and redistributionism returned in force from 2009 to 2011, as an $800 billion domestic spending stimulus package and up to $1.4 trillion deficit were key features of policy, complemented by a loose monetary policy that pumped trillions of dollars into the economy. Overall spending reached 24.4 percent of GDP in 2009, and in 2010 non-defense discretionary spending hit 4.7 percent of GDP and payments to

individuals reached 15.6 percent of GDP (the first was the highest since 1945, the second the highest since 1992, and the third the highest ever). The spending spree came to an end in 2011 after Republicans regained control of the House and forced spending restraint, bringing those numbers down to 20.9 percent, 3.2 percent, and 15.0 percent by 2016. Hearkening back to the Progressive and New Deal advocacy of "government by enlightened administration" (FDR), there was a new burst of policy making by bureaucracies that were deliberately designed to be insulated from public pressure. These included the Independent Payments Advisory Board (established in the Affordable Care Act) and the Consumer Financial Protection Board (created by Dodd-Frank). Regulation climbed throughout the Obama years, as pages in the *Federal Register* increased from 80,700 in 2008 to 97,110 in 2016, an all-time record.

Social welfare

The biggest change was passage of the Affordable Care Act in 2010, which faced numerous political and judicial challenges for the remainder of the Obama presidency. Part of the spending binge included big increases in social programs such as SNAP and Social Security disability benefits. The Department of Health and Human Services also issued new welfare guidelines allowing states to apply for waivers to reduce the work requirements stipulated in the 1996 welfare reform and its 2005 reauthorization, with an aim of increasing the number of people eligible for welfare.[26]

Civil rights

Obama promoted race-conscious preferential policies in school discipline and college admissions. Going in the other direction, the Supreme Court ended the fifty-year-old requirement that redistricting plans receive preclearance from the Justice Department. The Black Lives Matter movement focused attention on police shootings of African Americans.

Education

In higher education, the federal government took over all direct student loans and required colleges and universities to reduce procedural protections for people accused of sexual misconduct. In K–12 education, the administration backed the "Common Core" but also ultimately supported a bipartisan compromise to replace the No Child Left Behind Act (NCLB) with an alternative putting more power in local schools.

Environment

Obama's proposed cap-and-trade legislation did not pass the Senate, but his Environmental Protection Agency subsequently issued the Clean

Power Plan, an administrative regulatory substitute. Obama spent heavily on "green" technology, cut back on oil and gas leases, blocked two new pipelines, and signed on to the Paris Accords on climate change.

Federalism

In general, the trend toward centralization in the Bush administration accelerated in the Obama administration. Indeed, centralization of power in the federal government (and specifically the executive branch) was the theme of Obama policy making. Major areas of policy that had been the domain of state government were brought under federal jurisdiction, including health insurance regulation and marriage law, while the federal government edged closer to determining K–12 curriculum content. In other areas, formerly private functions were federalized, such as guaranteed student loans. The significant exceptions were in drug policy, where the federal government essentially stopped enforcing marijuana laws in states that had legalized it by state law, and in the Every Student Succeeds Act, a bipartisan enactment of Congress that seemed to turn back the process of educational centralization. In other ways, federalism was quite dynamic, as states were increasingly prone to challenge federal law and enforcement in a variety of contexts.

As usual, **people** mattered. A committed liberal, it was important that Obama rather than McCain or Romney was president. It also mattered that the president was Obama rather than Hillary Clinton, who came close to winning the 2008 Democratic presidential nomination. Just to cite one important example, given her experience in 1993–1994, it seems likely that Clinton would have proceeded more cautiously and incrementally on health care, and been more prone to heed the political warning signs in late 2009 and early 2010. The result might have been a more modest health care bill but smaller Democratic losses in the 2010 midterms. And had Democrats retained the House, the policy agenda going forward would have been very different.

The other key inputs also played their customary roles. Obama drew on an important (though recycled) set of political **ideas** (progressivism, New Deal liberalism, and Saul Alinsky), initially enjoyed a favorable **political environment** (large partisan majorities in Congress and substantial public goodwill), and was gifted significant opportunities by major **events** (unsatisfactory war in Iraq and, much more, economic disaster). A clear shift of policy to the left resulted, including major legislation such as the ACA and Dodd-Frank. But by 2011 that shift was stalled or dependent on administrative (or sometimes judicial) action. The political environment turned unfavorable, as public opinion turned against the president and Republicans gained control of Congress as well as most state governments. The Great Recession also turned from policy opportunity into liability, as economic recovery lagged.

Foreign affairs played a smaller role in domestic affairs than in the previous policy-making period. Where George W. Bush's domestic presidency was upended by 9/11, Obama downplayed the threat of terrorism. One exception was the successful raid against Osama bin Laden, the mastermind behind 9/11, in May 2011. Bin Laden's death had no direct effect on domestic policy but may have made the difference in Obama's narrow reelection the following year, which preserved the ACA and other Obama policy moves. (At home, Hurricane Sandy may also have helped push Obama past the finish line in 2012.) Conversely, the sudden sweep of ISIS to the edge of Baghdad in 2014 (after it was dismissed by Obama as the terrorist "jayvee team") undoubtedly contributed to the president's low approval ratings in the fall of 2014, which themselves contributed to the Democrats' loss of the Senate in those midterm elections.

Moreover, even big policies in 2009–2010 were significantly impacted by **"path dependency."** The ARRA was a multiplied successor to the spring 2008 stimulus package; interventionist recession-fighting policies like quantitative easing and TARP began in late 2008, before Obama took office; and even the Affordable Care Act built on existing structures such as Medicaid and employer-based health benefits.

The **policy agenda** included some items forced onto the agenda by events, such as fighting the recession; others that appeared as a result of a combination of events and new political pressures, such as the sharp growth of the deficit, the rise of the Tea Party movement, and the 2010 election results or the rise in inequality and the Occupy Wall Street movement; and some that were more discretionary items the president (and sometimes his opponents) chose to emphasize, such as health care and global warming.

Assessing the success of Obama's policies was complicated. His defenders noted that the recession ended in the summer of 2009, upon which the nation entered a period of economic growth that continued for the remainder of Obama's presidency. Unemployment, which peaked at over 10 percent, fell to 4.8 percent by January 2017.[27] Critics noted that the economic recovery was the weakest since World War II. In inflation-adjusted terms, the economy had grown more than 30 percent by the sixth year of Reagan's expansion, more than 20 percent under Clinton, almost 20 percent under Bush, and only about 10 percent under Obama.[28] Moreover, despite his goal of redistribution, income inequality grew and much of the new regulation seemed to hurt small companies more than big.[29] Some economists estimated that the average middle class family would have been nearly $12,000 a year better off by 2015 if incomes had grown as fast under Obama as in the average recovery.[30]

Similarly, the Affordable Care Act clearly benefited some Americans. The number of uninsured declined, and the ban on denying coverage for preexisting conditions was popular, as was the ability of parents to leave children on their health insurance policies until age 26. However, the ACA also produced several unfortunate examples of **unanticipated consequences**. Far fewer Americans were covered under Obamacare than had been predicted, millions lost their existing coverage despite the president's oft-repeated promise that "if you like your insurance, you can keep it," and the National Bureau of Economic Research estimated that the cost of insurance was nearly 25 percent higher than it would have been without the ACA.[31] Obamacare exchanges were struggling around the country, and critics argued the ACA was holding back hiring in the economy, as employers cut hours or employees to stay below the threshold that triggered the employer mandate.[32] The ACA as a whole remained unpopular to the end of Obama's tenure, and Republicans remained committed to repealing it.

THE TRUMP EXPERIMENT

Barack Obama's final act as president was to hand the keys to the White House over to Donald J. Trump, a more unexpected new occupant than any in the modern era. In the 2016 election, Trump had defeated Hillary Clinton, who had run as the logical successor to Obama. Unfortunately for Clinton, almost two-thirds of Americans held that the country was going in the wrong direction, and she had the additional burden of seeking a third consecutive presidential term for her party, a quest that has been successful only once since 1952 (George H. W. Bush in 1988).

Trump, a billionaire real estate developer and reality TV star who had been in the public eye for decades, ran as the consummate outsider and was the first president elected without having had any elected or appointed political experience or experience in the military.[33] He won the Republican presidential nomination by securing the support of a plurality of voters in what began as a 17-person field, despite the almost unified opposition of the party's elected officials and the intellectual organs of the conservative movement. When he faced Clinton in the fall of 2016, the two of them formed the least-liked pair of major-party presidential contenders in the history of polling.

In the end, Trump won by gaining a solid majority in the Electoral College despite trailing in the nationally aggregated popular vote by nearly three million votes. As in 2000 but to an even greater extent, the Democratic nominee piled up huge margins in a few big states while losing in most places. Trump won key swing states and surprised Clinton by flipping several midwestern states that had not voted for a Republican since the 1980s. At the same time, Republicans held on to their House and Senate majorities, albeit with small losses.[34]

Trump ran on a domestic policy platform that promised to shake up traditional coalitions. It was not clear that he operated on the basis of any coherent intellectual framework, though supporters at the new journal *American Greatness* worked hard to create one for him. In some ways, he hewed to traditional Republican themes, promising to repeal and replace Obamacare, cut taxes, protect religious liberty, be tough on crime, and appoint conservative Supreme Court justices. On the other hand, he rejected the long-standing Republican goal of reining in entitlement spending, promising instead to not reduce Social Security or Medicare. He also proposed a $1 trillion infrastructure program, promised trade protectionism to defend the manufacturing sector, and deemphasized the moral issues (though he said he had revised his previous pro-choice views on abortion). He also embraced a restrictionist immigration policy, which was not consistent with the immigration stands of Ronald Reagan or George W. Bush but was in line with the evolving views of most congressional Republicans over the last decade. In many ways, he sought to appeal to white working-class voters, especially in the center of the country, who had felt abandoned by political elites of both parties. In some ways, he mimicked Ross Perot's courting of the "radical center" from two decades before. Although his voters mostly consisted of the traditional Republican coalition, motivated as much by dislike of Clinton as by love of Trump, the voters who put him over the top were working-class voters in places like Wisconsin, Michigan, and Pennsylvania who had voted for Obama in 2008 and 2012 but felt betrayed. These voters had suffered a quiet erosion of well-being for a quarter century, though the recession and slow recovery had put an exclamation point on it.[35] For Trump, like Obama, the central event was the Great Recession and its aftermath, though what he drew from the event was quite different.

Trump took office at the head of unified Republican government, with a program that offered to break out of some of the ideological boxes that had developed in American politics. He was pugnacious and determined, a "fighter" who would not let his opponents roll over him. Some of his supporters posited that he might be in the process of realigning American politics, much as Obama's supporters believed their man was going to do when he was elected in 2008.[36] On the other hand, Trump suffered the burden of being a minority president, elected despite his opponent having received support from more Americans. His Senate majority was narrow; his House majority was divided, with a boisterous "Freedom Caucus" with Tea Party roots holding the balance; and he never received the customary "honeymoon" with either the press or public opinion. From the beginning of his presidency, he was also dogged by an investigation into whether his campaign "colluded" with Russia during the 2016 election, an investigation that steadily expanded with time. A significant percentage of Americans despised Trump because of his malign treatment of women, his reluctance to distance himself from white racial identity politics, his tendency to insult opponents in public remarks and ubiquitous Tweets, his policies on immigration, or some combination. Trump also suffered from being not terribly well informed or interested in policy, mercurial, and prone to step on his own successes with inflammatory comments. Consequently, despite Republican majorities in both houses of Congress until the 2018 elections, Trump's first two years were much like Obama's last six years. Legislatively, not much happened. Administratively, a great deal happened.

Trump's top two legislative priorities—that is, congressional Republicans' two legislative priorities—were tax reform and repeal of Obamacare. Repealing the ACA, a key promise of Republicans since 2010, proved more difficult than he anticipated. When the House finally approved a repeal and replace bill with much difficulty, the Senate could not act. In July 2017, supporters of a repeal bill lost a key vote when three Republican Senators would not sign on. Republicans then drafted an alternate approach, a reversion to federalism that would have decentralized Obamacare, putting resources in the states to find solutions. It also fell short, and the repeal effort was done. Democrats were adamantly opposed to the effort, and Republicans could not agree among themselves. Moreover, public opinion, which had long been opposed to the ACA, took a more favorable turn, demonstrating the potential effect of "loss aversion" on policy making—the phenomenon whereby people are more likely to fear the negative consequences of a change than to anticipate potential positive consequences.[37]

The embarrassment of the failed ACA repeal drive made success on the tax bill all the more important to Republicans. House Speaker Paul Ryan had long viewed tax reform as one of his own key policy priorities, and he shepherded a tax bill through the House. The Senate followed suit, and the Tax Cuts and Jobs Act was signed by Trump in December 2017. The bill was a tax cut for about 80 percent of taxpayers and the first major structural reform of the tax system since the Reagan tax reform of 1986. Key provisions included a cut in the corporate income tax rate, which had become one of the highest in the industrial world, from 35 percent to 21 percent, as well as reductions in individual tax rates, an increase in the standard deduction and family tax credits, and limitations on certain itemized deductions, notably the deduction for state and local taxes, which was capped at $10,000, a provision aimed at high-tax Democratic states such as California, New York, and New Jersey. Another key provision repealed the tax penalty attached to the individual mandate in the ACA, leaving the mandate technically intact but unenforced. Similarly, the bill included a provision long desired by Republicans opening a portion of the Arctic National Wildlife Refuge to oil exploration.[38]

The 2017 tax reform bill was emblematic of much that had changed in policy making over the previous three decades. Unlike the 1986 bill, which represented a many-sided compromise between Reagan and House and Senate Democrats and Republicans, the 2017 bill was carried almost entirely on the strength of Republican votes. In the pattern of Obama's ARRA, ACA, and Dodd-Frank, it was developed largely outside the committee structure by the majority party leadership working almost exclusively with majority party members. The tax bill was the one big legislative accomplishment of the first two years of the Trump presidency, and Republicans pinned their political hopes on it and on a strengthening economy that seemed finally to be breaking out of the post–Great Recession doldrums. (Those hopes proved misplaced, as polls showed most Americans were unpersuaded by the tax cut.) Otherwise, an infrastructure plan and other legislative proposals languished, though Congress did use the Congressional Review Act, passed by the 104th Congress, to assert legislative power and rescind a number of Obama-era regulations.[39]

Where the ARRA and other Obama spending decisions deliberately grew the federal deficit prior to 2011 as part of a Keynesian blueprint, Trump and the Republican Congress threatened to blow it up again by inattention. The $1.4 trillion/ten year tax cut was unaccompanied by any new effort at spending restraint, and the old spending restraints embodied in the 2011 sequestration deal were loosened considerably in a spring 2018 budget deal that ended a budget impasse by giving everyone more. Trump had run on a platform that deliberately eschewed limited government and fiscal restraint as a theme, and the fiscal picture would soon show the effects.

If few policy achievements came via Congress, Trump took a number of steps to administratively reverse Obama-era policies:[40]

- The Environmental Protection Agency rescinded much of the "Clean Power Plan," the climate-change regulation that Obama had imposed after losing the cap-and-trade battle in Congress, and Trump announced withdrawal from the Paris Accords.
- Trump reversed Obama's rulings against the Keystone XL and Dakota Access pipelines, and work began.
- The Department of Education rescinded the so-called Dear Colleague letter that had insisted colleges and universities impose a standard of "preponderance of evidence" rather than "clear and convincing evidence" in cases of alleged sexual assault. It also rescinded rules making it harder for for-profit universities to operate.

- Trump rescinded Obama's DACA memorandum, calling on Congress to assume its legislative responsibilities and reach a fix. (Through 2018, it had not done so.) More generally, Trump ordered immigration enforcement efforts to intensify, including issuing a "zero tolerance" policy requiring illegal immigrants to be tried for violating the law. (This order, in combination with a decree from the Ninth Circuit Court of Appeals, led to children of detainees being separated from their parents while judicial processes were underway, until a public outcry forced Trump to revise the policy.)
- The administration also used administrative means to chip away at the ACA. The Department of Health and Human Services rescinded the contraceptive mandate and, perhaps most importantly, began allowing insurance policies to be offered outside of the restrictions previously enforced to provide customers with more and cheaper options.
- The chair of the Consumer Financial Protection Bureau proposed new rules making the CFPB more transparent and accountable.
- Trump used trade authority delegated by Congress to impose tariffs on China, Europe, and Canada, sparking fears of a trade war but also leading to some trade concessions from the European Union and China and a renegotiation of NAFTA.
- Overall, the regulatory apparatus of the federal government slowed. Where the *Federal Register* published nearly 100,000 pages in Obama's last year, it only published 62,000 in Trump's first year, the fewest since 1990.

The conflict between federal versus state and local authorities, increasingly common in the Obama years, continued growing under Trump, though along different lines. Given Trump's restrictionist immigration policies, one key fault line was over state and local "sanctuary" status. Trump threatened to pull federal funding from sanctuary cities or states, though federal courts prevented it. States like California promised to conduct their own climate change policies. And a number of states sued to prevent HHS from redefining allowable insurance policies, claiming that the action was an illegal rewriting of the law.[41]

Trump hardly ever talked about the Constitution, and his constitutional knowledge was suspect (he once reportedly referred to Article XII of the Constitution, which only has seven articles). However, his actions in the beginning of his presidency generally had the tendency of unwinding the centralization and rule-by-expert-administrators promoted by Obama. He also was highly successful at appointing federal judges and two Supreme Court Justices who were endorsed by the conservative

Federalist Society. Over time, these appointments could shift the judiciary more in the direction of an "originalist" understanding of the Constitution, and perhaps a position more sympathetic to the states.

For most of 2017 and 2018, Trump's public approval rating held steady in the low to mid 40s—a historically mediocre level, but also the most stable approval ratings of any president in polling history.[42] Trump's level of public support was enough to sustain him for the time being, but probably not enough to propel an enduring change in politics or policy. Like Obama before him, he was holding his base but not expanding it, mobilizing the like-minded but not persuading. Trump may have made millions in real estate, but he was having difficulty transferring *The Art of the Deal* to Washington politics on health care, immigration, or other subjects.

In the 2018 elections, Republicans expanded their narrow Senate majority but lost 40 seats in the House, enough to give Democrats the majority there. Republicans lost heavily in affluent suburban districts, though they suffered an erosion of voters across the board.[43] Democrats promised to use their investigatory powers vigorously, and it seemed probable that policy making in Washington would be even more stalemated.[44] However, it was too early to compose a summary of policy in the Trump years, and anything could happen. The post-midterm election lame duck session of Congress demonstrated the range of possibilities. In late December, Congress overwhelmingly approved, on a bipartisan basis, the First Step Act, reducing federal criminal sentencing. The Trump administration, key Republican donors, libertarians, and civil rights organizations coalesced to support the legislation.[45] Days later, the same Congress and administration failed to achieve a budget compromise, launching the longest partial government shutdown in the nation's history.

Indeed, it is too early to render a final judgment on policy in either the Trump or Obama periods. Policy seeds planted in one era can grow into something more over time. Incrementalism can turn apparent stalemate into significant accomplishment, just as it can gradually erode what began as a towering achievement.

Conclusion

★ ★ ★

IF SOMEONE EXAMINING DOMESTIC PUBLIC POLICY in 1929 were
to look forward nine decades, the first thing that would probably strike
him or her would be the vast increase in the number and expense of federal policies and programs. Each policy enacted during that period was
enacted individually and must be examined on its own merits. Yet cumu-
latively, these policy changes have added up to a constitutional change.
The federal government might correctly have been described as a limited
government of enumerated powers in 1929. It would be difficult to call
it one today. The New Deal was a critical launching pad for the modern
welfare state, but it was only a beginning.

Throughout this period, policy debate has largely fallen into two
schools. One strand, taking its basic inspiration from the New Deal, has
advocated extending its logic to farther reaches. The other, skeptical of
the capacities of centralized government and fearful of its power, has
fought that extension. Since the 1960s or 1970s, another division has
arisen on social issues, with one stream of thinking pushing a liberaliza-
tion of social mores backed by permissive laws and the other resisting
what it sees as an assault on the moral foundations of society. These
divisions should not be seen simplistically. Often, political actors draw
from more than one well. Republican presidents (such as Richard Nixon
and George W. Bush) and congresses have expanded domestic government, while Democratic presidents (Jimmy Carter and Bill Clinton) have
sometimes cut domestic spending and reformed welfare. A president like
Barack Obama can generally favor centralization of power but still support specific moves toward decentralization, such as the Every Student
Succeeds Act.

Chart 1. Total Nondefense Spending Less Net Interest, 1940–2017 (as % of GDP)

Chart 2. Federal Register Page Count, 1936–2017

Year

The economy in general has remained a key issue on the public policy agenda throughout the years, although the particular form it takes changes (depression, inflation, stagflation, financial meltdown). And if government has grown, its growth has not been steady, but in fits and starts. As a percentage of GDP, domestic spending grew rapidly in the 1960s and early 1970s, leveled off in the late 1970s, fell to a lower level from 1980 to 2007 (though with bumps under both Bushes), followed by a big recession-Obama spurt, reaction, and stabilization at a level lower than the peak but higher than the 1980–2007 norm (see Chart 1). Similarly, pages in the *Federal Register*—a rough proxy for regulatory activity—exploded in the 1960s and 1970s, fell in the 1980s, grew slightly until the Obama years, then fell in Donald Trump's first year (Chart 2). Incrementalism surely describes the way most policy is made most of the time, but it is not the whole story. Bigger changes sometimes adjust the baseline—the New Deal, Great Society, and Obama era for big government, Reagan, the 104th Congress, and (at least in terms of regulation) Trump for more limited government. In a related vein, social welfare appeared in force in the 1930s and has remained relevant since then, though with varying degrees of priority and change. Federal social welfare policy was expansive and deliberately redistributive in the New Deal, Great Society, and Obama eras; in the 1980s and 1990s, the focus turned toward limiting expenditures, reinforcing individual responsibility, reducing welfare dependency, and shifting some power on social welfare policy back to the states.

Consider the following trends in other areas:

- Civil rights gained in prominence in the 1940s, became a high priority in the 1950s and 1960s, and subsequently fell back to a secondary issue. Movement toward civil rights protection started slowly, peaked with passage of the Civil Rights Act of 1964 and Voting Rights Act of 1965, and has been mired since the 1970s in debates over forced busing, affirmative action, and other race-based remedies.
- Federal environmental policy began with a focus on conservation, expanded to pollution control and cleanup in the 1960s and 1970s, and eventually included attempts to address global warming. After a burst of federal regulatory effort in the 1970s, policy has featured a persistent tug-of-war between advocates of stronger regulation and free-market opponents who fear overregulation has stifled economic growth. Environmental protection has intermittently competed with and complemented policies on energy production.
- K–12 education was never really a federal issue until Sputnik in 1957, but grew in importance in the Great Society; after a couple decades of relative dormancy, it returned when George H. W. Bush declared he would be the "education president," and it has frequently been high on the agenda since then. Original policy aims included funding for math and science instruction, funding for poor schools, and desegregation. Starting in the 1980s, attention turned to increasing educational standards and performance, though debate has continued over how strong a hand the federal government should assert in that drive.

- Though Prohibition was an issue in 1933, broad social consensus kept moral/cultural debates off the agenda until the 1960s; since then, school prayer, crime, drugs, abortion, gay rights, stem cell research, and other issues have formed the "culture wars." In waves, policy—often driven by federal courts—has shifted markedly toward the permissive or non-traditional pole.
- Starting with the New Deal, significant change took place in intergovernmental relations, moving from "layer cake federalism" to "marble cake federalism." In different ways, Richard Nixon and Ronald Reagan began moving policy back toward greater decentralization with different versions of a "new federalism," a trend that continued in the 1990s. More recently, policy has moved back toward centralization. Other constitutive issues, such as the role of the presidency and executive branch agencies, have been consistent questions since FDR, though they have only sometimes been raised intentionally.

As we have seen, whether the outputs of domestic policy are incremental or more fundamental depends on the nature of the inputs. Big events like the Great Depression, assassinations of political leaders, the crisis of stagflation, or a financial crisis are more likely to lead to big policy changes than less momentous events. However, even seemingly trivial contingencies—Newt Gingrich feeling snubbed on Air Force One, Monica Lewinsky delivering a pizza to Bill Clinton during a government shutdown—can alter the trajectory of policy making.

Another lesson from this study is just how often foreign events intrude into domestic policy making. The influence of World War II on government planning, health care, taxes, and race; the impact of Sputnik on education; the way the Cold War drove internal security concerns and influenced civil rights reforms; the way national security crises fueled Democratic election wins in 1962 and Republican election wins in 2002 and 2004 and the domestic policy consequences that flowed from those election results—all were examples. In addition, the relative prominence of foreign policy on the agenda can either suck the oxygen out of domestic policy efforts or can enhance them. World War II, Vietnam, and Iraq all negatively affected the president's ability to promote his domestic agenda by crowding out other priorities and (in Vietnam and Iraq) driving down the president's popularity and political leverage. The end of the Cold War meant that the public was focused almost wholly on domestic concerns in the 1990s for the first time since the 1930s.

Politics is another crucial input. Elections and the political power they confer can shift policy; public opinion and political mobilization in between elections can do the same thing. Policy-making eras are often inaugurated and brought to a close by elections. The elections of 1930, 1932, and 1934 ushered in the New Deal era of policy making; 1938 ended it. The elections of 1958 through 1964 were crucial to the Great Society; 1966 ended it. The Reagan Revolution could not have happened without the elections of 1978 and (especially) 1980, and was ended in stages by the elections of 1982 (which deprived Republicans of a working majority in the House) and 1986 (when the GOP lost control of the Senate). For Obama, 2006 and 2008 made possible some big legislation, while 2010 significantly changed the policy trajectory. Again, the political circumstances in which policy is made should not be viewed simply in partisan terms. Parties are more homogeneous and more polarized in some eras than in others. As David Mayhew pointed out in *Divided We Govern*, important policy can be made even when there is divided government—as attested by welfare reform in 1996.[1] And unified government is no guarantee of policy achievement, if other elements of the political picture and other inputs are not working in sync—as attested by the failures of health care reform in 1994 and Social Security reform in 2005. Even in today's more polarized environment, major legislation is rarely enacted without some bipartisan support; the Affordable Care Act and 2017 tax reform were exceptions.[2] Moreover, politics is more than just parties operating in the institutions of government. It is the political climate established by public opinion—what scholar John Kingdon called the "national mood"—and it includes political and social movements such as the American labor movement, movements supporting Charles Townsend and Father Coughlin, the civil rights movement, the conservative movement, the environmental movement, the religious right, and the Tea Party. Nevertheless, partisan or ideological majorities in Congress—preferably really big majorities—make big policy change more likely.

It is also clear that politics and policy can form a feedback loop. Not only does the political environment help produce policy, but policy shapes the political environment. Franklin Roosevelt's support for the Wagner Act helped cement the loyalty of labor unions to the Democratic Party. Policy makers are aware of this sort of process. Both George W. Bush and Barack Obama sought to use policy to change the political facts on the ground. Bush hoped that immigration reform would draw Hispanics into a new Republican coalition, while Social Security reform would shift the young into the Republican column. Obama clearly hoped, and conservatives openly feared, that health care reform and liberal immigration policies would structurally advance Democratic prospects.

Although ideas are largely impotent when standing alone, they can add tremendous power to events and politics. The ideas of populists, progressives, liberals like John Dewey, anti-laissez-faire economists like John Maynard Keynes, and even socialists like Eugene Debs laid the intellectual groundwork for the New Deal. Thought-provoking books by John Kenneth Galbraith, Michael Harrington, and Rachel Carson established an intellectual foundation for the Great Society. The Reagan Revolution was powered by the ideas of Friedrich Hayek, Milton Friedman, supply-side economists, Russell Kirk, and fusionist figures such as William F. Buckley and Barry Goldwater, who laid the foundation for an anti-statist politics and policy tying together the different strands of conservatism. Even policy-making eras of less import are often driven by ideas: The Democratic Leadership Council and the reinventing government ideas of David E. Osborne heavily influenced Bill Clinton, as the compassionate conservatism of Marvin Olasky and others did for George W. Bush.

Not least, when these three inputs have coincided, one still needs leadership from particular individuals in policy-making positions. Although the focus here has largely been on presidents, there are a multitude of individuals in the executive branch and Congress who can play a role. It does not take too much imagination to see that a different policy outcome would have resulted if one were to substitute John Nance Garner for Franklin Roosevelt, Howard Baker for Ronald Reagan, Ted Kennedy for Jimmy Carter, a more cautious bureaucrat for FDR's Labor Secretary Frances Perkins, a supply-side economist instead of Richard Darman as George H. W. Bush's budget director, or mild-mannered veteran lawmaker Bob Michel for the man who took his place as leader of House Republicans, Newt Gingrich. Indeed, congressional policy entrepreneurs from Robert F. Wagner to Jack Kemp were often crucial, and Congress as an institution was rarely irrelevant and frequently took the lead. The Supreme Court as a collective whole, and the individuals making it up, have also had considerable policy influence, whether by striking down and then accepting major portions of the New Deal, ordering desegregation of schools, mandating the legalization of abortion or same-sex marriage, or taking steps to restore the standing of the states.

Intergovernmental relations are often crucial to the development of national policy. The shifting form of American federalism, from "dual federalism" to "cooperative federalism" to "new federalism," has been a product of "constitutive policy," but has also driven policy in areas such as health care, welfare reform, and education.

Big policy changes have happened when ideas, events, politics, and people are aligned, as the multiple streams theory would anticipate. In particular, the "punctuation" of punctuated equilibrium has indeed been most likely when policy paradigms—the broad ideas or intellectual environment undergirding policy—shift substantially, as in the New Deal, the Great Society, and the Reagan Revolution. While the multiple streams and punctuated equilibrium models were developed to explain individual policy decisions or even just placement of issues on the agenda, they seem to be applicable as well to broad patterns of policy. When the inputs are not aligned, incrementalism will more than likely rule the day. Harry Truman and Dwight Eisenhower presided over a period of equilibrium because the politics were not right for anything else, they were personally unsuited for leading a successful major policy push, and events abroad pushed most domestic policy to the rear echelon of priorities. Nixon, Ford, and Carter likewise presided over a rough policy equilibrium in which the putatively conservative Nixon felt compelled to adopt a number of liberal policies while the Democrat Carter was compelled to declare that government could not solve every problem. George H. W. Bush and Clinton each had weaknesses and, in any event, mostly governed against an opposition Congress in a period of relative domestic calm. George W. Bush hoped a window was opening, but his majorities were too small and his mandate too tenuous; when dramatic events occurred, they either focused the attention of the nation abroad (9/11 and the Iraq War), or else made it harder for Bush to achieve domestic goals (Katrina, the Iraq War, and the financial crisis). A bigger window opened for Obama, and he took advantage to secure enactment of some major policies in his first two years. But his ambitions alienated enough Americans to change the politics and stall his project after November 2010. Bill Clinton and George W. Bush were propelled by ideas too small to drive non-incremental change, and Wilsonian progressivism and New Deal redux may have been too intellectually exhausted to sustain a major breakthrough in policy for Barack Obama, though it is too early to render a definitive judgment on policy change in that recent era.

Although policy eras may fit broadly within schemes of incrementalism or the change models of punctuated equilibrium or multiple streams, specific policy areas within those eras may step outside of the general tendency. At best, those models represent poles on a broad spectrum. Despite general movement in policy, the New Deal saw no breakthroughs in education, environment, or civil rights, while the Nixon equilibrium saw something of a breakthrough in environmental policy.

The public policy agenda has frequently shifted and significantly expanded since the New Deal. In 1933, the Depression was the biggest issue and almost the only issue. By 1946, the key issues included inflation, wartime economic controls, demobilization, and labor militancy, soon to be joined by civil rights and internal security. By the early 1960s, the issue was not scarcity for the bulk of society but affluence and what do with it, leading to both the War on Poverty and a host of quality of life questions. By the late 1970s, stagflation was on the top of the national mind, along with energy, moral issues such as abortion, and increasing fears of centralized government. In 1992, the question was how to restore growth, reduce the federal deficit, and align the country's economy for a global era in which the Cold War had been won. On September 10, 2001, the issue was what to do with the nation's new budget surplus, but the next day, attention turned back to the world. Surpluses became deficits, internal security returned as an issue, and energy grew increasingly prominent. In the fall of 2008, financial crisis and economic distress became the number one issue, though the new president soon also insisted on pushing health care reform and initiatives in energy and environment. Other issues come and go, or come and go and come back (such as immigration or energy).

What explains the churning of issues onto and off the policy agenda? Some changes in the agenda are traceable to each of the policy inputs. For example, it is obvious that events can instantly reshuffle the policy agenda. Energy became an issue with the Arab oil embargo of 1973–1974; 9/11 made defense against terrorism the key question of the moment; financial crisis put financial regulatory reform on the policy map. Shifting politics will also move issues onto or off the agenda. Loss of Congress by Democrats in 1994 took comprehensive health care reform off the national public policy agenda for a decade and a half; the Federal Marriage Amendment ceased to be a viable proposal after Republicans lost Congress in 2006. Individuals make a difference: Though they were from the same party and agreed on a number of issues, Ronald Reagan made an institutional defense of federalism a priority for his administration where George W. Bush did not. The recurrence of some issues on the policy agenda is owed to the importance some ideas hold within the parties. Universal health care has been an ideological commitment of liberal Democrats since FDR's Economic Bill of Rights, reflecting their deepest views on the purpose of government and the character of an empathetic society. This commitment has guaranteed that all subsequent Democratic presidents have sought to place health care high on the policy agenda, regardless of other circumstances. Likewise, keeping taxes low is a core ideological commitment of most Republicans, reflecting their deepest views on the purpose of government and the character of a free society. They can be counted on to make a priority out of tax relief in most circumstances.

Beyond the churning of issues, a noticeable feature since the New Deal has been the sheer expansion of the federal policy agenda. Some of this may be an artifact of taking the 1930s as the starting point. The Depression was such an overwhelming event that, for a brief time, nothing else much mattered. It was to be expected after the Depression ended that the policy agenda might be made up of a larger number of smaller issues competing for attention. However, the expansion of the agenda was also a real and self-perpetuating consequence of the growth of government activism, which created new expectations for policy, a lowering of barriers to federal policy making in one issue area after another, and an ever-growing set of feedback loops, flowing from both the successes and failures of policy ventures.

If a policy succeeds and the problem is solved to most people's satisfaction, the issue itself ceases to be high on the public policy agenda. Legally enforced segregation is no longer a major public policy concern because civil rights policies in the 1950s and 1960s succeeded in ending it. However, successful policy can invite imitation across related policy areas. Policy failure can either result in exhaustion leading to a downgrading of the issue, at least for a time, or it can also lead to a renewed push with a different policy approach. Some policies contain within them problems which virtually guarantee that the issue will be revisited from time to time. After the creation of Social Security old age pensions in 1935, policy makers revisited the issue several times through 1972 in order to expand eligibility or raise payments. After that, the automatic costs of the program and changing demographics meant that presidents Carter and Reagan had to "rescue" the program (in 1977 and 1983), and that presidents Clinton and Bush proposed new ways to rescue the program from potential financial ruin down the road. And, like Social Security, many policies have the potential to develop a clientele that will pressure policy makers for more. Thus more government can beget more government.

Throughout this study, problem definition has proved to be a very important area for contestation. When liberals succeeded in defining the Great Depression as a result of laissez-faire economics and private greed, the way was open for a vastly expanded role for government and diminution of the private sector. When conservatives succeeded in defining stagflation as a result of out-of-control government, they had the advantage in proposing a program of re-limited government and deregulation. In the 2008 campaign and his early presidency, Obama offered an interpretation of the financial crisis that (like FDR) emphasized deregulation and a greedy business sector as causes, while deemphasizing factors like Federal Reserve policy, government policies that encouraged lower lending standards, or the irresponsibility of individual borrowers. The policies flowing from his interpretation were predictably weighted toward enhanced government power, and were quite different than policies which might have flowed from an alternative interpretation. Of course, policy makers frequently fashion interpretations to support policies they already prefer—Obama was campaigning for more aggressive government intervention in the economy months before the financial crisis erupted—but to be able to enact those policies, they still must persuade Americans that the interpretation they are offering makes sense.

The battle over interpretation and problem definition is a prominent part of public policy making precisely because public policy is an imprecise science. Multiple interpretations of past policy outcomes are usually plausible, even if some are more plausible than others. It is often not even possible to achieve a consensus on whether a policy was "successful." Was the New Deal a success because the economy stabilized, democracy was preserved, and suffering was mitigated, or was it a failure because it did not end the Great Depression and it undermined important elements of a free Constitution? Was the Great Society a success because a raft of legislation was passed and the poverty rate fell, or a failure because much poverty not only remained but seemed to become more entrenched and dysfunctional? Was the Reagan Revolution a success because stagflation was tamed, the growth of government slowed, and federalism revitalized, or a failure because government was not significantly reduced and income inequality rose? It may be easier to assess a single program than a policy era, but not much. More than five decades after it was created, policy analysts cannot agree on whether Head Start has lasting positive effects for children. Did the 1981 Reagan tax cuts spur investment? How well did the Agricultural Adjustment Act work? What are the educational effects of charter schools? Was the Obama stimulus worth the cost? These questions also produce no consensus.

If it is difficult for policy analysts to interpret the past, it is that much more difficult for them to predict the future. Unanticipated consequences are a frequent occurrence in the policy world. A deepening Depression was surely not the objective of Congress when it passed the Smoot-Hawley tariff. When wage and price controls during World War II exempted fringe benefits, the goal was labor peace—the result was a health care system that is centered on employer-provided health insurance beyond the capacity of reformers of left or right to easily unwind. When the "luxury tax" was made part of the 1990 budget deal, the goal was deficit reduction (and perhaps a bit of redistributionism)—the result was a collapsing boat industry and a fiscal wreck. The Federal Reserve Board's policy of low interest rates after 9/11 aimed to revive a wounded economy, but may have contributed to the housing bubble and consequently the financial disaster of 2008. The Affordable Care Act of 2010 was meant to reduce the cost of insurance and add 30 million people to the ranks of the insured—but it covered far fewer than anticipated while, critics say, driving up the cost of insurance and inhibiting job growth.

It may be tempting to throw up one's hands at ever promoting sound policy, but the lesson one should take away is humility, not despair. Some policies *are* better than others for attaining their goals, though only democratic deliberation that takes into account the nature of the problem, the possible solutions, and the moral, political, and constitutional values of the nation can identify what goals are worthy. To be prepared to participate well in that discussion, it is important to know at least a brief history of public policy.

In the end, public policy matters. Imagine America with a different set of public policies. Alternatives to the New Deal included a Harding-Coolidge style response of minimal intervention, a full-scale (but democratic) socialist response, and a totalitarian response—three responses that would have produced three very different Americas than the one we now inhabit. The Great Society extended the federal "safety net," but also cost an estimated $22 trillion since 1964 in 2014 dollars—a hefty sum in a country with a $21 trillion debt. Could any alternative have been more effective and placed a lighter financial burden on future generations? There were alternatives to the Reagan Revolution on the left, center, and right; were there any that would also have ended stagflation and succeeded in slowing the course of centralization, without large deficits or growing inequality? Imagine life without unemployment insurance, interstate highways, the Clean Air Act, or employer-based health care—or *with* legal segregation, Swedish levels of confiscatory taxation, or 100,000 pages of new regulation every year.

Public policy will continue to matter. Important public policy challenges lie ahead, such as how to promote job creation, how to handle the exploding cost of the entitlement programs and national debt, what to do about immigration, how to address the rise of biotechnologies and artificial intelligence, whether and how to support crucial social institutions such as the family, and (as always) what to do about health care. Can liberals succeed in completing FDR's welfare state, making the United States more like a European social democracy? Can conservatives succeed in stopping them or even in restoring principles of limited government, federalism, and accountable administration in national policy? Will some new "third way" in politics and policy emerge from the "radical center?" Most of those challenges are extensions of policy issues that have been faced throughout history. As before, some combination of ideas, events, politics, and people will produce policies, even if sometimes the policy is to change nothing.

Notes

★　★　★

INTRODUCTION

1 Indices we will examine include domestic spending in real (inflation-adjusted) dollars; domestic spending as a percentage of the economy (GDP); spending on "discretionary" (or annually appropriated) domestic programs versus spending on "mandatory" domestic programs, or entitlement programs such as Social Security and Medicare; and pages in the *Federal Register*, the annual compilation of regulatory and executive activity. Sources will include Office of Management and Budget historical tables 1.3, 6.1, 8.2–8.4, 11.1 (https://www.whitehouse.gov/omb/historical-tables/) and also "Federal Register Pages Published Annually" (https://www.llsdc.org/assets/sourcebook/fed-reg-pages.pdf).

2 Theodore Lowi, "Four Systems of Policy, Politics, and Choice," *Public Administration Review*, 32(4; 1972), 298–310.

3 Frank Fischer, *Reframing Public Policy: Discursive Politics and Deliberative Practices* (New York: Oxford University Press, 2003), pp. 64–65.

4 Paul Pierson, "Increasing Returns, Path Dependence, and the Study of Politics," *American Political Science Review*, 94(2; June 2000), 251–67.

5 Herman Schwartz, "Down the Wrong Path: Path Dependence, Increasing Returns, and Historical Institutionalism," unpublished manuscript, 2004, https://pdfs.semanticscholar.org/f7a5/94a5709cc58cfc62ca7220af30d7cc9adc90.pdf.

6 David Kingdon, "Politicians, Self-Interest, and Ideas," in *Reconsidering the Democratic Public*, edited by Geosrge E. Marcus and Russell L. Hanson (University Park: Pennsylvania State University, 1993); Paul Sabatier, "An Advocacy Coalition Framework of Policy Change and the Role of Policy-Oriented Learning Therein," *Policy Sciences*, 21 (1988), 129–68.

7 John Kingdon, *Agendas, Alternatives, and Public Policies* (Boston: Little, Brown, 1984).

8 See Nicholaos Zahariadis, "Ambiguity, Time, and Multiple Streams," in *Theories of the Policy Process*, edited by Paul A. Sabatier (Boulder: Westview Press, 1999), p. 77.

9 Kingdon discusses "people" or policy makers both as a subset one of his three streams—administrative or legislative turnover (part of "politics")—and as policy entrepreneurs who are independent of the streams but are needed to join the streams into a coherent argument. Here we will treat "people" as a distinct "stream." Gary D. Brewer and Peter deLeon discuss "Personality" as one of the key elements to policy selection in *The Foundations of Policy Analysis* (Homewood, IL: Dorsey Press, 1983), p. 203.

10 David Braybrooke and Charles E. Lindblom, *A Strategy of Decision* (New York: Free Press, 1963).

11 Alan Abramowitz, *The Great Alignment* (New Haven: Yale University Press, 2018).

12 Alberto Alesina and Francesco Passarelli, "Loss Aversion in Politics," February 2017, https://scholar.harvard.edu/files/alesina/files/ap-lossaversion-8feb-2017-_002.pdf.

13 Thomas Kuhn, *The Structure of Scientific Revolutions*, 2nd ed. (Chicago: University of Chicago Press, 1970).

14 Matt Wilder, "What Is a Policy Paradigm? Overcoming Epistemological Hurdles in Cross-Disciplinary Conceptual Adaptation," in *Policy Paradigms in Theory and Practice: Studies in the Political Economy of Public Policy*, edited by J. Hogan and M. Howlett (London: Palgrave Macmillan, 2015), pp. 19–42.

15 James L. True, Bryan D. Jones, and Frank R. Baumgartner, "Punctuated-Equilibrium Theory: Explaining Stability and Change in American Policy Making," in *Theories of the Policy Process*, edited by Paul A. Sabatier (Boulder: Westview, 1999), pp. 97–116.

16 John Kingdon, *Agendas, Alternatives, and Public Policies* (Boston: Little, Brown, 1984).

17 Nicholaos Zahariadis, *Markets, States, and Public Policies: Privatization in Britain and France* (Ann Arbor: University of Michigan Press, 1995).

18 Bryan Jones, Frank Baumgartner, and James True, "Policy Punctuations: U.S. Budget Authority, 1947–1995," *Journal of Politics*, 60(February 1998), 1–33.

19 Another framework, called the "advocacy coalition" framework, also sees policy as a product of people, ideas, politics, and events, but seems to be limited to analysis of discrete policy decisions by policy subsystems. This framework sees policy as the result of competition between alternative coalitions—aggregations of large numbers of actors from different institutions at multiple levels of government (people) sharing a belief system and policy goals (ideas)—within policy subsystems (i.e., politics), driven by events. Paul A. Sabatier and Hank C. Jenkins-Smith, "The Advocacy Coalitions Framework," in *Theories of the Policy Process*, edited by Paul A. Sabatier (Boulder: Westview, 1999), pp. 117–66.

20 Eugene Bardach, *A Practical Guide for Policy Analysis: The Eightfold Path to More Effective Problem Solving* (New York: Chatham House, 2000), p. 1.

21 See Martha S. Feldman, *Order without Design: Information Production and Policy Making* (Palo Alto: Stanford University Press, 1989).

22 For an historical account favorable to this interpretation, see Arthur M. Schlesinger Jr., *The Crisis of the Old Order: The Age of Roosevelt, Vol. I, 1919–1933* (New York: Heineman, 1957).

23 See, for example, Milton Friedman and Anna Jacobson Schwartz, *The Great Contraction: 1929–1933,* new ed. (Princeton, NJ: Princeton University Press, 2008).

24 Mark Bovens and Paul 'T Hart, "Assessing Policy Outcomes: Social and Political Biases," *Understanding Policy Fiascoes* (New Brunswick, NJ: Transaction, 1996), pp. 21–51, http://www.downloads/usbo-spg_assessing_policy_outcomes%20(1).pdf.

25 Dylan Matthews, "Did the Stimulus Work? A Review of the Nine Best Studies on the Subject," *Washington Post,* August 24, 2011, https://www.washingtonpost.com/blogs/ezra-klein/post/did-the-stimulus-work-a-review-of-the-nine-best-studies-on-the-subject/2011/08/16/gIQAThbibJ_blog.html?utm_term=.b32f2405d84d.

26 Brewer and deLeon, *The Foundations of Policy Analysis,* p. 329.

27 See, for example, Martin Anderson, *Revolution*; Walter Williams, *Reaganism and the Death of Representative Democracy.*

28 Robert K. Merton, "The Unanticipated Consequences of Purposive Social Action," *American Sociological Review,* 1(6; December 1936), 894–904.

29 Agis Salpukas, "Falling Tax Would Lift All Yachts," *New York Times,* February 7, 1992, p. D1; James K. Glassman, "How to Sink an Industry and Not Soak the Rich," *Washington Post,* July 16, 1993, https://www.washingtonpost.com/archive/business/1993/07/16/how-to-sink-an-industry-and-not-soak-the-rich/08ea5310-4a4b-4674-ab88-fad8c42cf55b/?noredirect=on&utm_term=.6c38e759f52b.

30 Penn Wharton, University of Pennsylvania, "Effects of the $15 Minimum Wage in Seattle," https://publicpolicy.wharton.upenn.edu/live/news/2303-effects-of-the-15-minimum-wage-in-seattle/for-students/blog/news.php.

31 See Library of Congress, "The Civil Rights Act of 1964: A Long Struggle for Freedom," https://www.loc.gov/exhibits/civil-rights-act/world-war-ii-and-post-war.html; "Did World War II Launch the Civil Rights Movement?," https://www.history.com/news/did-world-war-ii-launch-the-civil-rights-movement.

32 David Mayhew, *Realignment: Critique of a Genre* (New Haven: Yale University Press, 2004).

33 For example, see the positive portrayal by Leonard Steinhorn, *The Greater Generation: In Defense of the Baby Boom Legacy* (New York: Thomas Dunne Books, 2007); for a negative appraisal, see Peter Collier and David Horowitz, *Destructive Generation: Second Thoughts about the 1960s* (New York: Encounter Books, 2005).

1: THE NEW DEAL

1 Paul Johnson, *Modern Times: From the Twenties to the Nineties,* rev. ed. (New York: HarperCollins, 1991), pp. 246–47.

2 See John D. Hicks, *The Populist Revolt* (Minneapolis: University of Minnesota Press, 1931); J. Rogers Hollingsworth, *The Whirligig of Politics: The Democracy of Cleveland and Bryan* (Chicago: University of Chicago Press, 1963); Lawrence Goodwyn, *The Populist Moment* (New York: Oxford Press, 1978).

3 Richard Hofstadter, *The Progressive Movement, 1900–1915* (Englewood Cliffs: Prentice-Hall, 1963); Lewis L. Gould, ed., *The Progressive Era* (Syracuse: Syracuse University Press, 1974).

4 Charles Merriam, *A History of American Political Theories* (New York: Macmillan, 1903), p. 307.

5 See, for example, Theodore Roosevelt, "The Right of the People to Rule," March 10, 1912.

6 See, for example, Woodrow Wilson, "The Meaning of Democracy," September 23, 1912, in *A Crossroads of Freedom: The 1912 Campaign Speeches*, edited by John W. Davidson (New Haven: Yale Press, 1956); Theodore Roosevelt, "The New Nationalism," in *An American Primer*, edited by Daniel J. Boorstin (New York: Penguin, 1966).

7 Socialist Party Platform of 1912, http://sageamericanhistory.net/progressive/docs/SocialistPlat1912.htm.

8 John Dewey, *The Public and Its Problems* (Athens: Ohio University Press, 1927).

9 See, for example, John Maynard Keyes, *The End of Laissez-Faire: The Consequences of the Peace* (Richmond, UK: Hogarth Press, 1926).

10 Among many biographies of Roosevelt, see Matthew Dallek, *Franklin Roosevelt: A Political Life* (New York: Viking, 2017); H. W. Brands, *Traitor to His Class: The Privileged Life and Radical Presidency of Franklin Delano Roosevelt* (New York: Doubleday, 2008).

11 Franklin Roosevelt, "Commonwealth Club Address," September 23, 1932.

12 Arthur M. Schlesinger Jr., *The Crisis of the Old Order* (New York: Mariner Books, 2003).

13 Johnson, *Modern Times*, pp. 243–46.

14 Milton Friedman and Anna Schwartz, *The Great Contraction 1929–1933* (Princeton: Princeton University Press, 1965).

15 Johnson, *Modern Times*, p. 246; Amity Schlaes, *The Forgotten Man: A New History of the Great Depression* (New York: HarperCollins, 2007), ch. 3 and 4.

16 James Grant, *The Forgotten Depression, 1921: The Depression That Cured Itself* (New York: Simon & Schuster, 2015).

17 See Alonzo L. Hamby, *For the Survival of Democracy: Franklin Roosevelt and the World Crisis of the 1930s* (New York: Free Press, 2004), ch. 1.

18 For a discussion of this period, see Hamby, *For the Survival of Democracy*, ch. 4 and 5; Arthur M. Schlesinger, *The Coming of the New Deal* (New York: Mariner, 2003).

19 Hamby, *For the Survival of Democracy*.

20 Schlaes, *The Forgotten Man*, ch. 6.

21 Thomas Patterson, "Franklin D. Roosevelt," http://users.skynet.be/fa101291/personen/roosevelt.htm.

22 Hamby, *For the Survival of Democracy*, pp. 262–68.

23 William E. Leuchtenburg, *Franklin D. Roosevelt and the New Deal 1932–1940* (New York: Harper & Row, 1963), p. 116.

24 Robert S. McElvaine, *The Great Depression: America 1929–1941* (New York: Times Books, 1984), p. 229.

25 For a discussion of this period, see Hamby, *For the Survival of Democracy*, ch. 8–9; Leuchtenburg, *Franklin D. Roosevelt and the New Deal 1932–1940*, ch. 6–8.

26 Hamby, *For the Survival of Democracy*, p. 172.

27 For a discussion of this period, see Hamby, *For the Survival of Democracy*, ch. 10; Leuchtenburg, *Franklin D. Roosevelt and the New Deal 1932–1940*, ch. 10–11.

28 James T. Patterson, *Congressional Conservatism and the New Deal* (Lexington: University of Kentucky Press, 1967).

29 Sean J. Savage, *Roosevelt: The Party Leader, 1932–1945* (Lexington: University of Kentucky Press, 1991), p. 159.

30 David Mayhew, "Innovative Midterm Elections," in *Midterm: The Elections of 1994 in Context*, edited by Philip A. Klinkner (Boulder: Westview Press, 1996).

31 For a discussion of this period, see Thomas Fleming, *The New Dealers' War: F.D.R. and the War within World War II* (New York: Basic Books, 2001).

32 Doris Goodwin, "The Way We Won: America's Economic Breakthrough during World War II," *The American Prospect*, fall 1992, https://prospect.org/article/way-we-won-americas-economic-breakthrough-during-world-war-ii.

33 Robert Higgs, "Wartime Origins of Modern Income-Tax Withholding," Foundation for Economic Education, November 1, 2007, https://fee.org/articles/wartime-origins-of-modern-income-tax-withholding/.

34 Aaron E. Carroll, "The Real Reason the U.S. Has Employer-Sponsored Health Insurance," *New York Times*, September 5, 2017, https://www.nytimes.com/2017/09/05/upshot/the-real-reason-the-us-has-employer-sponsored-health-insurance.html.

35 See Library of Congress, "The Civil Rights Act of 1964: A Long Struggle for Freedom," https://www.loc.gov/exhibits/civil-rights-act/world-war-ii-and-post-war.html; "Did World War II Launch the Civil Rights Movement?," https://www.history.com/news/did-world-war-ii-launch-the-civil-rights-movement.

36 For example, see the positive portrayal by Leonard Steinhorn, *The Greater Generation: In Defense of the Baby Boom Legacy* (New York: Thomas Dunne Books, 2007); for a negative appraisal, see Peter Collier and David Horowitz, *Destructive Generation: Second Thoughts about the 1960s* (New York: Encounter Books, 2005).

37 Franklin D. Roosevelt, "State of the Union Message to Congress." Online by Gerhard Peters and John T. Woolley, The American Presidency Project, https://www.presidency.ucsb.edu/node/210825.

38 Sidney M. Milkis and Michael Nelson, *The American Presidency: Origins and Development, 1776–2011*, 6th ed. (Washington, DC: Sage 2012), ch. 10.

39 Morton Grodzins, "The Federal System," in *American Government Readings and Cases*, edited by P. Woll (New York: Pearson Longman, 2004), pp. 74–78.

40 Michael Schuyler, "A Short History of Government Taxing and Spending in the United States," Tax Foundation, February 14, 2014, https://taxfoundation.org/short-history-government-taxing-and-spending-united-states/.

41 Robert Higgs, "The New Deal and the State and Local Governments," Foundation for Economic Education, March 1, 2008, https://fee.org/articles/the-new-deal-and-the-state-and-local-governments/.

42 Hamby, *For the Survival of Democracy*. See also Leuchtenburg, *Franklin D. Roosevelt and the New Deal 1932–1940*, James MacGregor Burns, *Roosevelt: The Lion and the Fox* (New York: Harcourt, Brace, and Company, 1956).

43 Schlaes, *The Forgotten Man*; Jim Powell, *FDR's Folly: How Roosevelt and His New Deal Prolonged the Great Depression* (New York: Crown Forum, 2004).

2: THE TRUMAN-EISENHOWER EQUILIBRIUM

1 Alonzo L. Hamby, *Man of the People: A Life of Harry S. Truman* (New York: Onford Press, 1995); David McCullough, *Truman* (New York: Simon & Schuster, 1992); Robert H. Ferrell, *Harry S. Truman* (Columbia: University of Missouri Press, 1994).

2 Stephen E. Ambrose, *Eisenhower: Soldier and President,* rev. ed. (New York: Simon & Schuster, 1991); Jean Edward Smith, *Eisenhower in War and Peace,* reprint ed. (New York: Random House, 2013).

3 Michael Barone, *Our Country: America from Roosevelt to Reagan* (New York: Free Press, 1990), ch. 20–24.

4 See Library of Congress, "The Civil Rights Act of 1964: A Long Struggle for Freedom," https://www.loc.gov/exhibits/civil-rights-act/world-war-ii-and-post-war.html; "Did World War II Launch the Civil Rights Movement?," https://www.history.com/news/did-world-war-ii-launch-the-civil-rights-movement.

5 United States Census Bureau, 1949 Statistical Abstract, http://www.census.gov/prod/www/abs/statab1901-1950.htm.

6 Harry S. Truman, "Special Message to the Congress Presenting a 21-Point Program for the Reconversion Period," September 6, 1945. Online by Gerhard Peters and John T. Woolley, The American Presidency Project, http://www.presidency.ucsb.edu/ws/?pid=12359.

7 Andrew E. Busch, *Horses in Midstream: U.S. Midterm Elections and Their Consequences, 1894–1998* (Pittsburgh: University of Pittsburgh Press, 1999), pp. 159–64.

8 Susan M. Hartmann, *Truman and the 80th Congress* (Columbia: University of Missouri Press, 1971).

9 See Michael B. Grossman, Martha Joynt Kumar, and Francis E. Rourke, "Second-Term Presidencies: The Aging of Administrations," in *The Presidency and the Political System,* 6th ed., edited by Michael Nelson (Washington, DC: CQ Press, 2000), p. 223.

10 Andrew E. Busch, *Truman's Triumphs: The 1948 Election and the Making of Postwar America* (Lawrence: University Press of Kansas, 2012).

11 Donald R. McCoy and Richard T. Ruetten, *Quest and Response: Minority Rights and the Truman Administration* (Lawrence: University Press of Kansas, 1973).

12 Robert J. Donovan, *The Future of the Republican Party* (New York: Signet, 1964), p. 61.

13 See Ambrose, *Eisenhower: Soldier and President*; Barone, *Our Country*.

14 James Sundquist, *Politics and Policy: The Eisenhower, Kennedy, and Johnson Years* (Washington, DC: Brookings Institution Press, 1968); Barone, *Our Country*, ch. 25–31.

15 The Presidential Papers of Dwight Eisenhower, http://web.archive.org/web/20051124190902/http://www.eisenhowermemorial.org/presidential-papers/first-term/documents/1147.cfm.

16 Geoffrey Kabaservice, "Leading as a True Conservative: Eisenhower, the GOP, and the Politics of Fiscal Responsibility," in *The Eisenhower Presidency: Lessons for the Twenty-First Century*, edited by Andrew J. Polsky (Lanham, MD: Lexington Books, 2015), p. 41.

17 John Lewis Gaddis, *Strategies of Containment: A Critical Appraisal of American National Security Policy during the Cold War,* rev. ed. (New York: Oxford, 2005), ch. 5.

18 David A. Nichols, *A Matter of Justice: Eisenhower and the Beginning of the Civil Rights Revolution* (New York: Simon & Schuster, 2007).

19 Sundquist, *Politics and Policy,* pp. 173–80.

20 Busch, *Horses in Midstream,* pp. 94–100.

21 Herbert Stein, *Presidential Economics: The Making of Economic Policy from Roosevelt to Clinton* (Washington, DC: AEI, 1994), pp. 75–87.

22 David Caute, *The Great Fear: The Anti-Communist Purge under Truman and Eisenhower* (New York: Simon & Schuster, 1978); Francis H. Collins, *The Frustration of Politics: Truman, Congress, and the Loyalty Issue* (Rutherford: Farleigh Dickinson University Press, 1979).

23 Allen Einstein, *Perjury: The Hiss-Chambers Case* (New York: Random House, 1997).

24 John Earl Haynes and Harvey Klehr, *Venona: Decoding Soviet Espionage in America,* new ed. (New Haven: Yale Press, 2000).

25 For a brief summary of these arguments, see "History and Cultural Impact of the Interstate Highway System," University of Vermont, http://www.uvm.edu/landscape/learn/impact_of_interstate_system.html.

3: THE NEW FRONTIER / GREAT SOCIETY

1 John Kenneth Galbraith, *The Affluent Society* (New York: Houghton Mifflin Harcourt, 1958).

2 Michael Harrington, *The Other America: Poverty in the United States* (New York: Macmillan, 1962).

3 Rachel Carson, *Silent Spring* (New York: Houghton Mifflin, 1962).

4 Gordon Tullock, "Did Nixon Beat Kennedy?" *New York Review of Books,* November 10, 1988, https://www.nybooks.com/articles/1988/11/10/did-nixon-beat-kennedy/.

5 Ted Sorensen, *Kennedy: The Classic Biography* (New York: Harper Perennial Political Classics, 2009).

6 John F. Kennedy, "Address of Senator John F. Kennedy Accepting the Democratic Party Nomination for the Presidency of the United States—Memorial Coliseum, Los Angeles," July 15, 1960. Online by Gerhard Peters and John T. Woolley, The American Presidency Project, http://www.presidency.ucsb.edu/ws/?pid=25966.

7 For a thorough examination of Johnson's life, see the three volume series by Robert Dallek and the four-volume series by Robert Caro. Dallek's appraisal is more positive; Caro's is more negative.

8 Randall Strahan, *Leading Representatives: The Agency of Leaders in the Politics of the U.S. House* (Baltimore: Johns Hopkins Press, 2007).

9 See Herbert Stein, *Presidential Economics: The Making of Economic Policy from Roosevelt to Clinton* (Washington, DC: AEI, 1994), ch. 4, esp. p. 95.

10 James N. Giglio, *The Presidency of John F. Kennedy,* 2nd rev. ed. (Lawrence: University Press of Kansas, 2006).

11 John F. Kennedy, "Inaugural Address." Online by Gerhard Peters and John T. Woolley, The American Presidency Project, https://www.presidency.ucsb.edu/node/234470.

12 Theodore C. Sorenson, *Kennedy* (New York: Harper & Row, 1965), p. 688.

13 Tom Wicker, "President Elated," *New York Times*, November 8, 1962, p. A1.

14 See Andrew E. Busch, *Horses in Midstream: U.S. Midterm Elections and Their Consequences, 1894–1998* (Pittsburgh: University of Pittsburgh Press, 1999), pp. 145–48.

15 Lyndon B. Johnson, Address before a Joint Session of the Congress, November 27, 1963.

16 William Ahern, "Comparing the Kennedy, Reagan and Bush Tax Cuts," Tax Foundation, http://www.taxfoundation.org/news/printer/323.html.

17 On this debate, see Stein, *Presidential Economics*, pp. 102–3; Bruce Bartlett, "Kennedy's Tax Cuts," National Center for Policy Analysis, January 27, 2004. http://www.ncpa.org/edo/bb/2004/bb-20040128.htm.

18 Lyndon B. Johnson, "Remarks at the University of Michigan," May 22, 1964. Online by Gerhard Peters and John T. Woolley, The American Presidency Project, http://www.presidency.ucsb.edu/ws/?pid=26262.

19 For subsequent discussion of Great Society policies, see John A. Andrews III, *Lyndon Johnson and the Great Society* (New York: Ivan R. Dee, 1999); Julian E. Zelizer, *The Fierce Urgency of Now: Lyndon Johnson, Congress, and the Battle for the Great Society* (New York: Penguin, 2015); Michael Barone, *Our Country: America from Roosevelt to Reagan* (New York: Free Press, 1990), ch. 37–42; James Sundquist, *Politics and Policy: The Eisenhower, Kennedy, and Johnson Years* (Washington, DC: Brookings, 1968).

20 For a detailed examination of the legislative and political process behind these measures, see Sundquist, *Politics and Policy*.

21 Wilbur J. Cohen, "1965: Year of Legislative Achievements in Health, Education, and Welfare," Archive.org, https://archive.org/stream/1965yearoflegisl-00gard/1965yearoflegisl00gard_djvu.txt.

22 Tanvi Misra, "How the 1965 Immigration Act Shaped America's Population," citylab, https://www.citylab.com/life/2015/09/how-the-1965-immigration-act-shaped-americas-population/407626/.

23 One can review the inside covers of the hardback edition of Lyndon Baines Johnson, *Vantage Point: Perspectives on the Presidency 1963–1969* (New York: Holt, Rinehart, and Winston, 1971).

24 *Report of the National Advisory Commission on Civil Disorders* (New York: Bantam Books, 1968).

25 "Vietnam War Casualties (1955–1975)," Military Factory, https://www.militaryfactory.com/vietnam/casualties.asp.

26 Stephen Daggett, "Costs of Major U.S. Wars," Congressional Research Service, June 29, 2010, https://fas.org/sgp/crs/natsec/RS22926.pdf, p. 2.

27 Busch, *Horses in Midstream*, pp. 100–106.

28 For example, see Joshua Zeitz, *Building the Great Society: Inside Lyndon Johnson's White House* (New York: Viking, 2018).

29 Mark Atwood Lawrence, "How Vietnam Killed the Great Society," *New York Times*, September 22, 2017, https://www.nytimes.com/2017/09/22/opinion/vietnam-war-great-society.html.

30 Daniel P. Moynihan, *Maximum Feasible Misunderstanding: Community Action in the War on Poverty*, new ed. (New York: Free Press, 1970).

31 James Capretta and Kevin Dyaratna, "Compelling Evidence Makes the Case for a Market-Driven Health Care System," The Heritage Foundation, December 20, 2013, https://www.heritage.org/health-care-reform/report/compelling-evidence-makes-the-case-market-driven-health-care-system.

32 Charles Murray, *Losing Ground: American Social Policy, 1950–1980* (New York: Basic Books, 1984). For a debate on this point between Murray and liberal sociologist Christopher Jencks, see Murray and Jencks, "'Losing Ground,' An Exchange," *New York Review of Books*, October 24, 1985, https://www.nybooks.com/articles/1985/10/24/losing-ground-an-exchange/?pagination=false.

33 An early example can be found in Ronald Reagan, *The Creative Society: Some Comments on Problems Facing America* (New York: Devin-Adair, 1968).

4: THE NIXON-FORD-CARTER EQUILIBRIUM

1 Michael Nelson, *Resilient America: Electing Nixon in 1968, Channeling Dissent, and Dividing Government* (Lawrence: University Press of Kansas, 2017).

2 F. Clifton White and William J. Gill, *Why Reagan Won: A Narrative History of the Conservative Movement 1964–1981* (Chicago: Regnery Gateway, 1981), pp. 122–23.

3 Kevin Phillips, *The Emerging Republican Majority* (New Rochelle, NY: Arlington House, 1969).

4 For biographies of Nixon, see Roger Morris, *Richard Milhous Nixon: The Rise of an American Politician* (New York: Holt, 1991); Richard Reeves, *President Nixon: Alone in the White House*, reprint ed. (New York: Simon & Schuster, 2002); John A. Farrell, *Richard Nixon: The Life* (New York: Doubleday, 2017).

5 Bryan Burrough, "The Bombings of America That We Forgot," *Time*, September 20, 2016, http://time.com/4501670/bombings-of-america-burrough/.

6 Richard M. Nixon, *RN: The Memoirs of Richard Nixon* (New York: Grossett and Dunlap, 1978).

7 Don Arthur, "Pedantic Fact Checking—Did Nixon Really Say 'We Are All Keynesians Now'?" Club Troppo, February 15, 2009, http://clubtroppo.com.au/2009/02/15/pedantic-fact-checking-did-nixon-really-say-we-are-keynesians-now/.

8 For a general discussion of policy in the Nixon years, see Michael Barone, *Our Country: America from Roosevelt to Reagan* (New York: Free Press, 1990), ch. 43–48; Herbert Stein, *Presidential Economics: The Making of Economic Policy from Roosevelt to Clinton* (Washington, DC: AEI, 1994), ch. 4.

9 Dennis S. Ippolito, *Congressional Spending* (Ithaca: Cornell University Press, 1981).

10 Richard Nixon, "Annual Message to the Congress on the State of the Union," January 22, 1971. Online by Gerhard Peters and John T. Woolley, The American Presidency Project, http://www.presidency.ucsb.edu/ws/?pid=3110.

11 Stein, *Presidential Economics*, p. 133.

12 Robert M. Ball, "Social Security Amendments of 1972: Summary and Legislative History," Social Security Administration, https://www.ssa.gov/history/1972amend.html.

13 "President Nixon Imposes Wage and Price Controls," http://www.econreview.com/events/wageprice1971b.htm.

14 See Daniel Griswold, "The Unhappy 40th Anniversary of Nixon's Wage and Price Controls," Cato Institute, August 15, 2011, https://www.cato.org/blog/unhappy-40th-anniversary-nixons-wage-price-controls.

15 James Cannon, *Gerald R. Ford: An Honorable Life* (Ann Arbor: University of Michigan Press, 2013); Scott Kaufman, *Ambition, Pragmatism, and Party: A Political Biography of Gerald R. Ford* (Lawrence: University Press of Kansas, 2017).

16 For example, Paul Maidment, "Gerald Ford: The Accidental President," Forbes, December 27, 2006, https://www.forbes.com/2006/12/27/notes-on-the-news-ford-biz-cx_pm_1227ford.html#ce28540554db.

17 Stuart E. Eizenstat, *President Carter: The White House Years* (New York: Thomas Dunne Books, 2018); Peter G. Bourne, *Jimmy Carter: A Comprehensive Biography from Plains to Post-Presidency* (New York: Scribner, 1997).

18 Andrew E. Busch, *Outsiders and Openness in the Presidential Nominating System* (Pittsburgh: University of Pittsburgh Press, 1997), pp. 143–47.

19 Andrew E. Busch, *Reagan's Victory: The 1980 Election and the Rise of the Right* (Lawrence: University Press of Kansas, 2005), ch. 1.

20 For an overall review, see Barone, *Our Country*, ch. 49–54.

21 Stein, *Presidential Economics*, ch. 6.

22 President Jimmy Carter, "Social Security Amendments of 1977," December 20, 1977, https://www.ssa.gov/history/carterstmts.html#77.

23 Jimmy Carter, "The State of the Union Address Delivered before a Joint Session of the Congress," January 19, 1978. Online by Gerhard Peters and John T. Woolley, The American Presidency Project, http://www.presidency.ucsb.edu/ws/?pid=30856.

24 John Berlau, "Ted Kennedy's Deregulatory Legacy on Airlines and Trucking," Competitive Enterprise Institute, August 26, 2009, https://cei.org/blog/ted-kennedys-deregulatory-legacy-airlines-and-trucking.

25 Stephen Skowronek, *Presidential Leadership in Political Time: Reprise and Reappraisal* (Lawrence: University Press of Kansas, 2008).

26 Samuel Beer, "In Search of a New Public Philosophy," in *The New American Political System*, edited by Anthony King (Washington, DC: American Enterprise Institute, 1978).

27 Michael A. Genovese, Todd L. Belt, and William W. Lammers, *The Presidency and Domestic Policy: Comparing Leadership Styles, FDR to Obama*, 2nd ed. (Boulder: Paradigm, 2014).

28 John E. Schwartz, *America's Hidden Success: A Reassessment of Public Policy from Kennedy to Reagan*, rev. ed. (New York: W. W. Norton, 1987).

29 See, for example, "Can Capitalism Survive?," *Time*, July 14, 1975, p. 52; Robert Heilbroner, "Does Capitalism Have a Future?," *New York Times Magazine*, August 5, 1982, p. 20.

30 Richard Neustadt, *Presidential Power: The Politics of Leadership from FDR to Carter*, 3rd ed. (New York: Wiley, 1980), p. 208.

31 Ben J. Wattenberg, "It's Time to Stop America's Retreat," *New York Times Magazine*, July 22, 1979.

5: THE REAGAN REVOLUTION

1 Friedrich Hayek, *The Road to Serfdom* (Chicago: University of Chicago Press, 1944).

2 Milton Friedman and Anna Schwartz, *The Great Contraction: 1929–1933* (Princeton: Princeton University Press, 1965).

3 For a review of Friedman's overall thinking, see *Capitalism and Freedom*, 40th anniversary ed. (Chicago: University of Chicago Press, 2002).

4 See Paul Craig Roberts, *The Supply-Side Revolution: An Insider's Account of Policymaking in Washington* (Cambridge: Harvard University Press, 1984); Brian Domitrovic, *Econoclasts: The Rebels Who Sparked the Supply-Side Revolution and Restored American Prosperity* (Wilmington, DE: ISI Books, 2009); Robert L. Bartley, *The Seven Fat Years ... And How to Do It Again* (New York: Free Press, 1992).

5 George Gilder, *Wealth and Poverty* (New York: Basic Books, 1981); Michael Novak, *The Spirit of Democratic Capitalism* (New York: Simon & Schuster, 1982).

6 Charles Murray, *Losing Ground: U.S. Social Policy, 1950–1980* (New York: Basic Books, 1984).

7 Russell Kirk, *The Conservative Mind: From Burke to Eliot*, 7th rev. ed. (New York: Gateway, 2001).

8 Samuel S. Hill and Dennis E. Owen, *The New Religious Political Right in America* (Nashville: Abingdon, 1982).

9 Peter Steinfels, *The Neoconservatives: The Men Who Are Changing America's Politics* (New York: Simon & Schuster, 1978).

10 Eric R. Crouse, *The Cross and Reaganomics: Conservative Christians Defending Ronald Reagan* (Lanham, MD: Lexington Books, 2013).

11 Andrew E. Busch, *Reagan's Victory: The Presidential Election of 1980 and the Rise of the Right* (Lawrence: University Press of Kansas, 2005), p. 24.

12 See Steven F. Hayward, *The Age of Reagan: The Fall of the Old Liberal Order: 1964–1980*, reprint ed. (New York: Crown Forum, 2009).

13 Andrew E. Busch, *Reagan's Victory: The 1980 Election and the Rise of the Right* (Lawrence: University Press of Kansas, 2005).

14 For biographies of Reagan, see Lou Cannon's *Governor Reagan: Rise to Power* (New York: Public Affairs, 2003) and *President Reagan: Role of a Lifetime*, rev. ed. (New York: Public Affairs, 2000); Edmund Morris, *Dutch: A Memoir of Ronald Reagan* (New York: Modern Library, 2000).

15 Ronald Reagan, *An American Life* (New York: Simon & Schuster, 1990), p. 129.

16 Reagan, *An American Life*, p. 333.

17 Martin Anderson, *Revolution* (New York: Harcourt, Brace, Jovanovich, 1988).

18 Ronald Reagan, "Inaugural Address." Online by Gerhard Peters and John T. Woolley, The American Presidency Project, https://www.presidency.ucsb.edu/node/246336.

19 Samuel Kernell, *Going Public: New Strategies of Presidential Leadership*, 2nd ed. (Washington, DC: Congressional Quarterly, 1993).

20 "Truth in Taxing," *New York Times*, March 10, 1983, p. 26.

21 Bruce Bartlett, "Kennedy's Tax Cuts," National Center for Policy Analysis, January 27, 2004. http://www.ncpa.org/edo/bb/2004/bb-20040128.htm.

22 See Jeffry H. Birnbaum and Alan S. Murray, *Showdown at Gucci Gulch: Lawmakers, Lobbyists, and the Unlikely Triumph of Tax Reform* (New York: Vintage, 1988).

23 See Andrew E. Busch, "Ronald Reagan and Economic Policy," in *The Reagan Presidency: Assessing the Man and His Legacy*, edited by Paul Kengor and Peter Schweizer (Lanham, MD: Rowman & Littlefield, 2005), p. 32.

24 Lou Cannon, *President Reagan: The Role of a Lifetime* (New York: Simon and Schuster, 1991), p. 277.

25 Lawrence Lindsey, *The Growth Experiment* (New York: Basic Books, 1990), pp. 118–20; Richard Nadler, "Special(k)," *National Review*, April 19, 1999, pp. 52–54.

26 Paul C. Light, "The Crisis Last Time: Social Security Reform," Brookings Institution, March 5, 2005, https://www.brookings.edu/opinions/the-crisis-last-time-social-security-reform/.

27 Reagan, *An American Life*, p. 335.

28 For a review of this debate, see Andrew E. Busch, *Ronald Reagan and the Politics of Freedom* (Lanham, MD: Rowman & Littlefield, 2001), pp. 211–17.

29 Arun Venugopal, "Black Leaders Once Championed the Strict Drug Laws They Now Seek to Dismantle," WNYC, August 15, 2013, https://www.wnyc.org/story/312823-black-leaders-once-championed-strict-drug-laws-they-now-seek-dismantle/.

30 Busch, *Ronald Reagan and the Politics of Freedom*, p. 160.

31 Steven K. Wisensale, "Family Policy During the Reagan Years: The Private Side of the Conservative Agenda," in *Ronald Reagan's America*, vol. 1, edited by Eric J. Schmertz, Natalie Datlof, and Alexej Ugrinsky (Westport, CT: Greenwood, 1997), pp. 283–84.

32 Linda Lyons, "The Gallup Brain: Prayer in Public Schools," December 10, 2002, https://news.gallup.com/poll/7393/Gallup-Brain-Prayer-Public-Schools.aspx.

33 Ronald Reagan, "Address Accepting the Presidential Nomination at the Republican National Convention in Detroit." Online by Gerhard Peters and John T. Woolley, The American Presidency Project, https://www.presidency.ucsb.edu/node/251302.

34 Dinesh D'Souza, *Ronald Reagan: How an Ordinary Man Became an Extraordinary Leader* (New York: Free Press, 1997), p. 118.

35 Busch, *Ronald Reagan and the Politics of Freedom*, ch. 2–3.

36 Richard Neustadt, *Presidential Power and the Modern Presidents: The Politics of Leadership from Roosevelt to Reagan* (New York: Free Press, 1990), pp. 269–70.

37 See President Ronald Reagan, Remarks at the investiture of Chief Justice William H. Rehnquist and Associate Justice Antonin Scalia at the White House, September 26, 1986, Washington, DC, *The Great Debate: Interpreting Our Written Constitution* (Washington, DC: The Federalist Society, 1986), pp. 53–56.

38 Richard Nathan, "Institutional Change Under Reagan," in *Perspectives on the Reagan Years*, edited by John L. Palmer (Washington, DC: Urban Institute, 1986), p. 125.

39 Busch, *Ronald Reagan and the Politics of Freedom*, pp. 33–40.

40 Alice M. Rivlin, *Reviving the American Dream* (Washington, DC: Brookings, 1992), p. 109.

41 David M. O'Brien, "The Reagan Judges: His Most Enduring Legacy?," in *The Reagan Legacy: Promise and Performance*, edited by Charles O. Jones (Chatham, NJ: Chatham House, 1988), p. 62.

42 Andrew E. Busch, *The Constitution on the Campaign Trail: The Surprising Career of America's Founding Document* (Lanham, MD: Rowman & Littlefield, 2007).

43 Andrew Balls, "How Deregulation Spurs Growth," National Bureau of Economic Research, January 24, 2019, https://www.nber.org/digest/sep03/w9560.html.

44 Jeremy D. Mayer, "Reagan and Race: Prophet of Color Blindness, Baiter of the Backlash," in *Deconstructing Reagan: Conservative Mythology and America's Fortieth President*, edited by Kyle Longley, Jeremy D. Mayer, Michael Schaller, and John W. Sloan (New York: M. E. Sharpe, 2007), pp. 70–89; Nicholas Laham, *The Reagan Presidency and the Politics of Race: In Pursuit of Color-Blind Justice and Limited Government* (Westport, CT: Praeger, 1998).

45 The National Commission on Excellence in Education, *A Nation at Risk: The Imperative for Educational Reform*, April 1983, https://www2.ed.gov/pubs/NatAtRisk/risk.html.

46 Marc Landy and Sidney M. Milkis, *Presidential Greatness* (Lawrence: University Press of Kansas, 2000), p. 219.

47 "The New Tilt," *Newsweek*, November 20, 1978, p. 44.

48 Busch, *Ronald Reagan and the Politics of Freedom*, pp. 82–87. For an overall defense of Reagan's economic policies, see Anderson, *Revolution*; Bartley, *Seven Fat Years*; Lindsey, *The Growth Experiment*.

49 Kimberly Amadeo, "Savings and Loan Crisis Explained," The Balance, January 24, 2019, https://www.thebalance.com/savings-and-loans-crisis-causes-cost-3306035. For overall critiques of Reagan's economic policies, see Anthony S. Campagna, *The Economy in the Reagan Years: The Economic Consequences of the Reagan Administrations* (Westport, CT: Greenwood, 1994); Donald L. Bartlett and James B. Steele, *America: What Went Wrong?* (Kansas City: Andrews and McNeel, 1990).

50 Bureau of the Census, "Money Incomes of Households, Families, and Persons, 1990," p. 202.

51 Herbert Stein, *Presidential Economics: The Making of Economic Policy from Roosevelt to Clinton* (Washington, DC: AEI, 1994), ch. 7–8.

52 Busch, *Ronald Reagan and the Politics of Freedom*, ch. 5.

53 Busch, *Ronald Reagan and the Politics of Freedom*, ch. 6.

54 Gerald M. Pomper, "The Presidential Election," in *Election of 1988: Reports and Interpretations*, edited by Gerald M. Pomper (Chatham, NJ: Chatham House, 1989).

6: THE BUSH-CLINTON EQUILIBRIUM

1 For biographies of Bush, see John Meacham, *Destiny and Power: The American Odyssey of George Herbert Walker Bush* (New York: Random House, 2015); Timothy Naftali, *George H. W. Bush: The American Presidents Series: The 41st President, 1989–1993* (New York: Times Books, 2007).

2 On the election of 1988, see Gerald M. Pomper, ed., *The Election of 1988: Reports and Interpretations* (Chatham, NJ: Chatham House, 1989).

3 "1990 Budget Enforcement Act," Bancroft Library, http://bancroft.berkeley.edu/ROHO/projects/debt/budgetenforcementact.html.

4 In the House, Democrats supported the deal by a margin of 181–74, while Republicans opposed by 126–47; in the Senate, Democrats supported by 35–20, while Republicans opposed by 25–19. William J. Eaton, "Congress Passes $490-Billion Cut in Deficit; Bush to Sign Bill," *Los Angeles Times*, October 28, 1990, http://articles.latimes.com/1990–10-28/news/mn-5023_1_budget-plan.

5 Meacham, *Destiny and Power*; John Robert Greene, *The Presidency of George H. W. Bush* (Lawrence: University Press of Kansas Press).

6 In 1993, the liberal-leaning *Atlantic Monthly* published a cover story by sociologist Barbara Dafoe Whitehead entitled "Dan Quayle Was Right." Barbara Dafoe Whitehead, "Dan Quayle Was Right," *The Atlantic*, April 1993, https://www.theatlantic.com/magazine/archive/1993/04/dan-quayle-was-right/307015/.

7 George Bush, "Address before a Joint Session of the Congress on the State of the Union," January 28, 1992. Online by Gerhard Peters and John T. Woolley, The American Presidency Project, http://www.presidency.ucsb.edu/ws/?pid=20544.

8 James W. Ceaser and Andrew E. Busch, *Upside Down and Inside Out: The Elections of 1992 and American Politics* (Lanham, MD: Rowman & Littlefield, 1993).

9 For biographies of Bill Clinton, see David Maraniss, *First in His Class: A Biography of Bill Clinton* (New York: Simon & Schuster, 1996); Michael Tomaskey, *Bill Clinton: The American Presidents Series: The 42nd President, 1993–2001* (New York: Times Books, 2017).

10 Kenneth S. Baer, *Reinventing Democrats* (Lawrence: University Press of Kansas, 2000).

11 For a review of policy in this era, see Bob Woodward, *The Agenda: Inside the Clinton White House* (New York: Simon & Schuster, 1994); Colin Campbell and Bert A. Rockman, ed., *The Clinton Legacy* (Chatham, NJ: Chatham House, 2000); Steven Schier, ed., *Postmodern Presidency: Bill Clinton's Legacy in U.S. Politics* (Pittsburgh: University of Pittsburgh Press, 2000); James W. Ceaser and Andrew E. Busch, *Losing to Win: The 1996 Elections and American Politics* (Lanham, MD: Rowman & Littlefield, 1997).

12 David Osborne and Ted Gaebler, *Reinventing Government: How the Entrepreneurial Spirit Is Transforming Government* (New York: Plume, 1993).

13 John Kamensky, "A Brief History," https://govinfo.library.unt.edu/npr/whoweare/history2.html.

14 J. Peter Grace, *War on Waste: President's Private Sector Survey on Cost Control* (New York: Macmillan, 1984).

15 For a history and examination of policy flowing from the Contract, see Major Garrett, *The Enduring Revolution: How the Contract with America Continues to Shape the Nation* (New York: Crown Forum, 2005). For an overall

review of policy, see Campbell and Rockman, ed., *The Clinton Legacy*; Schier, ed., *Postmodern Presidency*; Dick Morris, *Behind the Oval Office* (New York: Random House, 1997).

16 Randall Strahan, *Leading Representatives: The Agency of Leaders in the Politics of the U.S. House* (Baltimore: Johns Hopkins University Press, 2007), ch. 5.

17 William J. Clinton, "Address before a Joint Session of the Congress on the State of the Union," January 23, 1996. Online by Gerhard Peters and John T. Woolley, The American Presidency Project, http://www.presidency.ucsb.edu/ws/?pid=53091.

18 Strahan, *Leading Representatives*, ch. 5.

19 Jerry Gray, "104th Congress Falls Short of Revolution," *New York Times*, September 30, 1996, https://www.nytimes.com/1996/09/30/us/104th-congress-falls-short-of-revolution.html.

20 Ceaser and Busch, *Losing to Win*.

21 Andrew E. Busch, *Horses in Midstream: U.S. Midterm Elections and Their Consequences, 1894–1998* (Pittsburgh: University of Pittsburgh Press, 1999), pp. 149–52.

22 Bert A. Rockman, "Cutting with the Grain: Is There a Clinton Leadership Legacy?," in *The Clinton Legacy*, edited by Colin Campbell and Bert A. Rockman (Chatham, NJ: Chatham House, 1999), p. 293.

23 *The Outcomes of 1996 Welfare Reform*, Congressional Budget Office, July 19, 2006.

24 Agis Salpukas, "Falling Tax Would Lift All Yachts," *New York Times*, February 7, 1992, p. D1; James K. Glassman, "How to Sink an Industry and Not Soak the Rich," *Washington Post*, July 16, 1993, https://www.washingtonpost.com/archive/business/1993/07/16/how-to-sink-an-industry-and-not-soak-the-rich/08ea5310-4a4b-4674-ab88-fad8c42cf55b/?noredirect=on&utm_term=.6c38e759f52b.

25 Robert Kuttner, "The Alarming Parallels between 1929 and 2007," *American Prospect*, October 2, 2007, https://prospect.org/article/alarming-parallels-between-1929-and-2007.

26 On this debate, see Jordan Weissman, "The Failure of Welfare Reform," Slate, June 1, 2016, https://slate.com/news-and-politics/2016/06/how-welfare-reform-failed.html; Scott Winship, "Was Welfare Reform a Success?," Manhattan Institute, June 21, 2016, https://www.manhattan-institute.org/html/issues-2016-welfare-reform-9001.html; Ron Haskins, "Welfare Reform, Success or Failure? It Worked," Brookings Institution, March 15, 2006, https://www.brookings.edu/articles/welfare-reform-success-or-failure-it-worked/.

27 Scott Hodge, Mark Wilson, and William Beach, "Is There a Clinton Crunch?: How the 1993 Budget Plan Affected the Economy," Heritage Foundation, April 1, 1996, https://www.heritage.org/budget-and-spending/report/there-clinton-crunch-how-the-1993-budget-plan-affected-the-economy.

28 For a summary of these arguments, see Joshua Gordon, "Looking Back 20 Years at the 1997 Balanced Budget Agreement," Concord Coalition, August 8, 2017, https://www.concordcoalition.org/blog-post/looking-back-20-years-1997-balanced-budget-agreement.

29 On this debate, see Andrew E. Busch, *Ronald Reagan and the Politics of Freedom* (Lanham, MD: Rowman & Littlefield, 2001), pp. 105–8.

7: GEORGE W. BUSH AND THE REPUBLICAN NON-BREAKOUT

1 On the 2000 election, see James W. Ceaser and Andrew E. Busch, *The Perfect Tie: The True Story of the 2000 Presidential Election* (Lanham, MD: Rowman & Littlefield, 2001).

2 Marvin Olasky, *The Tragedy of American Compassion* (Wheaton, IL: Crossway, 1992).

3 James W. Ceaser and Andrew E. Busch, *Red over Blue: The 2004 Elections and American Politics* (Lanham, MD: Rowman & Littlefield, 2005).

4 For an overall view of policy in the George W. Bush period, see *The George W. Bush Legacy*, edited by Colin Campbell, Bert A. Rockman, and Andrew Rudalevige (Washington, DC: CQ Press, 2008); Steven E. Schier, ed., *High Risk and Big Ambition: Presidency of George W. Bush* (Pittsburgh: University of Pittsburgh Press, 2004); Gary L. Gregg II and Mark J. Rozell, ed., *Considering the Bush Presidency* (New York: Oxford, 2004).

5 Patrick J. McGuinn, *No Child Left Behind and the Transformation of Federal Education Policy, 1965–2005* (Lawrence: University Press of Kansas, 2006).

6 William Ahern, "Comparing the Kennedy, Reagan and Bush Tax Cuts," Tax Foundation, http://www.taxfoundation.org/news/printer/323.html.

7 Department of Homeland Security, Allgov, http://www.allgov.com/departments/department-of-homeland-security?detailsDepartmentID=571.

8 See Fred Barnes, *Rebel in Chief: Inside the Bold and Controversial Presidency of George W. Bush*, reprint ed. (New York: Three Rivers Press, 2006). Barnes coined the phrase "big government conservatism" to describe Bush's program.

9 John J. Diulio, *Godly Republic: A Centrist Blueprint for America's Faith-Based Future—A Former White House Official Explodes Ten Polarizing Myths about Religion and Religion in America Today* (Berkeley: University of California Press, 2007).

10 Dan Balz, "Bush's Ambitious Second-Term Agenda Hits Reality," in *Second-Term Blues: How George W. Bush Has Governed*, edited by John C. Fortier and Norman J. Ornstein (Washington, DC: Brookings/AEI, 2007), pp. 17–38.

11 Richard Stevenson, "Confident Bush Outlines Ambitious Plan for 2nd Term," *New York Times*, November 5, 2004, http://www.nytimes.com/2004/11/05/politics/campaign/05bush.html.

12 Jeffrey M. Jones, "Public Sends Mixed Messages on Social Security Reform," Gallup, April 6, 2005, https://news.gallup.com/poll/15538/public-sends-mixed-messages-social-security-reform.aspx.

13 See Balz, "Bush's Ambitious Second-Term Agenda Hits Reality," pp. 35–36; Fred I. Greenstein, "George W. Bush: The Man and His Leadership," in *Second-Term Blues*, pp. 57–58.

14 See Christopher H. Foreman Jr., "The Braking of the President: Shifting Context and the Bush Domestic Agenda," in *The George W. Bush Legacy*, edited by Colin Campbell, Bert A. Rockman, and Andrew Rudalevige (Washington, DC: CQ Press, 2008), pp. 274–79.

15 Foreman, "The Braking of the President," p. 280.

16 Congressional Research Service, "Welfare Reauthorization in the 109th Congress: An Overview," January 23, 2007, https://www.everycrsreport.com/reports/RL33418.html.

17 Will Kenton, "Troubled Asset Relief Program—TARP," Investopedia, January 30, 2018, https://www.investopedia.com/terms/t/troubled-asset-relief-program-tarp.asp.

18 Andrew E. Busch, *The Constitution on the Campaign Trail: The Surprising Political Career of America's Founding Document* (Lanham, MD: Rowman & Littlefield, 2007), p. 191.

19 Jacob Weisberg, "The Bush Who Got Away," *New York Times*, January 28, 2008, https://www.nytimes.com/2008/01/28/opinion/28weisberg.html.

20 Bruce Bartlett, *Impostor: How George W. Bush Bankrupted America and Betrayed the Reagan Legacy* (New York: Doubleday, 2006).

21 Michael A. Genovese, Todd L. Belt, and William W. Lammers, *The Presidency and Domestic Policy: Comparing Leadership Styles, FDR to Obama* (Boulder: Paradigm, 2014).

22 Robert Kuttner, "The Alarming Parallels between 1929 and 2007," *American Prospect*, October 2, 2007, https://prospect.org/article/alarming-parallels-between-1929-and-2007.

23 Lauren Carroll, "Bill Clinton: Glass-Steagall Repeal Had Nothing to Do with Financial Crisis," Politifact, August 19, 2015, https://www.politifact.com/truth-o-meter/statements/2015/aug/19/bill-clinton/bill-clinton-glass-steagall-had-nothing-do-financi/.

24 See John A. Allison, *The Financial Crisis and the Free Market Cure: How Destructive Banking Reform Is Killing the Economy* (New York: McGraw Hill, 2013), esp. pp. 17–65.

25 Andrew Kahr, "Who's to Blame for the Crisis? The Consumer," American Banker, February 20, 2012, https://www.americanbanker.com/opinion/whos-to-blame-for-the-crisis-the-consumer.

8: NEW DIRECTIONS IN THE WAKE OF THE GREAT RECESSION? THE OBAMA AND TRUMP "TRANSFORMATIONS"

1 Carol E. Lee, "Obama Makes FDR Comparison," Politico, May 27, 2009, https://www.politico.com/story/2009/05/obama-makes-fdr-comparison-023031.

2 Viveca Novak, "Bum Rap for Rahm," FactCheck.org, January 13, 2011, https://www.factcheck.org/2011/01/bum-rap-for-rahm/.

3 James W. Ceaser, Andrew E. Busch, and John J. Pitney, *Epic Journey: The 2008 Elections and American Politics* (Lanham, MD: Rowman & Littlefield, 2009).

4 Exit Polls, CNN ElectionCenter 2008, http://www.cnn.com/ELECTION/2008/results/polls/#val=USP00p3.

5 David Jackson, "Ten Years Ago: Obama Makes National Debut," *USA Today*, July 27, 2014, https://www.usatoday.com/story/theoval/2014/07/27/barack-obama-2004-democratic-convention-john-kerry-john-edwards/13236077/.

6 David J. Garrow, *Rising Star: The Making of Barack Obama* (New York: HarperCollins, 2017).

7 Thomas Piketty, *The Economics of Inequality* (Cambridge: Belknap, 2015).

8 See Andrew E. Busch, "The Limits of Governmental Accomplishment: Obama's Domestic Policies," in *Debating the Obama Presidency*, edited by Steven

E. Schier (Lanham, MD: Rowman & Littlefield, 2016), pp. 196–97; Stanley A. Renshon, *Barack Obama and the Politics of Redemption* (New York: Routledge, 2012), pp. 240–43.

9 Justin Wolfers, "The Fed Has Not Stopped Trying to Stimulate the Economy," *New York Times*, October 29, 2014.

10 See Garrow, *Rising Star*, pp. 1053, 1058, 1060, 1067, 1075; Busch, "The Limits of Governmental Accomplishment," pp. 203–8; Ruth O'Brien, "Progress and Good Governance in Domestic Policy," in *Debating the Obama Presidency*, edited by Steven E. Schier (Lanham, MD: Rowman & Littlefield, 2016), pp. 172–75.

11 Busch, "The Limits of Governmental Accomplishment," pp. 197–98.

12 Bryan Walsh, "Why the Climate Bill Died," *Time*, July 26, 2010, http://science.time.com/2010/07/26/why-the-climate-bill-died/.

13 Theda Skocpol and Vanessa Williamson, *The Tea Party and the Remaking of Republican Conservatism* (New York: Oxford, 2013); Elizabeth Price Foley, *The Tea Party: Three Principles* (New York: Cambridge, 2012).

14 Alan Abramowitz, *The Great Alignment* (New Haven: Yale, 2018).

15 Chantal da Silva, "Has Occupy Wall Street Changed America?," *Newsweek*, September 19, 2018, https://www.newsweek.com/has-occupy-wall-street-changed-america-seven-years-birth-political-movement-1126364.

16 Paul Krugman, "Krugman and Obama's Dangerous Austerity Myths," *Huffington Post*, January 11, 2013, https://www.huffingtonpost.com/william-k-black/krugman-austerity-myth_b_2458906.html.

17 James W. Ceaser, Andrew E. Busch, and John J. Pitney Jr., *After Hope and Change: The 2012 Elections and American Politics*, post midterm election ed. (Lanham, MD: Rowman & Littlefield, 2015).

18 For policy in this period, see Busch, "The Limits of Governmental Accomplishment."

19 Department of Justice, "Department of Justice Report Regarding the Criminal Investigation into the Shooting Death of Michael Brown by Ferguson, Missouri Police Officer Darren Wilson," March 4, 2015, https://www.justice.gov/sites/default/files/opa/press-releases/attachments/2015/03/04/doj_report_on_shooting_of_michael_brown_1.pdf.

20 Victor Davis Hanson, "A Tale of Two Shootings," PJ Media, November 9, 2015, http://pjmedia.com/victordavishanson/tale-of-two-shootings/?print=1

21 Department of Education, "Every Student Succeeds Act (ESSA)," https://www.ed.gov/essa.

22 Busch, "The Limits of Governmental Accomplishment," pp. 212–13.

23 Renshon, *Barack Obama and the Politics of Redemption*, p. 231.

24 Norm Ornstein, "Yes, Polarization Is Asymmetric—and Conservatives Are Worse," *The Atlantic*, June 14, 2014, https://www.theatlantic.com/politics/archive/2014/06/yes-polarization-is-asymmetric-and-conservatives-are-worse/373044/; "Political Polarization in the American Public," Pew Research Center, June 12, 2014, http://www.people-press.org/2014/06/12/political-polarization-in-the-american-public/.

25 Bill Scher, "Obama vs. FDR, Year Seven," RealClearPolitics, February 9, 2015, https://www.realclearpolitics.com/articles/2015/02/09/obama_vs_fdr_year_seven_125526.html.

26 Molly Ball, "What Obama Really Did to Welfare Reform," *The Atlantic*, August 9, 2012, https://www.theatlantic.com/politics/archive/2012/08/what-obama-really-did-to-welfare-reform/260931/.

27 Paul Krugman, "The Obama Boom," *New York Times*, January 16, 2017, https://www.nytimes.com/2016/01/11/opinion/the-obama-boom.html.

28 Kate Davidson, "Economy Grows But Stays in Its Rut," *Wall Street Journal*, July 31, 2015, p. A1, 2.

29 Jeb Hensaerling, "After Five Years, Dodd-Frank Is a Failure," *Wall Street Journal*, July 20, 2015, p. A15; Matt O'Brien, "The Middle Class Is Poorer Than It Was in 1989," *Washington Post*, October 1, 2014, https://www.washington-post.com/news/wonk/wp/2014/10/01/the-middle-class-is-poorer-today-than-it-was-in-1989/?noredirect=on&utm_term=.69d695c90ab6.

30 Phil Gramm, "What's Wrong with the Golden Goose?," *Wall Street Journal*, April 21, 2015, p. A19.

31 Sally Pipes, "Unhappy Birthday, Obamacare: Five Years after Its Signing, the Affordable Care Act Is Failing to Live Up to Its Promise," *New York Daily News*, March 23, 2015, http://www.nydailynews.com/opinion/sally-pipes-unhap-py-birthday-obamacare-article-1.2157297.

32 "Businesses Eliminated Hundreds of Thousands of Full-Time Jobs to Avoid Obamacare Mandate," MarketWatch, November 24, 2017, https://www.market-watch.com/story/businesses-eliminated-hundreds-of-thousands-of-full-time-jobs-to-avoid-obamacare-mandate-2017–11-24.

33 David Cay Johnston, *The Making of Donald Trump* (London: Melville House, 2017).

34 James W. Ceaser, Andrew E. Busch, and John J. Pitney Jr., *Defying the Odds: The 2016 Elections and American Politics* (Lanham, MD: Rowman & Littlefield, 2017).

35 Charles Murray, *Coming Apart: The State of White America, 1960–2010* (New York: Crown, 2012).

36 See Selena Zito and Brad Todd, *The Great Revolt*.

37 Dylan Scott and Sarah Kliff, "Why Obamacare Repeal Failed," Vox, July 31, 2017, https://www.vox.com/policy-and-politics/2017/7/31/16055960/why-obamacare-repeal-failed; M. J. Lee and Lauren Fox, "Bruised Republicans Regroup after Obamacare Repeal Fail," CNN, September 27, 2017, https://www.cnn.com/2017/09/27/politics/bruised-republicans-regroup-after-obamacare-re-peal-fail/index.html.

38 Preliminary Details and Analysis of the Tax Cuts and Jobs Act, The Tax Foundation, December 18, 2017, https://taxfoundation.org/final-tax-cuts-and-jobs-act-details-analysis/.

39 House Republican Conference, "Signed into Law: Congressional Review Act (CRA) Resolutions," June 1, 2018, https://www.gop.gov/cra/.

40 For an examination of Trump's efforts here in just his first year in office, see Juliet Eilperin and Darla Cameron, "How Trump Is Rolling Back Obama's Legacy," *Washington Post*, January 20, 2018, https://www.washingtonpost.com/graphics/politics/trump-rolling-back-obama-rules/?utm_term=.884eda1d2005.

41 Christian Farias, "A New Romance: Trump Has Made Progressives Fall in Love with Federalism," *New York Magazine*, August 24, 2017, http://nymag.com/intelli-gencer/2017/08/trump-has-made-progressives-fall-in-love-with-federalism.html.

42 Jeffrey M. Jones, "Trump Approval More Stable Than Approval for Prior Presidents," Gallup, December 21, 2018, https://news.gallup.com/opinion/polling-matters/245567/trump-approval-stable-approval-prior-presidents.aspx.

43 James W. Ceaser, Andrew E. Busch, and John J. Pitney Jr., *Defying the Odds: The 2016 Elections and American Politics*, post-midterm election ed. (Lanham, MD: Rowman & Littlefield, 2019).

44 Andrew Prokop, "Trump's Free Ride from Congress Just Ended," Vox, November 7, 2018, https://www.vox.com/2018/11/6/18025036/election-results-democrats-win-house-trump-investigations-analysis.

45 Sophie Tatum, "Bipartisan Criminal Justice Bill Clears Congress," CNN, December 20, 2018, https://www.cnn.com/2018/12/20/politics/house-pass-criminal-justice-first-step-bill/index.html.

CONCLUSION

1 David Mayhew, *Divided We Govern: Party Control, Lawmaking, and Investigations, 1946–2002*, 2nd ed. (New Haven: Yale, 2005).

2 James R. Curry and Frances Lee, "Congress Is Far More Bipartisan Than Headlines Suggest," *Washington Post*, December 20, 2016, https://www.washingtonpost.com/news/monkey-cage/wp/2016/12/20/congress-is-far-more-bipartisan-than-headlines-suggest/?noredirect=on&utm_term=.67d25968b097.

Bibliography

★ ★ ★

Abramowitz, Alan. *The Great Alignment*. New Haven: Yale University Press, 2018.

Ahern, William. "Comparing the Kennedy, Reagan and Bush Tax Cuts," Tax Foundation, http://www.taxfoundation.org/news/printer/323.html.

Alesina, Alberto, and Francesco Passarelli. "Loss Aversion in Politics," February 2017, https://scholar.harvard.edu/files/alesina/files/ap-lossaversion-8feb-2017-_002.pdf.

Allison, John A. *The Financial Crisis and the Free Market Cure: How Destructive Banking Reform Is Killing the Economy*. New York: McGraw Hill, 2013.

Amadeo, Kimberly. "Savings and Loan Crisis Explained," The Balance, January 24, 2019, https://www.thebalance.com/savings-and-loans-crisis-causes-cost-3306035.

Ambrose, Stephen E. *Eisenhower: Soldier and President*, rev. ed. New York: Simon & Schuster, 1991.

Anderson, Martin. *Revolution*. New York: Harcourt, Brace, Jovanovich, 1988.

Andrews, John A., III. *Lyndon Johnson and the Great Society*. New York: Ivan R. Dee, 1999.

Arthur, Don. "Pedantic Fact Checking—Did Nixon Really Say 'We Are All Keynesians Now'?" Club Troppo, February 15, 2009, http://clubtroppo.com.au/2009/02/15/pedantic-fact-checking-did-nixon-really-say-we-are-keynesians-now/.

Baer, Kenneth S. *Reinventing Democrats*. Lawrence: University Press of Kansas, 2000.

Ball, Molly. "What Obama Really Did to Welfare Reform," *The Atlantic*, August 9, 2012, https://www.theatlantic.com/politics/archive/2012/08/what-obama-really-did-to-welfare-reform/260931/.

Ball, Robert M. "Social Security Amendments of 1972: Summary and Legislative History," Social Security Administration, https://www.ssa.gov/history/1972amend.html.

Balls, Andrew. "How Deregulation Spurs Growth," National Bureau of Economic Research, January 24, 2019, https://www.nber.org/digest/sep03/w9560.html.

Balz, Dan. "Bush's Ambitious Second-Term Agenda Hits Reality," in *Second-Term Blues: How George W. Bush Has Governed*, edited by John C. Fortier and Norman J. Ornstei. Washington, DC: Brookings/AEI, 2007. pp. 17–38.

Bardach, Eugene. *A Practical Guide for Policy Analysis: The Eightfold Path to More Effective Problem Solving*. New York: Chatham House, 2000.

Barnes, Fred. *Rebel in Chief: Inside the Bold and Controversial Presidency of George W. Bush*, reprint ed. New York: Three Rivers Press, 2006.

Barone, Michael. *Our Country: America from Roosevelt to Reagan*. New York: Free Press, 1990.

Bartlett, Bruce. *Impostor: How George W. Bush Bankrupted America and Betrayed the Reagan Legacy*. New York: Doubleday, 2006.

Bartlett, Bruce. "Kennedy's Tax Cuts," National Center for Policy Analysis, January 27, 2004. http://www.ncpa.org/edo/bb/2004/bb-20040128.htm.

Bartlett, Donald L., and James B. Steele, *America: What Went Wrong?* Kansas City: Andrews and McNeel, 1990.

Bartley, Robert L. *The Seven Fat Years ... And How to Do It Again*. New York: Free Press, 1992.

Beer, Samuel. "In Search of a New Public Philosophy," in *The New American Political System*, edited by Anthony King. Washington, DC: American Enterprise Institute, 1978.

Berlau, John. "Ted Kennedy's Deregulatory Legacy on Airlines and Trucking," Competitive Enterprise Institute, August 26, 2009, https://cei.org/blog/ted-kennedys-deregulatory-legacy-airlines-and-trucking.

Birnbaum, Jeffry H., and Alan S. Murray. *Showdown at Gucci Gulch: Lawmakers, Lobbyists, and the Unlikely Triumph of Tax Reform*. New York: Vintage, 1988.

Bourne, Peter G. *Jimmy Carter: A Comprehensive Biography from Plains to Post-Presidency*. New York: Scribner, 1997.

Bovens, Mark, and Paul 'T Hart. "Assessing Policy Outcomes: Social and Political Biases," *Understanding Policy Fiascoes*. New Brunswick, NJ: Transaction, 1996.

Brands, H. W. *Traitor to His Class: The Privileged Life and Radical Presidency of Franklin Delano Roosevelt*. New York: Doubleday, 2008.

Braybrooke, David, and Charles E. Lindblom. *A Strategy of Decision*. New York: Free Press, 1963.

Burns, James MacGregor. *Roosevelt: The Lion and the Fox*. New York: Harcourt, Brace, and Company, 1956.

Burrough, Bryan. "The Bombings of America That We Forgot," *Time*, September 20, 2016, http://time.com/4501670/bombings-of-america-burrough/.

Busch, Andrew E. *The Constitution on the Campaign Trail: The Surprising Career of America's Founding Document*. Lanham, MD: Rowman & Littlefield, 2007.

Busch, Andrew E. *Horses in Midstream: U.S. Midterm Elections and Their Consequences, 1894–1998*. Pittsburgh: University of Pittsburgh Press, 1999.

Busch, Andrew E. "The Limits of Governmental Accomplishment: Obama's Domestic Policies," in *Debating the Obama Presidency*, edited by Steven E. Schier. Lanham, MD: Rowman & Littlefield, 2016. pp. 196–97.

Busch, Andrew E. *Outsiders and Openness in the Presidential Nominating System*. Pittsburgh: University of Pittsburgh Press, 1997.

Busch, Andrew E. *Reagan's Victory: The 1980 Election and the Rise of the Right*. Lawrence: University Press of Kansas, 2005.

Busch, Andrew E. "Ronald Reagan and Economic Policy," in *The Reagan Presidency: Assessing the Man and His Legacy*, edited by Paul Kengor and Peter Schweizer. Lanham, MD: Rowman & Littlefield, 2005. p. 32.

Busch, Andrew E. *Ronald Reagan and the Politics of Freedom*. Lanham, MD: Rowman & Littlefield, 2001.

Busch, Andrew E. *Truman's Triumphs: The 1948 Election and the Making of Postwar America*. Lawrence: University Press of Kansas, 2012.

Bush, George. "Address before a Joint Session of the Congress on the State of the Union," January 28, 1992. Online by Gerhard Peters and John T. Woolley, The American Presidency Project, http://www.presidency.ucsb.edu/ws/?pid=20544.

Campagna, Anthony S. *The Economy in the Reagan Years: The Economic Consequences of the Reagan Administrations*. Westport, CT: Greenwood, 1994.

Campbell, Colin, and Bert A. Rockman, eds. *The Clinton Legacy*. Chatham, NJ: Chatham House, 2000.

Campbell, Colin, Bert A. Rockman, and Andrew Rudalevige. *The George W. Bush Legacy*. Washington, DC: CQ Press, 2008.

Cannon, James. *Gerald R. Ford: An Honorable Life*. Ann Arbor: University of Michigan Press, 2013.

Cannon, Lou. *Governor Reagan: Rise to Power*. New York: Public Affairs, 2003.

Cannon, Lou. *President Reagan: The Role of a Lifetime*. New York: Simon and Schuster, 1991.

Capretta, James, and Kevin Dyaratna. "Compelling Evidence Makes the Case for a Market-Driven Health Care System," The Heritage Foundation, December 20, 2013, https://www.heritage.org/health-care-reform/report/compelling-evidence-makes-the-case-market-driven-health-care-system.

Carroll, Aaron E. "The Real Reason the U.S. Has Employer-Sponsored Health Insurance," *New York Times*, September 5, 2017, https://www.nytimes.com/2017/09/05/upshot/the-real-reason-the-us-has-employer-sponsored-health-insurance.html.

Carroll, Lauren. "Bill Clinton: Glass-Steagall Repeal Had Nothing to Do with Financial Crisis," Politifact, August 19, 2015, https://www.politifact.com/truth-o-meter/statements/2015/aug/19/bill-clinton/bill-clinton-glass-steagall-had-nothing-do-financi/.

Carson, Rachel. *Silent Spring*. New York: Houghton Mifflin, 1962.

Carter, Jimmy. "Social Security Amendments of 1977," December 20, 1977, https://www.ssa.gov/history/carterstmts.html#77.

Carter, Jimmy. "The State of the Union Address Delivered before a Joint Session of the Congress," January 19, 1978. Online by Gerhard Peters and John T. Woolley, The American Presidency Project, http://www.presidency.ucsb.edu/ws/?pid=30856.

Caute, David. *The Great Fear: The Anti-Communist Purge under Truman and Eisenhower*. New York: Simon & Schuster, 1978.

Ceaser, James W., and Andrew E. Busch. *Losing to Win: The 1996 Elections and American Politics*. Lanham, MD: Rowman & Littlefield, 1997.

Ceaser, James W., and Andrew E. Busch. *The Perfect Tie: The True Story of the 2000 Presidential Election*. Lanham, MD: Rowman & Littlefield, 2001.

Ceaser, James W., and Andrew E. Busch. *Red over Blue: The 2004 Elections and American Politics*. Lanham, MD: Rowman & Littlefield, 2005.

Ceaser, James W., and Andrew E. Busch. *Upside Down and Inside Out: The Elections of 1992 and American Politics*. Lanham, MD: Rowman & Littlefield, 1993.

Ceaser, James W., Andrew E. Busch, and John J. Pitney Jr. *After Hope and Change: The 2012 Elections and American Politics*, post midterm election ed. Lanham, MD: Rowman & Littlefield, 2015.

Ceaser, James W., Andrew E. Busch, and John J. Pitney Jr. *Defying the Odds: The 2016 Elections and American Politics*. Lanham, MD: Rowman & Littlefield, 2017.

Ceaser, James W., Andrew E. Busch, and John J. Pitney Jr. *Epic Journey: The 2008 Elections and American Politics*. Lanham, MD: Rowman & Littlefield, 2009.

Clinton, William J. "Address before a Joint Session of the Congress on the State of the Union," January 23, 1996. Online by Gerhard Peters and John T. Woolley, The American Presidency Project, http://www.presidency.ucsb.edu/ws/?pid=53091.

Cohen, Wilbur J. "1965: Year of Legislative Achievements in Health, Education, and Welfare," Archive.org, https://archive.org/stream/1965yearoflegisl00gard/1965yearoflegisl00gard_djvu.txt.

Collier, Peter, and David Horowitz. *Destructive Generation: Second Thoughts about the 1960s*. New York: Encounter Books, 2005.

Collins, Francis H. *The Frustration of Politics: Truman, Congress, and the Loyalty Issue*. Rutherford: Farleigh Dickinson University Press, 1979.

Congressional Research Service, "Welfare Reauthorization in the 109th Congress: An Overview," January 23, 2007, https://www.everycrsreport.com/reports/RL33418.html.

Crouse, Eric R. *The Cross and Reaganomics: Conservative Christians Defending Ronald Reagan*. Lanham, MD: Lexington Books, 2013.

Curry, James R., and Frances Lee. "Congress Is Far More Bipartisan Than Headlines Suggest," *Washington Post*, December 20, 2016, https://www.washingtonpost.com/news/monkey-cage/wp/2016/12/20/congress-is-far-more-bipartisan-than-headlines-suggest/?noredirect=on&utm_term=.67d25968b097.

Daggett, Stephen. "Costs of Major U.S. Wars," Service, June 29, 2010, https://fas.org/sgp/crs/natsec/RS22926.pdf.

Dalle, Matthew. *Franklin Roosevelt: A Political Life*. New York: Viking, 2017.

Davidson, Kate. "Economy Grows But Stays in Its Rut," *Wall Street Journal*, July 31, 2015, p. A1, 2.

Department of Education, "Every Student Succeeds Act (ESSA)," https://www.ed.gov/essa.

Department of Justice, "Department of Justice Report Regarding the Criminal Investigation into the Shooting Death of Michael Brown by Ferguson, Missouri Police Officer Darren Wilson," March 4, 2015, https://www.justice.gov/sites/default/files/opa/press-releases/attachments/2015/03/04/doj_report_on_shooting_of_michael_brown_1.pdf.

Dewey, John. *The Public and Its Problems*. Athens: Ohio University Press, 1927.

Dilulio, John J. *Godly Republic: A Centrist Blueprint for America's Faith-Based Future—A Former White House Official Explodes Ten Polarizing Myths about Religion and Government in America Today*. Berkeley: University of California Press, 2007.

Domitrovic, Brian. *Econoclasts: The Rebels Who Sparked the Supply-Side Revolution and Restored American Prosperity*. Wilmington, DE: ISI Books, 2009.

D'Souza, Dinesh. *Ronald Reagan: How an Ordinary Man Became an Extraordinary Leader*. New York: Free Press, 1997.

Eaton, William J. "Congress Passes $490-Billion Cut in Deficit Bush to Sign Bill," *Los Angeles Times*, October 28, 1990, http://articles.latimes.com/1990–10-28/news/mn-5023_1_budget-plan.

Eilperin, Juliet, and Darla Cameron. "How Trump Is Rolling Back Obama's Legacy," *Washington Post*, January 20, 2018, https://www.washington-post.com/graphics/politics/trump-rolling-back-obama-rules/?utm_term=.884eda1d2005.

Einstein, Allen. *Perjury: The Hiss-Chambers Case*. New York: Random House, 1997.

Eizenstat, Stuart E. *President Carter: The White House Years*. New York: Thomas Dunne Books, 2018.

Farias, Christian. "A New Romance: Trump Has Made Progressives Fall in Love with Federalism," *New York Magazine*, August 24, 2017, http://nymag.com/intelligencer/2017/08/trump-has-made-progressives-fall-in-love-with-federalism.html.

Farrell, John A. *Richard Nixon: The Life*. New York: Doubleday, 2017.

Feldman, Martha S. *Order without Design: Information Production and Policy Making*. Palo Alto: Stanford University Press, 1989.

Ferrell, Robert H. *Harry S. Truman*. Columbia: University of Missouri Press, 1994.

Fischer, Frank. *Reframing Public Policy: Discursive Politics and Deliberative Practices*. New York: Oxford University Press, 2003.

Fleming, Thomas. *The New Dealers' War: F.D.R. and the War within World War II*. New York: Basic Books, 2001.

Foreman, Christopher H., Jr. "The Braking of the President: Shifting Context and the Bush Domestic Agenda," in *The George W. Bush Legacy*, edited by Colin Campbell, Bert A. Rockman, and Andrew Rudalevige. Washington, DC: CQ Press, 2008. pp. 274–79.

Friedman, Milton, and Anna Jacobson Schwartz. *The Great Contraction: 1929–1933*, new ed. Princeton, NJ: Princeton University Press, 2008.

Gaddis, John Lewis. *Strategies of Containment: A Critical Appraisal of American National Security Policy During the Cold War*, rev. ed. New York: Oxford, 2005.

Galbraith, John Kenneth. *The Affluent Society*. New York: Houghton Mifflin Harcourt, 1958.

Garrett, Major. *The Enduring Revolution: How the Contract with America Continues to Shape the Nation*. New York: Crown Forum, 2005.

Garrow, David J. *Rising Star: The Making of Barack Obama*. New York: HarperCollins, 2017.

Genovese, Michael A., Todd L. Belt, and William W. Lammers. *The Presidency and Domestic Policy: Comparing Leadership Styles, FDR to Obama*, 2nd ed. Boulder: Paradigm, 2014.

Giglio, James N. *The Presidency of John F. Kennedy*, 2nd rev. ed. Lawrence: University Press of Kansas, 2006.

Gilder, George. *Wealth and Poverty*. New York: Basic Books, 1981.

Glassman, James K. "How to Sink an Industry and Not Soak the Rich," *Washington Post*, July 16, 1993, https://www.washingtonpost.com/archive/business/1993/07/16/how-to-sink-an-industry-and-not-soak-the-rich/08ea5310-4a4b-4674-ab88-fad8c42cf55b/?noredirect=on&utm_term=.6c38e759f52b.

Goodwin, Doris. "The Way We Won: America's Economic Breakthrough during World War II," *The American Prospect*, Fall 1992, https://prospect.org/article/way-we-won-americas-economic-breakthrough-during-world-war-ii.

Goodwyn, Lawrence. *The Populist Moment*. New York: Oxford Press, 1978.

Gordon, Joshua. "Looking Back 20 Years at the 1997 Balanced Budget Agreement," Concord Coalition, August 8, 2017, https://www.concordcoalition.org/blog-post/looking-back-20-years-1997-balanced-budget-agreement.

Gould, Lewis L. ed. *The Progressive Era*. Syracuse: Syracuse University Press, 1974.

Grace, J. Peter. *War on Waste: President's Private Sector Survey on Cost Control*. New York: Macmillan, 1984.

Gramm, Phil. "What's Wrong with the Golden Goose?," *Wall Street Journal*, April 21, 2015, p. A19.

Grant, James. *The Forgotten Depression, 1921: The Depression That Cured Itself*. New York: Simon & Schuster, 2015.

Gray, Jerry. "104th Congress Falls Short of Revolution," *New York Times*, September 30, 1996, https://www.nytimes.com/1996/09/30/us/104th-congress-falls-short-of-revolution.html.

Greene, John Robert. *The Presidency of George H. W. Bush*. Lawrence: University Press of Kansas.

Greenstein, Fred I. "George W. Bush: The Man and His Leadership," in *Second-Term Blues: How George W. Bush Has Governed*, edited by John C. Fortier and Norman J. Ornstei. Washington, DC: Brookings/AEI, 2007. pp. 57–58.

Gregg, Gary L., II, and Mark J. Rozell, ed. *Considering the Bush Presidency*. New York: Oxford, 2004.

Griswold, Daniel. "The Unhappy 40th Anniversary of Nixon's Wage and Price Controls," Cato Institute, August 15, 2011, https://www.cato.org/blog/unhappy-40th-anniversary-nixons-wage-price-controls.

Grodzins, Morton. "The Federal System," in *American Government Readings and Cases*, edited by P. Woll. New York: Pearson Longman, 2004. pp. 74–78.

Grossman, Michael B., Martha Joynt Kumar, and Francis E. Rourke. "Second-Term Presidencies: The Aging of Administrations," in *The Presidency and the Political System*, 6th ed. edited by Michael Nelson. Washington, DC: CQ Press, 2000. p. 223.

Hamby, Alonzo L. *For the Survival of Democracy: Franklin Roosevelt and the World Crisis of the 1930s*. New York: Free Press, 2004.

Hamby, Alonzo L. *Man of the People: A Life of Harry S. Truman*. New York: Onford Press, 1995.

Hanson, Victor Davis. "A Tale of Two Shootings," PJ Media, November 9, 2015, http://pjmedia.com/victordavishanson/tale-of-two-shootings/?print=1.

Harrington, Michael. *The Other America: Poverty in the United States*. New York: Macmillan, 1962.

Hartmann, Susan M. *Truman and the 80th Congress*. Columbia: University of Missouri Press, 1971.

Haskins, Ron. "Welfare Reform, Success or Failure? It Worked," Brookings Institution, March 15, 2006, https://www.brookings.edu/articles/welfare-reform-success-or-failure-it-worked/.

Hayek, Friedrich. *The Road to Serfdom*. Chicago: University of Chicago Press, 1944.

Haynes, John Earl, and Harvey Klehr. *Venona: Decoding Soviet Espionage in America*, new ed. New Haven: Yale Press, 2000.

Hayward, Steven F. *The Age of Reagan: The Fall of the Old Liberal Order: 1964–1980*, reprint ed. New York: Crown Forum, 2009.

Heilbroner, Robert. "Does Capitalism Have a Future?," *New York Times Magazine*, August 5, 1982, p. 20.

Hensaerling, Jeb. "After Five Years, Dodd-Frank Is a Failure," *Wall Street Journal*, July 20, 2015, p. A15.

Hicks, John D. *The Populist Revolt*. Minneapolis: University of Minnesota Press, 1931.

Higgs, Robert. "The New Deal and the State and Local Governments," Foundation for Economic Education, March 1, 2008, https://fee.org/articles/the-new-deal-and-the-state-and-local-governments/.

Higgs, Robert. "Wartime Origins of Modern Income-Tax Withholding," Foundation for Economic Education, November 1, 2007, https://fee.org/articles/wartime-origins-of-modern-income-tax-withholding/.

Hill, Samuel S., and Dennis E. Owen, *The New Religious Political Right in America*. Nashville: Abingdon, 1982.

Hodge, Scott, Mark Wilson, and William Beach, "Is There a Clinton Crunch?: How the 1993 Budget Plan Affected the Economy," Heritage Foundation, April 1, 1996, https://www.heritage.org/budget-and-spending/report/there-clinton-crunch-how-the-1993-budget-plan-affected-the-economy.

Hofstadter, Richard. *The Progressive Movement, 1900–1915*. Englewood Cliffs: Prentice-Hall, 1963.

Hollingsworth, J. Rogers. *The Whirligig of Politics: The Democracy of Cleveland and Bryan*. Chicago: University of Chicago Press, 1963.

House Republican Conference, "Signed into Law: Congressional Review Act. CRA. Resolutions," June 1, 2018, https://www.gop.gov/cra/.

Ippolito, Dennis S. *Congressional Spending*. Ithaca: Cornell University Press, 1981.

Jackson, David. "Ten Years Ago: Obama Makes National Debut," *USA Today*, July 27, 2014, https://www.usatoday.com/story/theoval/2014/07/27/barack-obama-2004-democratic-convention-john-kerry-john-edwards/13236077/.

Johnson, Lyndon B. "Remarks at the University of Michigan," May 22, 1964. Online by Gerhard Peters and John T. Woolley, The American Presidency Project, http://www.presidency.ucsb.edu/ws/?pid=26262.

Johnson, Lyndon B. *Vantage Point: Perspectives on the Presidency 1963–1969.* New York: Holt, Rinehart, and Winston, 1971.

Johnson, Paul. *Modern Times: From the Twenties to the Nineties,* rev. ed. New York: HarperCollins, 1991.

Johnston, David Cay. *The Making of Donald Trump.* London: Melville House, 2017.

Jones, Bryan, Frank Baumgartner, and James True. "Policy Punctuations: U.S. Budget Authority, 1947–1995," *Journal of Politics,* 60(February 1998), 1–33.

Jones, Jeffrey M. "Public Sends Mixed Messages on Social Security Reform," Gallup, April 6, 2005, https://news.gallup.com/poll/15538/public-sends-mixed-messages-social-security-reform.aspx.

Jones, Jeffrey M. "Trump Approval More Stable Than Approval for Prior Presidents," Gallup, December 21, 2018, https://news.gallup.com/opinion/polling-matters/245567/trump-approval-stable-approval-prior-presidents.aspx.

Kabaservice, Geoffrey. "Leading as a True Conservative: Eisenhower, the GOP, and the Politics of Fiscal Responsibility," in *The Eisenhower Presidency: Lessons for the Twenty-First Century,* edited by Andrew J. Polsky. Lanham, MD: Lexington Books, 2015. p. 41.

Kahr, Andrew. "Who's to Blame for the Crisis? The Consumer," American Banker, February 20, 2012, https://www.americanbanker.com/opinion/whos-to-blame-for-the-crisis-the-consumer.

Kamensky, John. "A Brief History," https://govinfo.library.unt.edu/npr/whoweare/history2.html.

Kaufman, Scott. *Ambition, Pragmatism, and Party: A Political Biography of Gerald R. Ford.* Lawrence: University Press of Kansas, 2017.

Kennedy, John F. "Address of Senator John F. Kennedy Accepting the Democratic Party Nomination for the Presidency of the United States—Memorial Coliseum, Los Angeles," July 15, 1960. Online by Gerhard Peters and John T. Woolley, The American Presidency Project, http://www.presidency.ucsb.edu/ws/?pid=25966.

Kennedy, John F. "Inaugural Address." Online by Gerhard Peters and John T. Woolley, The American Presidency Project, https://www.presidency.ucsb.edu/node/234470.

Kenton, Will. "Troubled Asset Relief Program—TARP," Investopedia, January 30, 2018, https://www.investopedia.com/terms/t/troubled-asset-relief-program-tarp.asp.

Kernell, Samuel. *Going Public: New Strategies of Presidential Leadership,* 2nd ed. Washington, DC: Congressional Quarterly, 1993.

Keyes, John Maynard. *The End of Laissez-Faire: The Consequences of the Peace.* Hogarth Press, 1926.

Kingdon, David. "Politicians, Self-Interest, and Ideas," in *Reconsidering the Democratic Public,* edited by George E. Marcus and Russell L. Hanson. University Park: Pennsylvania State University, 1993.

Kingdon, John. *Agendas, Alternatives, and Public Policies*. Boston: Little, Brown, 1984.

Kirk, Russell. *The Conservative Mind: From Burke to Eliot*, 7th rev. ed. New York: Gateway, 2001.

Krugman, Paul. "Krugman and Obama's Dangerous Austerity Myths," *Huffington Post*, January 11, 2013, https://www.huffingtonpost.com/william-k-black/krugman-austerity-myth_b_2458906.html.

Krugman, Paul. "The Obama Boom," *New York Times*, January 16, 2017, https://www.nytimes.com/2016/01/11/opinion/the-obama-boom.html.

Kuhn, Thomas. *The Structure of Scientific Revolutions*, 2nd ed. Chicago: University of Chicago Press, 1970.

Kuttner, Robert. "The Alarming Parallels between 1929 and 2007," *American Prospect*, October 2, 2007, https://prospect.org/article/alarming-parallels-between-1929-and-2007.

Laham, Nicholas. *The Reagan Presidency and the Politics of Race: In Pursuit of Color-Blind Justice and Limited Government*. Westport, CT: Praeger, 1998.

Landy, Marc, and Sidney M. Milkis, *Presidential Greatness*. Lawrence: University Press of Kansas, 2000. p. 219.

Lawrence, Mark Atwood. "How Vietnam Killed the Great Society," *New York Times*, September 22, 2017, https://www.nytimes.com/2017/09/22/opinion/vietnam-war-great-society.html.

Lee, Carol E. "Obama Makes FDR Comparison," Politico, May 27, 2009, https://www.politico.com/story/2009/05/obama-makes-fdr-comparison-023031.

Lee, M. J., and Lauren Fox. "Bruised Republicans Regroup after Obamacare Repeal Fail," CNN, September 27, 2017, https://www.cnn.com/2017/09/27/politics/bruised-republicans-regroup-after-obamacare-repeal-fail/index.html.

Leuchtenburg, William E. *Franklin D. Roosevelt and the New Deal 1932–1940*. New York: Harper & Row, 1963.

Library of Congress, "The Civil Rights Act of 1964: A Long Struggle for Freedom," https://www.loc.gov/exhibits/civil-rights-act/world-war-ii-and-post-war.html.

Light, Paul C. "The Crisis Last Time: Social Security Reform," Brookings Institution, March 5, 2005, https://www.brookings.edu/opinions/the-crisis-last-time-social-security-reform/.

Lindsey, Lawrence. *The Growth Experiment*. New York: Basic Books, 1990.

Lowi, Theodore. "Four Systems of Policy, Politics, and Choice," *Public Administration Review*, 32(4; 1972), 298–310.

Lyons, Linda. "The Gallup Brain: Prayer in Public Schools," December 10, 2002, https://news.gallup.com/poll/7393/Gallup-Brain-Prayer-Public-Schools.aspx.

Maidment, Paul. "Gerald Ford: The Accidental President," Forbes, December 27, 2006, https://www.forbes.com/2006/12/27/notes-on-the-news-ford-biz-cx_pm_1227ford.html#ce28540554db.

Maraniss, David. *First in His Class: A Biography of Bill Clinton*. New York: Simon & Schuster, 1996.

Matthews, Dylan. "Did the Stimulus Work? A Review of the Nine Best Studies on the Subject," *Washington Post*, August 16, 2011, https://www.washington-post.com/blogs/ezra-klein/post/did-the-stimulus-work-a-review-of-the-nine-best-studies-on-the-subject/2011/08/16/gIQAThbibJ_blog.html?utm_term=.b32f2405d84d.

Mayer, Jeremy D. "Reagan and Race: Prophet of Color Blindness, Baiter of the Backlash," in *Deconstructing Reagan: Conservative Mythology and America's Fortieth President*, edited by Kyle Longley, Jeremy D. Mayer, Michael Schaller, and John W. Sloan. New York: M. E. Sharpe, 2007. pp. 70–89.

Mayhew, David. *Divided We Govern: Party Control, Lawmaking, and Investigations, 1946–2002*, 2nd ed. New Haven: Yale, 2005.

Mayhew, David. "Innovative Midterm Elections," in *Midterm: The Elections of 1994 in Context*, edited by Philip A. Klinkner. Boulder: Westview Press, 1996.

Mayhew, David. *Realignment: Critique of a Genre*. New Haven: Yale University Press, 2004.

McCoy, Donald R., and Richard T. Ruetten. *Quest and Response: Minority Rights and the Truman Administration*. Lawrence: University Press of Kansas, 1973.

McCullough, David. *Truman*. New York: Simon & Schuster, 1992.

McElvaine, Robert S. *The Great Depression: America 1929–1941*. New York: Times Books, 1984.

McGuinn, Patrick J. *No Child Left Behind and the Transformation of Federal Education Policy, 1965–2005*. Lawrence: University Press of Kansas, 2006.

Meacham, John. *Destiny and Power: The American Odyssey of George Herbert Walker Bush*. New York: Random House, 2015.

Merriam, Charles. *A History of American Political Theories*. New York: Macmillan, 1903.

Merton, Robert K. "The Unanticipated Consequences of Purposive Social Action," American Sociological Review, 1(6; December 1936), 894–904.

Milkis, Sidney M., and Michael Nelson. *The American Presidency: Origins and Development, 1776–2011*, 6th ed. Washington, DC: Sage 2012.

Misra, Tanvi. "How the 1965 Immigration Act Shaped America's Population," citylab, https://www.citylab.com/life/2015/09/how-the-1965-immigration-act-shaped-americas-population/407626/.

Morris, Dick. *Behind the Oval Office*. New York: Random House, 1997.

Morris, Edmund. *Dutch: A Memoir of Ronald Reagan*. New York: Modern Library, 2000.

Morris, Roger. *Richard Milhous Nixon: The Rise of an American Politician*. New York: Holt, 1991.

Moynihan, Daniel P. *Maximum Feasible Misunderstanding: Community Action in the War on Poverty*, new ed. New York: Free Press, 1970.

Murray, Charles. *Coming Apart: The State of White America, 1960–2010*. New York: Crown, 2012.

Murray, Charles. *Losing Ground: American Social Policy, 1950–1980*. New York: Basic Books, 1984.

Nadler, Richard. "Special(k)" *National Review*, April 19, 1999, pp. 52–54.

Naftali, Timothy. *George H. W. Bush: The American Presidents Series: The 41st President, 1989–1993*. New York: Times Books, 2007.

Nathan, Richard. "Institutional Change Under Reagan," in *Perspectives on the Reagan Years*, edited by John L. Palmer. Washington, DC: Urban Institute, 1986. p. 125.

National Commission on Excellence in Education, *A Nation at Risk: The Imperative for Educational Reform*, April 1983, https://www2.ed.gov/pubs/NatAtRisk/risk.html.

Nelson, Michael. *Resilient America: Electing Nixon in 1968, Channeling Dissent, and Dividing Government*. Lawrence: University Press of Kansas, 2014.

Neustadt, Richard. *Presidential Power and the Modern Presidents: The Politics of Leadership from Roosevelt to Reagan*. New York: Free Press, 1990.

Nichols, David A. *A Matter of Justice: Eisenhower and the Beginning of the Civil Rights Revolution*. New York: Simon & Schuster, 2007.

Nixon, Richard M. *RN: The Memoirs of Richard Nixon*. New York: Grossett and Dunlap, 1978.

Nixon, Richard M. "Annual Message to the Congress on the State of the Union," January 22, 1971. Online by Gerhard Peters and John T. Woolley, The American Presidency Project, http://www.presidency.ucsb.edu/ws/?pid=3110.

Novak, Michael. *The Spirit of Democratic Capitalism*. New York: Simon & Schuster, 1982.

Novak, Viveca. "Bum Rap for Rahm," FactCheck.org, January 13, 2011, https://www.factcheck.org/2011/01/bum-rap-for-rahm/.

O'Brien, David M. "The Reagan Judges: His Most Enduring Legacy?," in *The Reagan Legacy: Promise and Performance*, edited by Charles O. Jones. Chatham, NJ: Chatham House, 1988. p. 62.

O'Brien, Matt. "The Middle Class Is Poorer Than It Was in 1989," *Washington Post*, October 1, 2014, https://www.washingtonpost.com/news/wonk/wp/2014/10/01/the-middle-class-is-poorer-today-than-it-was-in-1989/?noredirect=on&utm_term=.69d695c90ab6.

O'Brien, Ruth. "Progress and Good Governance in Domestic Policy," in *Debating the Obama Presidency*, edited by Steven E. Schier. Lanham, MD: Rowman & Littlefield, 2016. pp. 172–75.

Olasky, Marvin. *The Tragedy of American Compassion*. Wheaton, IL: Crossway, 1992.

Ornstein, Norm. "Yes, Polarization Is Asymmetric—and Conservatives Are Worse," *The Atlantic*, June 14, 2014, https://www.theatlantic.com/politics/archive/2014/06/yes-polarization-is-asymmetric-and-conservatives-are-worse/373044/.

Osborne, David, and Ted Gaebler. *Reinventing Government: How the Entrepreneurial Spirit Is Transforming Government*. New York: Plume, 1993.

Patterson, James T. *Congressional Conservatism and the New Deal*. Lexington: University of Kentucky Press, 1967.

Phillips, Kevin. *The Emerging Republican Majority*. New Rochelle, NY: Arlington House, 1969.

Pierson, Paul. "Increasing Returns, Path Dependence, and the Study of Politics," *American Political Science Review*, 94(2; June 2000), 251–67.

Piketty, Thomas. *The Economics of Inequality*. Cambridge: Belknap, 2015.

Pipes, Sally. "Unhappy Birthday, Obamacare: Five Years after Its Signing, the Affordable Care Act Is Failing to Live Up to Its Promise," *New York Daily News*, March 23, 2015, http://www.nydailynews.com/opinion/sally-pipes-unhappy-birthday-obamacare-article-1.2157297.

Pomper, Gerald M., ed. *The Election of 1988: Reports and Interpretations*. Chatham, NJ: Chatham House, 1989.

Powell, Jim. *FDR's Folly: How Roosevelt and His New Deal Prolonged the Great Depression*. New York: Crown Forum, 2004.

Price Foley, Elizabeth. *The Tea Party: Three Principles*. New York: Cambridge, 2012.

Prokop, Andrew. "Trump's Free Ride from Congress Just Ended," Vox, November 7, 2018, https://www.vox.com/2018/11/6/18025036/election-results-democrats-win-house-trump-investigations-analysis.

Reagan, Ronald. "Address Accepting the Presidential Nomination at the Republican National Convention in Detroit." Online by Gerhard Peters and John T. Woolley, The American Presidency Project, https://www.presidency.ucsb.edu/node/251302.

Reagan, Ronald. *An American Life*. New York: Simon & Schuster, 1990.

Reagan, Ronald. *The Creative Society: Some Comments on Problems Facing America*. New York: Devin-Adair, 1968.

Reagan, Ronald. "Inaugural Address." Online by Gerhard Peters and John T. Woolley, The American Presidency Project, https://www.presidency.ucsb.edu/node/246336.

Reeves, Richard. *President Nixon: Alone in the White House*, reprint ed. New York: Simon & Schuster, 2002.

Renshon, Stanley A. *Barack Obama and the Politics of Redemption*. New York: Routledge, 2012.

Report of the National Advisory Commission on Civil Disorders. New York: Bantam Books, 1968.

Rivlin, Alice M. *Reviving the American Dream*. Washington, DC: Brookings, 1992.

Roberts, Paul Craig. *The Supply-Side Revolution: An Insider's Account of Policymaking in Washington*. Cambridge: Harvard University Press, 1984.

Rockman, Bert A. "Cutting with the Grain: Is There a Clinton Leadership Legacy?," in *The Clinton Legacy*, edited by Colin Campbell and Bert A. Rockman. Chatham, NJ: Chatham House, 1999. p. 293.

Roosevelt, Theodore. "The New Nationalism," in *An American Primer*, edited by Daniel J. Boorstin. New York: Penguin, 1966.

Roosevelt, Franklin D. "State of the Union Message to Congress." Online by Gerhard Peters and John T. Woolley, The American Presidency Project, https://www.presidency.ucsb.edu/node/210825.

Sabatier, Paul. "An Advocacy Coalition Framework of Policy Change and the Role of Policy-Oriented Learning Therein," *Policy Sciences*, 21(1988), 129–68.

Sabatier, Paul A., and Hank C. Jenkins-Smith. "The Advocacy Coalitions Framework," in *Theories of the Policy Process*, edited by Paul A. Sabatier. Boulder: Westview, 1999. pp. 117–66.

Salpukas, Agis. "Falling Tax Would Lift All Yachts," *New York Times*, February 7, 1992, p. D1.

Savage, Sean J. *Roosevelt: The Party Leader, 1932–1945*. Lexington: University of Kentucky Press, 1991.

Scher, Bill. "Obama vs. FDR, Year Seven," RealClearPolitics, February 9, 2015, https://www.realclearpolitics.com/articles/2015/02/09/obama_vs_fdr_year_seven_125526.html.

Schier, Steven, ed. *Postmodern Presidency: Bill Clinton's Legacy in U.S. Politics*. Pittsburgh: University of Pittsburgh Press, 2000.

Schier, Steven E. ed. *High Risk and Big Ambition: Presidency of George W. Bush*. Pittsburgh: University of Pittsburgh Press, 2004.

Schlaes, Amity, *The Forgotten Man: A New History of the Great Depression*. New York: HarperCollins, 2007.

Schlesinger, Arthur M. Jr. *The Crisis of the Old Order*. New York: Mariner Books, 2003.

Schlesinger, Arthur M., Jr. *The Coming of the New Deal*. New York: Mariner, 2003.

Schlesinger, Arthur M., Jr. *The Crisis of the Old Order: The Age of Roosevelt, Vol. I, 1919–1933*. New York: Heineman, 1957.

Schuyler, Michael. "A Short History of Government Taxing and Spending in the United States," Tax Foundation, February 14, 2014, https://taxfoundation.org/short-history-government-taxing-and-spending-united-states/.

Schwartz, Herman. "Down the Wrong Path: Path Dependence, Increasing Returns, and Historical Institutionalism," unpublished manuscript, 2004, https://pdfs.semanticscholar.org/f7a5/94a5709cc58cfc62ca7220af30d7c-c9adc90.pdf.

Schwartz, John E. *America's Hidden Success: A Reassessment of Public Policy from Kennedy to Reagan*, rev. ed. New York: W. W. Norton, 1987.

Scott, Dylan, and Sarah Kliff. "Why Obamacare Repeal Failed," Vox, July 31, 2017, https://www.vox.com/policy-and-politics/2017/7/31/16055960/why-obamacare-repeal-failed.

Silva, Chantal da. "Has Occupy Wall Street Changed America?," *Newsweek*, September 19, 2018, https://www.newsweek.com/has-occupy-wall-street-changed-america-seven-years-birth-political-movement-1126364.

Skocpol, Theda, and Vanessa Williamson. *The Tea Party and the Remaking of Republican Conservatism*. New York: Oxford, 2013.

Skowronek, Stephen. *Presidential Leadership in Political Time: Reprise and Reappraisal*. Lawrence: University Press of Kansas, 2008.

Smith, Jean Edward. *Eisenhower in War and Peace*, reprint ed. New York: Random House, 2013.

Sorensen, Ted. *Kennedy: The Classic Biography*. New York: Harper Perennial Political Classics, 2009.

Stein, Herbert. *Presidential Economics: The Making of Economic Policy from Roosevelt to Clinton*. Washington, DC: AEI, 1994.

Steinfels, Peter. *The Neoconservatives: The Men Who Are Changing America's Politics*. New York: Simon & Schuster, 1978.

Steinhorn, Leonard. *The Greater Generation: In Defense of the Baby Boom Legacy*. New York: Thomas Dunne Books, 2007.

Stevenson, Richard. "Confident Bush Outlines Ambitious Plan for 2nd Term," *New York Times*, November 5, 2004, http://www.nytimes.com/2004/11/05/politics/campaign/05bush.html.

Strahan, Randall. *Leading Representatives: The Agency of Leaders in the Politics of the U.S. House*. Baltimore: Johns Hopkins Press, 2007.

Sundquist, James. *Politics and Policy: The Eisenhower, Kennedy, and Johnson Years*. Washington, DC: Brookings Institution Press, 1968.

Tatum, Sophie. "Bipartisan Criminal Justice Bill Clears Congress," CNN, December 20, 2018, https://www.cnn.com/2018/12/20/politics/house-pass-criminal-justice-first-step-bill/index.html.

Tomaskey, Michael. *Bill Clinton: The American Presidents Series: The 42nd President, 1993–2001*. New York: Times Books, 2017.

True, James L., Bryan D. Jones, and Frank R. Baumgartner. "Punctuated-Equilibrium Theory: Explaining Stability and Change in American Policy Making," in *Theories of the Policy Process*, edited by Paul A. Sabatier. Boulder: Westview, 1999. pp. 97–116.

Truman, Harry S. "Special Message to the Congress Presenting a 21-Point Program for the Reconversion Period," September 6, 1945. Online by Gerhard Peters and John T. Woolley, The American Presidency Project, http://www.presidency.ucsb.edu/ws/?pid=12359.

Tullock, Gordon. "Did Nixon Beat Kennedy?" New York Review of Books, November 10, 1988, https://www.nybooks.com/articles/1988/11/10/did-nixon-beat-kennedy/.

United States Census Bureau. 1949 Statistical Abstract, http://www.census.gov/prod/www/abs/statab1901-1950.htm.

Venugopal, Arun. "Black Leaders Once Championed the Strict Drug Laws They Now Seek to Dismantle," WNYC, August 15, 2013, https://www.wnyc.org/story/312823-black-leaders-once-championed-strict-drug-laws-they-now-seek-dismantle/.

Walsh, Bryan. "Why the Climate Bill Died," *Time*, July 26, 2010, http://science.time.com/2010/07/26/why-the-climate-bill-died/.

Wattenberg, Ben J. "It's Time to Stop America's Retreat," *New York Times Magazine*, July 22, 1979.

Weisberg, Jacob. "The Bush Who Got Away," *New York Times*, January 28, 2008, https://www.nytimes.com/2008/01/28/opinion/28weisberg.html.

Weissman, Jordan. "The Failure of Welfare Reform," Slate, June 1, 2016, https://slate.com/news-and-politics/2016/06/how-welfare-reform-failed.html.

Wharton, Penn. "Effects of the $15 Minimum Wage in Seattle," University of Pennsylvania, https://publicpolicy.wharton.upenn.edu/live/news/2303-effects-of-the-15-minimum-wage-in-seattle/for-students/blog/news.php.

White, F. Clifton, and William J. Gill. *Why Reagan Won: A Narrative History of the Conservative Movement 1964–1981*. Chicago: Regnery Gateway, 1981.

Whitehead, Barbara Dafoe. "Dan Quayle Was Right," *The Atlantic*, April 1993, https://www.theatlantic.com/magazine/archive/1993/04/dan-quayle-was-right/307015/.

Wicker, Tom. "President Elated," *New York Times*, November 8, 1962, p. A1.

Wilder, Matt. "What Is a Policy Paradigm? Overcoming Epistemological Hurdles in Cross-Disciplinary Conceptual Adaptation," in *Policy Paradigms in Theory and Practice: Studies in the Political Economy of Public Policy*, edited by J. Hogan and M. Howlett. London: Palgrave Macmillan, 2015. pp. 19–42.

Wilson, Woodrow. "The Meaning of Democracy—September 23, 1912," in *A Crossroads of Freedom: The 1912 Campaign Speeches*, edited by John W. Davidson. New Haven: Yale Press, 1956.

Wisensale, Steven K. "Family Policy During the Reagan Years: The Private Side of the Conservative Agenda," in *Ronald Reagan's America*, vol. 1, edited by Eric J. Schmertz, Natalie Datlof, and Alexej Ugrinsky. Westport, CT: Greenwood, 1997. pp. 283–84.

Wolfers, Justin. "The Fed Has Not Stopped Trying to Stimulate the Economy," *New York Times*, October 29, 2014.

Woodward, Bob. *The Agenda: Inside the Clinton White House*. New York: Simon & Schuster, 1994.

Zahariadis, Nicholaos. "Ambiguity, Time, and Multiple Streams," in *Theories of the Policy Process*, edited by Paul A. Sabatier. Boulder: Westview Press, 1999. p. 77.

Zahariadis, Nicholaos. *Markets, States, and Public Policies: Privatization in Britain and France*. Ann Arbor: University of Michigan Press, 1995.

Zeitz, Joshua. *Building the Great Society: Inside Lyndon Johnson's White House*. New York: Viking, 2018.

Zelizer, Julian E. *The Fierce Urgency of Now: Lyndon Johnson, Congress, and the Battle for the Great Society*. New York: Penguin, 2015.

Index

★ ★ ★